We

Won't

Go

We

PERSONAL ACCOUNTS

Won't

OF WAR OBJECTORS

Go

COLLECTED BY

ALICE LYND

BEACON PRESS : BOSTON

"But if

two and two

and fifty

make a million. . . ."

ACKNOWLEDGMENTS

I WOULD particularly like to thank attorneys Ann Fagan Ginger, Eleanor Norton, Francis Heisler, Marvin Karpatkin, Leonard Boudin, and especially Stanley Faulkner who gave his time to read the entire manuscript, for information, suggestions, and encouragement; Joseph S. Tuchinsky for patient reading, expert advice, and helpful corrections; many, many individuals, among them Paul Salstrom and Fred Moore, who generously sent material for the book; my husband, Staughton, and my children, Barbara and Lee, for forbearance and a shared sense that the work was important, and Martha, who as a baby likes to play with books and papers too.

ACKNOWLEDGMENTS

WE WON'T GO

INTRODUCTION

THE UNEASINESS about the war in Vietnam which led students at Yale and elsewhere to begin formulating "We Won't Go" pledges in the fall of 1966 led also to the idea for this book.

Students meeting in our living room to discuss the draft raised questions that were being asked across the country. Concerned to stop the war, they were troubled by their sheltered position in relation to the draft. They knew they could not participate in the war but felt impotent to stop it.

In one discussion, a girl who had a friend in prison asked, what good does it do to let them put you away like that? When I realized that hardly anyone else in the room had ever heard of her friend I thought, what a waste! This person had experienced so much that might be pertinent to others. Someone should write a book about the unknown men who had tried to answer with their lives the questions about effectiveness and personal sacrifice being asked by many individuals and little groups.

Since that time draft resistance has mushroomed. Draft information and counseling are much more available. More and more young people are responding to the tension between what is and what could be by saying to themselves, *you* are the agent for change. Resistance organizers regard the draft as a single aspect of a larger problem. Ending the war in Vietnam is not in itself a solution; those who refuse to fight in Vietnam will need to continue to struggle for justice and to resist the arbitrary use of power wherever it occurs.

Those who say "We won't go" draw the line at different points. This line is drawn according to values and priorities which claim their first allegiance. There is a question for anyone faced with the draft—what am I willing to die for?

Here is a collection of accounts by men who wrote about what they had to grapple with and what they did as they confronted the dilemmas of conscience which military participation poses.

It is not a book of answers but of questions and examples of attempts to deal with them.

The forms of activity described and the rationales for them may soon seem dated. But some of these concepts and experiences are recurrent because they are rooted in eternal conflicts between power and justice, individual conscience and responsibility to common humanity, means and ends.

The contributors were asked to write freely or to use the following questions as a guide.

1. What did you do to resist or avoid military service?
2. How did you decide what you would do? (What influenced you? What choices did you have to make? What pressures did you feel?)
3. Were you part of a group concerned with the draft? If so, please describe and evaluate the group experience. [This question was added to later inquiries only.]
4. What happened to you as a result of acting on your beliefs?
5. How do you feel now about what you have been through?
6. What issues seem most important to you? What do you want your action to make people think about?
7. Is there anything you would like to say to others who are trying to decide what they should do about the draft or military service?

Contributors were also asked to send copies of statements, letters, or other material which they thought would be useful. A few of the accounts were transcribed and edited from tape-recorded interviews. Several were drawn exclusively from personal letters. Most of the accounts were pieced together from different kinds of sources, such as letters to draft boards, replies to questions on the Special Form for Conscientious Objector (Form 150), and published articles or fliers. Formal statements have largely been eliminated or cut in favor of descriptions of the decision-making process. Whenever possible, the accounts were designed to show how a person's views developed in relation to what he experienced. Some of the men are still in midstream.

This collection is not fully representative. Most noticeably absent from the book but existing in substantial numbers are objectors who engaged in combat in Vietnam, deserters in Europe or other countries, draft evaders who have "gone underground," those who have discovered personal solutions, and dropouts who are not deliberately taking any principled position. Perhaps most important among the missing are those who were badly hurt by what they did, have retreated, and do not want to talk about it. It is hoped that this book can forestall grief by affording a little more opportunity to anticipate what may be involved in following or not following one's commitment. And apologies are due not so much for failing to represent certain elements or leaning too much stress on others, but for presuming to touch men at this point in their lives where past and future hopes and dreams are brought to a focus and tested by a dire and immediate reality.

To those who wonder, "Why would a person do a thing like that?", this book may afford some insight into views very different from their own. They may be perplexed as they see a young man going off and doing something which seems not to fit with the way he grew up, or in defiance of the law, or without regard for the feelings of others or his family responsibilities, or risking his future in ways he cannot foresee. Yet he still *is* that person whom they love and it may well be that some of the things they love in him are prompting him to do what hurts and puzzles them so much. For most men, where they are now is the result of many steps, decisions, and evaluations interacting with experience. Those who have sketched their development can help us to understand how people, like some we know, were able to do what they did.

It is critical that wives and girl friends be involved in their partner's searchings and decisions about the draft. Both members of a couple will have consequences to bear. It is not helpful to a mutual relationship for one member to stand apart and say, in effect, "You do what you have to do and somehow I'll do what I can to live with it." If a life is to be built together the basis for decisions needs to be shared and differences recognized and understood.

Every man who is faced with induction makes a choice as to whether or not he will go when called. If he goes into the armed forces he is choosing not to say "No." If he comes to think that he has made the wrong choice he can still find ways to honor the dictates of conscience, but the consequences under military law are usually far more severe. This book may serve as background for young men to sift out their thoughts and make choices on the basis of their own convictions.

There are some problems which adequate counseling can prevent but others which emerge only through experience and no one can convey to another person what they will mean. It need not be personally undermining or a breach of faith to change one's mind. Under new circumstances, a new decision may be more realistic than maintaining a position which no longer seems relevant or true. In an area fraught with contradictions and counterpressures, it is nevertheless important that one's feelings and intellectual picture be together, that one take only those voluntary steps which one feels ready to take.

Viktor Frankl, a psychiatrist who survived Nazi concentration camps, observed in *Man's Search for Meaning* (Beacon Press, 1963) that it is normal to react abnormally in an abnormal situation. Self-doubt, uncertainty, confusion, aloneness, depression, irritability, sleeplessness, and a variety of ailments are common as confrontations approach. But some men never feel clearer in their lives. A release of energy and conquering of fear come to them when doing what they think is right. Times of inaction or compromise are usually the hardest. It may make some difference to see oneself as a human being facing inhuman demands.

It is easier to give up security in the present if that which one is choosing has a quality of affirmation. There is something about religious beliefs or political convictions or a sense that "this is what has to be done" which gives strength. The example of another person may help. Ammon Hennacy spent seven and a half months in solitary confinement for refusal to register at the time of World War I. Crouching by the door of his cell on sunny mornings, he could see the top of the head of an anarchist who he knew had spent three and a half years in solitary. This man had been in prison since before Ammon was born and had "a fighting spirit that jails could not kill." It gave Ammon courage.

The men who tell their stories here are not heroes with qualities of character above what the rest of us can attain. They are everyday people like you and me. Rather than measure ourselves as less worthy we need to have faith that there is something in humanness or in relatedness which has tremendous untapped resources and that when circumstances require it ordinary people with hang-ups and quirks may be able to act with a dignity of which mankind can be proud.

To the "two and two and fifty" who contributed to this book, thanks.

ALICE LYND
February 1968

We

Won't

Go

Tom Gardner

MANPOWER UNCHANNELED

By the use of deferments as inducements and induction as a threat, the Selective Service System exerts an inescapable influence on men of draft age. Phrases from the Selective Service document on "Channeling," such as "the club of induction," "pressurized guidance," "to force his choice," and "the national interest," convey to young men a lack of confidence that their own perceptions of what they can contribute to the world are worth considering. "Manpower channeling" has become a highly resented term because it so aptly expresses the putting of systems ahead of men. The response Tom Gardner slowly evolved was that "it's mostly important not to be intimidated out of what you think you should be doing."

Distaste for jail did not deter him from being jailed repeatedly after the events related in this account, for attempting to bring his views on foreign policy and the draft to students on Southern campuses. The Southern Student Coordinating Committee with which he works:

> . . . *affirms the right of each individual to participate in the decision-making processes in those social, economic, and political areas which directly influence his life. We envision a world dedicated to free speech and unfettered inquiry; a community of love and cooperation in an economy of abundance.*

WITH THE MAINTENANCE of the "Peacetime" draft, the government outlines for young men certain alternatives (such as, kill or go to prison), and to most the ultimatum is a compelling one. But the final decision still rests with us. It is wrong to say that we are "forced" into the army or "forced" to fight in a war. Many of us, at one point or another, are saying "No."

It is not even enough to say "I won't go." There are many different ways to refuse to join the military or fight in a war. Among those of us who have made the basic decision not to go, there is a constant debate concerning which method of refusal is the most moral, effective, or successful.

I have found it impossible to formulate a position in relation to the Selective Service System without considering much broader questions. Is the singular, moral witness the best way personally to affect history? Should effectiveness be considered at all? In light of the present war and pending disaster, don't we have a moral duty to be effective? How can we act most effectively to end the war, abolish the draft, and change the American system that breeds imperialism? Should I go out of my way to help Uncle Sam lock me up? Is that "resistance"? What personal course will contribute the most toward building a popular resistance movement? Am I personally ready to act on the basis of my political and moral decisions? To what extent are my decisions political and moral decisions? To what extent are my decisions political and to what extent are they rationalizations for personal shortcomings?

I don't pretend to have the answers to these questions, nor will I attempt to deal with all of them here. In the hope that my experience may assist at least one other person, I would like to review some of the decisions I have made and discuss how and why my position has changed.

I have, until recently, lived a fairly normal, middle-class life. My father is a career dental officer in the Navy, and most of my nomadic life has been spent in the South. A Kennedy-Peace Corps admirer, I enrolled at the University of Virginia, planning to enter the foreign service and enrolled in Air Force ROTC. I quickly dropped out of ROTC. Through contact with activists in the civil rights and campus reform movements, and after discovering some facts about our foreign policy, I became active in anti-war organizing. The comparative emptiness of the "education" I was receiving in college, and a desire to do something significant compelled me toward my first confrontation with the selective slavery system. I call it a confrontation not because I received any orders from my local board, but because the probable threat of induction if I were to drop out of school forced me to consider the draft while deciding whether or not to drop out. The obvious conflict was between what I wanted to do and what the Selective Service System would want me to do.

There were three main factors that influenced me to drop out in spite of the draft. One factor was that a best friend had withdrawn from the University of Virginia in order to work with the Virginia Students' Civil Rights Committee in southside Virginia, while I was still in school. His example affected me for two reasons: one, I respected his courage and commitment; and, two, he was living testimony to the fact that it was possible to drop out of school and still avoid or delay induction.

The second factor was my exposure to the moral absolutist position. When we organized a state-wide demonstration in support of Beardall, Keith, and Rodd, who were imprisoned at Petersburg Federal Reformatory, I publicly read Tom Rodd's statement to Judge Rosenberg. That gave me a stronger feeling of identity with the noncooperators. John Buenfil of Charlottesville, Virginia, was the first person to ever articulate the noncooperator position to me. At that time, I didn't completely agree with the absolutists' position, but their witness would have made me ashamed to stay in college rather than risk prison.

The third factor, probably the decisive one, was my strong personal resentment and rebellion against the idea of some distant group of old men presuming to control my life. I grew up believing in democracy and the sanctity of the individual conscience—you know, Thomas Paine, Jefferson, Adams, Thoreau, Jesus Christ, etc. (or, by antithetical example, Adolph Eichmann) —and it was just too late for all those old people who taught me those things to reverse themselves and tell me: "Forget all that conscience stuff, don't think, just follow orders—kill, kill, kill!!" Not only was I so much of a Christian, American, "democrat" that I wouldn't let them order me to kill a stranger, but I also didn't think that they should be able to force me to go to college.

So, I decided that regardless of the eventual consequences, I would leave college because I wanted to—period. I also intended to use whatever semi-legitimate evasive tactics I could, so that I could continue to work in the movement. Being by now a convinced pacifist, I felt I would eventually apply for conscientious objector status. If possible, I wanted to avoid a direct confrontation while doing the organizing work that I wanted to do. To stay in college to avoid that confrontation would not have been evasive; for me, it would have been total prostitution and humiliation.

After leaving the University, working with the Virginia Students' Civil Rights Committee, and then coming on the staff of the USNSA [National Student Association] Southern Project, I began to question whether I could accept certain deferments or exemptions or whether I should be a total noncooperator. During this period of indecision, I was what the SSS calls a delinquent, i.e., I ignored the draft board, not informing them of my work or address. I could have applied for an occupational deferment (II-A), since NSA was, as is now obvious, "essential to the national safety." Since I didn't consider myself to be part of NSA's national defense scheme, the very thought of being classified as essential to Johnson's definition of "the national safety or interest" was too repugnant to consider. Also, at an early meeting of the advisory committee of the Southern Project, the National Affairs Vice-President of NSA was asked what NSA is doing on the draft. His reply was, "To be honest with you, we (the officers and staff) all have occupational deferments and we don't want to do anything too drastic because we're afraid we'll lose them." That was the kind of statement that pushed me closer toward noncooperation.

In September of 1966, in an effort to think through my position, I wrote myself a short diatribe. Part of it follows:

> The draft—to take a purely moral stand, or to be effective? It's difficult to divide those two satisfactorily so that you can actually choose one from the other. For instance, I tend to have more respect for those who take a seemingly moral stand rather than thinking primarily of effectiveness. On the other hand, I also begin to get the feeling that wanting just to wipe one's own moral slate clean is a rather selfish

goal when you consider the moral imperative of needing to end the war. In other words, you can't divide "moral" from "effective" when you consider that with thousands of people being killed, you have a moral duty to be effective. But then, what is "being effective"? How the hell are we going to end this war-drunk world's spiral toward disaster? How can we just end the war in Vietnam? If I feel that the only way I can work toward that is by urging others not to fight, and if I feel that the best way to protest the draft is for myself and others to refuse allegiance even to its alternative service, then how can I continue to pussy-foot around about my own status? And if I rationalize staying out of jail so that I can build a larger draft resistance movement, what the hell am I doing working for NSA which, like the schools it wants to change, is more responsive to its ownership, foundations, and government, than to its constituency—students? Should I burn my card? Apply for I-O? Ask for asylum in Cuba? Go to Canada? What?

I want to work full-time on learning and talking with people about relating to other people, about love and peace, hate and war, freedom and FREEDOM. I want to help people overcome what the system is doing to them. I want to love and help build bridges between people and maybe nations. Is that so evil or dangerous? Well, I guess it may be to those who have a vested interest in keeping people hating and killing each other. But, I'm going to do it anyway; I'm tired of that word "later." I'm tired of allowing my life to be ruled by a machine which I have no influence over. To quote Mrs. Fannie Lou Hamer, "All my life I've been sick and tired, and now I'm sick and tired of being sick and tired!" All of us have so many chains wrapped around us, we're slaves; but most of us are cringing inside those chains, trying to roll ourselves into insignificant little balls of flesh so that we won't even be touched by the cold iron that surrounds us. Other people have been in that situation; most of them also cringed frightened, but some have stood up and pushed against the chains that bound them—with their whole bodies, with their feet, with their songs, with their lives. Whether the chains broke or remained, those men and women were declaring themselves free and were, in fact,

close to FREEDOM, by virtue of having lost their fear of the
consequences and standing up and asserting their manhood
or womanhood. Through that kind of involvement, one *can*
declare his own freedom, and only by doing so can he be
maximally and individually both effective and moral. It is the
persons who have taken that kind of stand who have had a
stronger effect on history than those who have compromised
their principles as a price for effectiveness. Now, how about
me?

Sounds good doesn't it, but before I attended the Noncooperators' Conference in New York [October 1966], I still had two
major reservations about noncooperation: one, how effective
would it be?; and two, is the fact of my nominal affiliation, registration, or classification with the SSS so immoral in itself that I
am willing to go to prison in an attempt to sever it? At the conference, I don't really think I resolved those questions, but I was
overwhelmingly impressed with the courage and moral clarity of
the men who had chosen noncooperation. They were beautiful
people and I wanted to be part of them. But even as I joined, two
lingering impressions bothered me (slightly, then, but more
later); considering the dominant air of self-righteousness (which
is possibly inherent in martyrdom), many of the noncooperators
seemed disproportionately politically naïve, especially about the
probable short-range effect of their own act of refusal. It was to
me a convincing point that for a person to live an effective life he
must have a consistent record of having stood up for what he
believes in. However, that appraisal of one's lifelong effectiveness
should not lead one to an unrealistic overestimation of the immediate political effect of burning or returning a draft card, or, as
some see it, volunteering for prison. Anyone deciding to risk
prison should distinguish between the long and the short range
effectiveness arguments, and decide for himself how each of them
relates specifically to him.

I then decided to join the long line of revolutionary zealots
and sign the statement: "Saying No to Military Conscription."

*We, the undersigned men of draft age (18–35), believe that
all war is immoral and ultimately self-defeating. We believe*

that military conscription is evil and unjust. Therefore, we will not cooperate in any way with the Selective Service System.

We will not register for the draft.

If we have registered, we will sever all relations with the Selective Service System.

We will carry no draft cards or other Selective Service certificates.

We will not accept any deferment, such as 2-S.

We will not accept any exemption, such as 1-O or 4-D.

We will refuse induction into the armed forces.

We urge and advocate that other young men join us in non-cooperating with the Selective Service System.

We are in full knowledge that these actions are violations of the Selective Service laws punishable by up to 5 years imprisonment and/or a fine of $10,000.

On my way back South, I went by my home at Camp Lejeune, North Carolina, and found waiting for me a I-A classification card. I immediately wrote the following letter, carried it around for a couple of weeks, and finally dropped it in the mailbox, along with my draft card.

Dear Board Members,

I recently received a card from you indicating my classification as I-A. In recent months, I have spent much time considering my relation to the system of conscription. . . .

I have decided to refuse cooperation with conscription for several reasons. . . . I know of the alternatives within the System, and I imagine I could avoid having to kill by asking for alternative "service." I also realize, however, that I would have a chance of qualifying for one of the alternatives: I've had a formal education; I've been exposed to the varying philosophies of pacifism and can articulate my beliefs; I could afford appeals and lawyers; and I'm white. I realize also that there are a lot of men who couldn't avoid military service because their environment makes the military look to them like a positive step by comparison; or because they lack the same financial resources; or, regardless of other

qualifications, because they are Black. Am I going to work
with my brothers in a common struggle, and then at the
danger point step "up" and use my "privileged" position? If
I were to accept a privileged position under the draft law, I
would, in a very real sense, be recognizing the right of the
regime to gobble up my brethren, and I don't recognize that
right. I feel that in order to be of service to my "country,"
which is Humanity, and to be loyal to my god, whom I call
Love, and to participate in my religion, which I define as
action, I must sever all connections with the system of destruction which wishes to induct me into its services. I hereby
consider myself no longer connected with the system of military conscription, and under no circumstances will I accept
induction.

I received no reply other than an order to report for my physical on December 14. I didn't intend to report (I discovered later
that the Justice Department had been notified so that they could
arrest me when I failed to show), but on December 8, I was
sentenced by a kind North Carolina judge to thirty days in jail
for criminal contempt, thereby making it impossible for me to
report for my physical, even if I had wanted to.

I was in Greensboro, North Carolina, helping a recently indicted nonregistrant find a lawyer. While attending the court sessions, I met two other fellows who were charged with refusing
induction. The one with whom I had a chance to speak had withdrawn from Appalachian State Teachers College. He had never
read any of the standard peace literature or heard of any of the
peace organizations. He said he wasn't a conscientious objector—
he was "just sick of the whole mess"; he was just a calm, ordinary
guy who had decided he wasn't going. In court, this registrant refused to make a statement. He had written his board: "I don't feel
a need to justify my action in anyone's mind." Nobody in the courtroom, not the D.A., the FBI agent, nor the judge could figure out
what possible reason this young man could have for not wanting
to kill people. So the judge, scratching his head and saying, "I
wish there were something else I could do," sentenced him to two
years in prison. The other draft refuser was also sentenced to two
years.

At recess, when the command was given, "Everyone rise," having little respect for that court to indicate by rising, I remained seated. When the court reconvened, the judge declared that I had been "disrespectful and contemptuous of the court" and that I had planned to "disrupt the order and decorum of the court and obstruct the administration of justice." I was then hauled off to Forsyth County jail in Winston-Salem, North Carolina, without being given a chance to speak. I was released after sixteen days so that I could enjoy Christmas at home.

My jail term in North Carolina was the first chance I had to just read and think. I learned as much about myself as I did about our "just society." It was in jail where my position regarding the SSS began to modify itself toward a more personally realistic one. The following excerpt out of my thick file of prison notes relates a couple of my most important realizations.

> I was thinking, in regards to noncooperation, that one of the valuable things would be to confront the Judge and other officials with the burden of having to imprison me, etc. After watching Judge Gordon throw two guys away for two years and imprison me, as I sit here in jail, I can't help but give more pensive thought to the possibility of a two- to five-year term. Judge Gordon was not affected in the slightest, nor were any of the spectators. I am just now seeing more vividly that they . . . have absolute power, and that it's somewhat ridiculous to let them put me away for four damn years (that's forty-eight times as long as I'm serving now). . . . I'm just not sure it's worth it.
>
> Secondly, I'm just not sure that with the doubts I have, I could fabricate the daily consolation that going to prison for conscience sake requires. Going to jail for absolutism means that if one expects to maintain his sanity, one must be an absolutist in his decision. That means that one has to be able to look at the entire world and domestic situation—at everything that's happening socially, politically, economically, technologically—at the way people think, at the alternatives available and then decide that the best place for him is jail for 5 yrs. I don't think I can say that now, I just don't think I can.

. . . What this means practically, I guess, is that I would be willing to apply for CO and take alternative service . . . Goddamn, Gardner, don't be so defensive, everyone has a right to grow or change his mind.

More specifically, with the world spiraling toward destruction and America marching toward fascism . . . I felt a lot more pessimistic about the possible short-range effectiveness of my noncooperation. I wanted to be outside, talking to people, organizing with them where they are *at*. What could I do in prison? Who would understand? Who is going to join a "Go to Prison" movement? Why should I help the enemy take me out of commission for several years? Perhaps I also learned about myself (as Thomas More says in *A Man for All Seasons*), that, "This is not the stuff from which martyrs are made." I decided to apply for conscientious objector status—at least to give me more time to think, although I didn't rule out the possibility of doing alternative service. Since receiving a I-O from the state appeal board, I have not received an order to report for alternative service, as of this writing.

So, what conclusions have I drawn and what is my present position? One point is that a guy may be influenced to drop out of school and/or resist the draft just as much by the example of someone escaping both the draft and prison as by the example of an imprisoned noncooperator. Another point is that it would be a good idea for everyone contemplating noncooperation to spend just a few days in the pokey so that they could make a more realistic appraisal of the consequences of their act. A decision to noncooperate after one has experienced imprisonment is likely to be more personally realistic.

I think that the major weakness of my original act of noncooperation was that it was not real enough for me to stand on. I wasn't yet really refusing or responding to any final orders from Selective Service, nor had I exhausted all the possibilities for delaying or completely avoiding induction. I was waging an offensive against the SSS, the major issue being whether or not I was registered with them. When pressed on the point, I decided that it really didn't make any difference what my board thought my status was or whether or not they considered me to be a registrant. (It is impossible in that sense to be "unregistered," since even if you go to prison, the warden can register you with the SSS.) What really mattered was whether in the end *I* would grant the draft system any influence over the direction of my life.

Perhaps the issue of disaffiliation is not the best issue around which to organize a resistance movement; although, acts of total noncooperation do help add to a general sense of rebellion and thus contribute toward building a resistance movement. Essentially, though, the point at which guys will more readily resist is the point at which the draft comes into their lives and attempts to coerce their bodies into slavery. There are basically two ways that the SSS attempts to enter our lives. One way is through induction into the military—hopefully more and more young men will at this point say "No." The other way, which is just as much an essential function of the SSS as the former one, is through the granting of various deferments and exemptions (II-S, II-A, I-O, IV-D, etc.) that are designed "to channel people into the occupations that are defined by those in government as critical" and to buy off potential resisters. The important point here for me has been to decide what I want to do, not considering the draft, and then go ahead and do it.

The question arises, what if what I really want to do would entitle me to a deferment anyway? This, of course, must be resolved personally. I haven't completely resolved it for myself, but if I *really* wanted to return to college, I would probably accept a II-S. What would be important would be not to let that II-S be the decisive factor for keeping me in school. And if I *really* wanted to work for the American Friends Service Committee, or work in a hospital for two years, then I would probably let the draft board call it "alternative service." However, since I plan to keep working with the Southern Student Organizing Committee for at least the next several years, and since SSOC is not recognized as alternative service, I am reaching a point at which I will have to decide whether I will do what I want to do or what "they" want me to do. If I were to state here and now exactly what I intend to do, that would only indicate that I have learned nothing from my past experience. I do not know what I am going to do. How far can one bend and still call himself a man? For myself, I suspect, not much further.

Gene Keyes

AN ARREST OF ONE
IS AN ARREST OF ALL

The pact which Gene Keyes and two friends carried out in the early 1960's was a forerunner of the acts of solidarity envisioned by the Resistance in 1967. (See account, pp. 238–243.)

Charlotte Keyes, Gene's mother, wrote an article for *McCall's* magazine, October 1966, entitled "Suppose They Gave a War and No One Came." Reprinted and widely distributed, this article describes in fuller detail the human story behind her son's early actions.

The account presented here was written for this book prior to the massive return of draft cards planned by the Resistance for October 16, 1967.

HOW *MUCH* do you oppose the draft? What are you going to do about it?

There are already enough of us against the draft, in principle, to rock the Selective Service System. But so far the catch is that too many of us have been afraid of prison. So we've dodged the issue, or postponed it, or clung to a II-S, or let some other influence pressure us out of resisting the draft.

Once you've decided to go to prison instead of collaborating with the draft law, what can you do to have something to show for all that time you'll be locked up? This is what I began asking myself by January 1962. I didn't want to sit around and let the law take me in its own good time. I didn't want to be just another negligible statistic when there were only a few guys each year who got busted for draft resistance. How could Selective Service be challenged, at times and places of my own choosing, as dramatically as possible?

I was always a Quaker-type pacifist. In October 1959 I had registered for the draft, intending to do alternate service. . . .

With the magic word "Quaker" I'd have no trouble getting a I-O and getting it over with.

But filling out that form made me begin to think harder about the nuclear facts of life. I started getting on mailing lists and talking to people already giving their lives to peace work: Bob Pickus, A. J. Muste, Bob Swann, and Brad Lyttle, among others. By February 1961, I decided that the most important thing in the world that anyone could do was to stop whatever else he was doing and start to work full time in nonviolent action against the war machine.

That month I dropped out of Harvard, midway through my second year, and went to New London, Connecticut, where the New England Committee for Nonviolent Action had set up a permanent base of operations focusing on the Polaris missile system. I got busy manning the mimeograph, hitting the peace-march trail, and going limp in front of Polaris submarines.

I began to meet more people who already saw that the Selective Service System, like any other arm of the war machine, should be resisted completely instead of used for personal advantage. That system had one purpose and one purpose only: the army. Registering had been a mistake, and I realized this most clearly when I began to read the text of the law itself and some of the literature the system put out to describe itself. "The first step in the procurement of military manpower is registration," General Hershey had written. Well, I had taken one step too many.

And what about alternate service under the draft? That's just the trouble: "under the draft." The Military Selective Service Act is not a social service act. All the hospital work a conscientious objector could do in two years would not make up for a single day of napalm and pellet bombs. A law which gives a special privilege to a few CO's makes everyone else pull the trigger, and helps ease resistance to the draft itself.

Back in those days the draft age was twenty-three, and since I was just twenty, I had a little time to decide how to resist. Eventually I carried out two public challenges to the draft, one on my own and one as part of a group.

First, I used my draft card to light a candle at midnight, Christmas Eve, 1963, in front of the local board office in Champaign, Illinois.

Then in May 1964, Barry Bassin, Russ Goddard, and I entered a pact saying that "an arrest of one is an arrest of all." When Russ was convicted for draft resistance in St. Louis in July 1964, the other two of us stood up in court and got ourselves six-month sentences for contempt, on top of our own draft sentences which were still to come.

As it turned out, both of these events got unusual publicity; but they would have happened anyway, with or without the fanfare. Neither the candle scene nor the pact developed overnight. In the rest of this narrative I'll try to sketch in a little of the process they were a part of.

I

Better to Light One Draft Card than Curse the Darkness

In the summer of 1962, I mapped out a campaign for my own case of draft resistance, to culminate with civil disobedience against the draft law by the fall or winter of 1963. But if I was going to urge abolition of the draft and the armed forces, I thought I should first spend some more time studying how we can defend ourselves without them. I was at Pendle Hill, a Quaker study center, from September 1962 to June 1963, reading more about pacifism and nonviolent defense and draft resistance.

In my countdown, I thought I should at least go through the formality of trying to get the draft law repealed before I had to disobey it, so I read a prepared statement to a subcommittee of two senators when the law was absent-mindedly renewed in March 1963. I mentioned that I would have to resist the law if it were not taken off the books. . . . I also suggested that free men should not be forced to carry draft cards, and that free men should volunteer to defend their country. I said that we must never surrender in the cause of defending liberty, but that we must seek to maintain that defense by any means consistent with nonviolence, morality, and honor. . . . They ignored any threat and passed the law anyway.

From Pendle Hill I went to work at the New York office of the Committee for Nonviolent Action in June 1963. By now, Local Board No. 10 had sent me the first of three Current Information Questionnaires. Each time I sent back a letter saying I wouldn't fill it out. Then on October 3, I canceled my application for CO status. Back came a I-A on November 12. I wrote back a letter saying I wouldn't accept it and asked for a hearing in December, when I would be visiting my family in Champaign anyway.

December was my deadline for action because Christmas would be a logical time to mount a radical anti-war demonstration. For several weeks beforehand I had been wondering how best to act. Should I burn my card? Give it back personally? Tear it and tape the halves on the door? Block a train to the induction center?

Way back in the March 1960 *Student Peace Union Bulletin,* Karl Meyer had written that "To cry out the truth in the streets of our time is a vocation to truth, to poverty and to prison. . . . Beyond this it is an ultimate prayer to God to save the people." When the inspiration came in late November I decided the demonstration itself could be a prayer for peace, since a prayer is an earnest or humble request. What's more, it being Christmas, I could light my draft card with a candle—or better yet, light a candle with my draft card. At midnight Christmas Eve. And try for a twenty-four-hour fast and vigil in front of the local board office. No: twelve hours would be more realistic. Without fasting.

A slogan for the vigil sign emerged in the same spirit: TO LIGHT THIS CANDLE WITH A DRAFT CARD—A PRAYER FOR PEACE ON EARTH. Some artist friends lettered a Christmas-card-like sign well in advance.

The December 19 hearing at the local board wasn't really necessary, but it was to make my draft resistance as personal as possible, not just a file folder for them to forward to the Justice Department. I could even give them back one of my draft cards in person and still have one left to burn.

The secretary was young and polite. The several anonymous

board members looked glum, except for the chairman who smiled sadly. The clerk of the Urbana-Champaign Friends Meeting gave me a character reference. Then it was my turn.

Face to face confrontation is one of my weak points. My statement was simply a recital of what I had done to defy the draft law. I had wanted to ask them point-blank to resign rather than participate in a bad system, yet could barely muster the nerve to say it. I must have managed to indicate that I was asking for *no* classification, or, that if they didn't resign, they'd have to classify me I-A Delinquent. I also gave them copies of my Senate testimony (which they were as likely to read as *Pravda*). I concluded by laying my registration card on the table, and announced my candle ceremony of five days hence.

The chairman asked for questions, but the others just exchanged blank stares. Someone asked where I was employed. I told them. He exhaled and threw up his hands. The chairman said that I knew the consequences of my action. I mumbled back that I did.

I sent a letter to the editors of the two local papers, explaining my stand ahead of time.

The night before the vigil, I tested a piece of cardboard to make sure it would burn on a cold windy night; it didn't burn very well. A little candle wax smeared on it improved its flammability.

My girl friend was visiting the family over the Christmas holiday and she kept the vigil with me much of the time. Other friends and acquaintances dropped by during the vigil to walk or chat. Late in the evening my parents brought me a grilled cheese sandwich and french fries.

Midnight drew near. By now a throng of two or three dozen had assembled, family and friends as well as reporters and curiosity-seekers. I had a bayberry candle in a silver candlestick ready and a pocket lighter and a pair of tongs to hold the waxed draft card. Suddenly, floodlights went on for movie and TV cameras, and flashbulbs went off. The card flickered and took flame. Jane held the candle. We left it alight for a few minutes; then we blew it out and went home.

By "coincidence," on the day of the vigil the local board issued an order for me to report for the pre-induction physical. But I was getting ready to return to New York to earn some money— and finish work on the pact.

II

In the summer of 1961, some Antioch and Oberlin students tried to talk up a draft-card-return by 500 or 1,000 demonstrators, but the idea quietly expired when there were only a dozen or so who were even vaguely interested. I didn't see much more interest in 1963 either, so I thought mainly in terms of a one-man collision with Selective Service. I had several friends who would resist the draft sooner or later, but they had other plans for now and prosecution depended on the whims of different local boards. Group action seemed like wishful thinking; mass action a dream.

In November 1963, a month before I actually burned my draft card, Russ Goddard came to New York for a meeting of the Committee for Nonviolent Action. He was a friend I'd met the year before at the New England CNVA training program (he and his wife, Joan, had stayed to become staff members). He had personally given back his draft card to a local board in suburban St. Louis the previous March. Meanwhile, another peace-march friend of ours, Dennis Weeks, had just published a letter in *The Peacemaker* refusing induction. Since the arrest of any of us was only a matter of time, Russ suggested he might want to picket his local board in sympathy if Dennis or I were arrested before he was.

Now here was a possibility for joint action against the draft! How about an agreement among the three of us to demonstrate in solidarity for whoever is the first to be arrested? Or an arrest-me-too demonstration? Or, go to jail in solidarity with whoever got the longest sentence? We could even sign a pact in advance.

I jotted down some ideas and discussed them with Russ, who was enthusiastic. We contacted Dennis, but he was more non-committal. Then Barry Bassin, who was a full-time volunteer at CNVA, heard us talking about it and expressed interest.

Dennis eventually decided not to join and the pact was the product of Russ, Barry, and myself. As early as December 8, we were already in provisional agreement that two of us would jail-in for whoever was the first to be "snarfed up," but it was not until April 9, 1964, that we put our initials on the actual text of the pact, and it was June 10 by the time we formally signed a printed copy of it—with only a week to spare.

I believe our painstaking preparation was well worth it. To perform a federal felony on one another's behalf was not something to do in a lighthearted moment.

After discussion, the focus of the pact came to be "immediate prosecution of all" rather than equal sentences. We would be demanding release for all rather than arrest, but we couldn't count on release.

We sought advice from Arlo Tatum of the Central Committee for Conscientious Objectors, among others. He reminded us not to get so tightly bound that there would be an emotional setback or loss of friendship if any of us had to ease out of the pact at some point. He and A. J. Muste agreed to sign as witnesses.

My proposed text was long and legalistic. Russ boiled it down to half a page and we all jiggled it a little more till each of us approved it word for word. We also exchanged memos and working papers. For example, Barry researched a three-page paper on contempt of court—one of the hazards we hoped to avoid. I did a memo, trying to relate the pact to the mainstream of the peace movement because the draft was almost a forgotten issue compared to Cuba, the test-ban, and the advisors in Vietnam. Russ did much of the work of designing the layout and typography for the pact [see page 22].

Next we spent quite a while writing and designing a six-page brochure to explain the pact. It too was a perfect collaboration among the three of us.

These were parts of our statement:

WHY TRY TO GET INTO JAIL? CAN'T YOU DO MORE GOOD OUTSIDE, EVEN IF SOME OF YOUR FRIENDS ARE ARRESTED?
We don't want to go to jail any more than most military

WE, THE UNDERSIGNED, who are opposed to all institutions of military power, nuclear threat, and violent conflict

> *being subject to the provisions of the Universal Military Training and Service Act*
>
> *having noted that the purpose of the Act is to "increase the strength of the armed forces of the United States"*
>
> *believing that the voice of conscience must be followed even when in conflict with the law*

who have therefore declared individually our independence of the requirements of the Universal Military Training and Service Act

> *seeing our friends imprisoned for their principled refusal to follow the dictates of Selective Service*
>
> *knowing that we may soon be prosecuted at the convenience of the Government*
>
> *wishing to be responsible to one another for our shared convictions*

and who do now commit ourselves to honorable, open, and nonviolent resistance to the enforcement of the Universal Military Training and Service Act

HEREBY RESOLVE

that the arrest of any one of the undersigned for violation of one or more of the provisions of the Universal Military Training and Service Act will be considered an arrest of all, and the remaining members of this pact will publicly assert equal liability and will take necessary steps to secure equal treatment — either immediate release of the first arrested or prosecution of all.

Barry Bassin   *Russ Goddard*   *Gene Keyes*

Witnesses: May 18, 1964

A. J. Muste

Neil Haworth

strategists want a thermonuclear war. Like them, we are dealing with a reality—in our case, that the government can send whom it chooses, when it pleases, to prison, for refusing to kill. To challenge this power, enough people must say "us too" when necessary—and follow through—so that jail can no longer be used as a deterrent to the exercise of freedom.

If we try to avoid arrest, or are content to let our friends be arrested instead of ourselves, we hand over to the government the key to deter everyone by jailing a few.

It would be quite a vision if we could foresee many pacts like this—whether written or not. Hundreds—or even tens of people—who declare at the critical moment: "You've arrested him; now arrest us. Either let him go, or do your duty to all of us." While the three of us are not that mass strategy, a jail-in by even one person looks toward such a concept.

That's the vision. Far from reality today perhaps. But meanwhile, friends of ours, and people who believe the same things we do about war and killing, are being arrested and imprisoned. We have watched helplessly one time too many.

No longer.

We knew time was growing short. On January 1, 1964, Barry had written his draft board declaring independence from them as a New Year's resolution. On January 30, I had ignored my physical. On February 28, Russ had received an induction notice for March 19, and sent the board a letter stating he wouldn't even sign an escape-clause form showing that he was a married father. On April 10, Barry got a I-A notice, scrawled "refused" on it, sent it back. April 29 brought me a five-count delinquency notice from the local board—theoretically good for twenty-five years in prison if someone wanted to throw the book at me. Then on May 15, I got my induction notice for May 26.

On May 26, I addressed telegrams to General Hershey, President Johnson, Attorney General Kennedy, and Local Board No. 10. The message was: "THERE IS NO MORAL VALIDITY TO ANY PART OF ANY LAW WHOSE PURPOSE IS TO TRAIN PEOPLE TO KILL ONE ANOTHER. I HEREBY REJECT THE ORDER TO REPORT FOR INDUCTION."

Arlo Tatum had told us to estimate about ten weeks between an order to report for induction and the arrest. So Russ would be entering the danger zone late in May. Sure enough, it was just then that the FBI requested a voluntary interview with Russ at its New York headquarters. There would probably be no arrest yet, but we couldn't be sure. We put on our suits and slipped handcuffs into our pockets. Barry and I lounged in the waiting room reading FBI handouts while Russ answered questions. No action, and it was quite a relief because that week we were not quite prepared for the major demonstration.

A few days later, the Goddards left for St. Louis, intending to get Joan's arrangements made for prison widowhood and to interpret Russ's action to friends, relatives, officials, and the mass media. They arrived on June 17. The next day Russ was arrested.

Now came the crunch. On Saturday morning, June 20, Joan and Julie met Barry and me at the St. Louis airport. Russ was at the St. Louis City Jail and his arraignment was scheduled for that Monday, June 22.

Barry and I set off to explore midtown St. Louis. Should we sit in at the DA's office? At the FBI office in the brand-new Federal Building? Stand up in court? What about East St. Louis, Illinois, across the river, where I would otherwise be prosecuted? We were already worn out from the strain of having events get ahead of us; and the heat was at its St. Louis summer worst. We plodded from one place to the next, wondering if our presence could possibly be worth it.

Monday arrived. Russ had been indicted for refusing to report for induction. How did he plead? Guilty.

Then Judge Roy W. Harper began a soft-spoken little monologue about wanting Russ to be sure he knew what would happen. If Russ had been denied alternate service by the draft board, Harper would arrange for Russ to do two years of hospital work if he wanted to. But otherwise, the judge said, he always handed down five-year sentences for the draft. It would be such a black mark against Joan and Julie, the judge said, if Russ went to prison, so he would release Russ for two weeks to think it over, and let him change his mind if he wished; but if not—

Five years!

The stiffest sentence in recent years for a draft resister. Ostensibly, the judge wanted actual days in prison to be nearly as many as if Russ were a draftee, and parole could be obtained when a sentence was one-third completed—twenty months of a five-year sentence. But parole was problematic and time off for good behavior might still leave Russ forty months in prison, as well as under restriction the remaining twenty.

Just after the court session, two polite FBI agents recognized us. "Are you Barry Basin and Gene Keys?" We voluntarily gave them all the information, chapter and verse, incriminating ourselves about our several and repeated violations of the draft law, and gave them copies of the pact brochure.

How best to use the next two weeks? We spent a good bit of time in strategy discussions on how to provoke the arrest. We had decided we would stay in St. Louis rather than carry the action to Washington or to our own separate districts. The stiff five-year sentence would underscore our solidarity if we sought to face the same judge in the same area as Russ. We would try, at first, to avoid getting deflected into disorderly conduct or contempt of court by not sitting down in the courtroom itself, for example.

We decided to focus the demonstration on Judge Harper himself, who had passed the five-year sentence, rather than any other federal official. A judge has the power to reduce a sentence within sixty days; if we sat in at his office for at least that long we would probably get some kind of reaction. That would make the aim of our demonstration as clear-cut as possible, even if the judge dodged the issue and convicted us on something other than our flagrant draft violations. We would be focusing on his power to release Russ, and a sixty-day fast and vigil at his office would be a very quiet but unavoidable moral confrontation.

Over the July 4 weekend we split up for farewell home visits; the others went to visit Joan's family in Columbia, Missouri, and I went to see my family in Champaign, Illinois. (A separate essay needs to be written about pressure from families, wives, girl friends. Karl Meyer speaks of "trial by parents" as "the most

horrendous ordeal a young radical can face." For the most part,
I had great moral support from my parents, and, for the most
part, Barry and Russ didn't.)

On July 5, we reassembled at a motel in St. Louis. There to
greet us also was Paul Salstrom, just released from the federal
pen at Springfield, Missouri, after two years there for draft
resistance.

I will now lean on Paul Salstrom's account of the court session
on Monday, July 6, from a report he wrote shortly afterward.

When the case was announced, about 10:30 A.M., Russ
stood and stepped forward—followed by Julie, who had
scrambled off her seat and tottered along, ten feet behind.
But Julie hadn't enough nerve to follow her father through
the swinging gate. She ran back to her mother's arms and
gave way to tears.

After the case had been presented, and Russ had again,
as on June 22, pled guilty, he spoke for ten to fifteen minutes about the beliefs which had brought him to where he
stood. His five main points were: (1) his opposition to the
whole system of military defense, and to Selective Service
as a part of that system; (2) that though it might be legitimate to argue that one could work more effectively for peace
and disarmament if he is free instead of in prison, his purpose is broader than merely to work for good causes—that
"all our fine plans for a better world are as nothing if they are
not based upon the individual's personal responsibility and
determination to stand up for what he believes in; jail must
not deter us from principled action"; (3) that the possible
injustice to one's wife and child when one must go to prison
"is relatively small compared with the great injustice against
women and children everywhere, which modern militarism
constitutes"; (4) that the job of resisting conscription by
going to jail should not be left to young and single men
alone, just as in wartime there are married men among those
who, believing in military defense, risk their lives in battle;
and (5) that true freedom is based not on military defense
but on willingness to act even in the face of severe penalties;
therefore he would not back down from his stand against the
Selective Service System.

Judge Harper then spoke for ten to fifteen minutes. He asked Russ if he thought he might change his position if given another two weeks to think it over, to which Russ answered No. The judge then made a series of comments centering around the theme that "if everyone were to believe as you do those who have sacrificed their lives in the past to defend the country would, I believe, have died in vain," that "I love children and so am mainly concerned about the black mark your conviction and sentence will leave on your daughter, who is helpless to do anything about it," and that "I am grateful to live in a country where you can hold the beliefs you do."

And then pronounced sentence of five years.

Barry and I stood up. In crisis situations I can hardly speak or think well on my feet. I was going to make a forceful and ringing announcement of solidarity, but it got lost somewhere in a cotton-throated mumble. According to the newspaper, what I said was, "We have violated the draft law also and deserve the same penalty. Goddard should not be sentenced to prison alone." I wanted to say it better but that would have to do. Salstrom continues:

. . . the judge said, "Just a minute, are you the fellows who sent me those letters?"

Barry then said, "Yes, we're not going to let Russ accept the penalty for draft refusal without doing all we can to secure his release, or else equal treatment"—to which the judge replied, "The only power I could have over you would be the power of a contempt citation."

Gene said, "We are prepared to wait indefinitely in your chambers for our cases to be brought to a conclusion."

Judge Harper threatened again to hold us in contempt immediately, so we left the courtroom and proceeded down the corridor to the anteroom of the chambers. There was a leather couch in front of a low partition, just beyond which was the secretary at her desk. We sat down on the couch and glanced at the clock. It was perhaps 11:20 or so. Our companions waited nearby.

Around noon, Judge Harper returned. He looked disapprovingly at us through his half-moon glasses, once again argued that he had no jurisdiction over us, and warned that we couldn't stay after he and the secretary left for lunch. He went into his office.

At 12:30, Harper came out of his office in civilian clothes. He looked a little flustered and could not seem to decide whether we should be arrested or just thrown out.

> . . . the judge walked down the hallway and summoned the marshals. With them at his side, he addressed Barry and Gene, "If you don't leave right now I'll have you arrested for contempt—OK, take them and throw them on the front steps, and if they come back in the building, arrest them." When he saw that they would not walk voluntarily he said they'd be arrested right away. Gene and Barry then stated flatly that they would not leave voluntarily, and the judge said, "These fellows will carry you out. We don't want to have to hurt you." And to the marshals, "Just pick them up and throw them out on the front steps."

If you have ever tried to carry a mattress somewhere, I suppose you can imagine the difficulty and frustration of carrying inert pacifists. They twisted and maneuvered us out into the hall, got us to the elevator, then off at the main floor and finally, to the outside steps. Barry had been hustled along by an arm lock. "Walk or I'll twist it off," the marshal had said. We were left on the front steps.

> . . . caught an elevator down with eight or ten newsmen and we found the two fellows picking themselves up outside the front door. After a brief interview they reentered and talked themselves past a confrontation with the marshals in the lobby. Back upstairs, the judge's office was found to be locked, and more interviews followed.

The wait that time lasted from 12:40 to 2 P.M. Then the judge returned and stated that unless the friends of the two sit-inners left the building within fifteen minutes, all would be arrested. . . . Joanne Collier felt it a matter of principle that she stay, which she did—throughout Judge Harper's subsequent series of threats to cite her for contempt, along with Barry and Gene.

Joanne wrote in *Liberation* magazine, August 1964:

[Judge Harper] is intellectual and courteous. He doesn't want to sentence "the boys" but he has to. He quickly takes an opportunity to get off the subjects of conscription and mass murder, to discuss civil rights and the courts. When he shows me out, his voice and mood change suddenly: "If you get in the way out there, don't think it's going to bother me to have you arrested. You're married and have a family, but that's not going to make any difference. I won't lose a minute's sleep over it."

Joanne was afraid that with nobody to watch, the marshals would twist us worse. As they did. This time we were hauled to the courtroom. I think two or three of them had my arm in a half-nelson and were carrying me, like a suitcase, by the belt. I was looking at the floor most of the time while trying all at once to relax, not to howl, and to minimize whatever torsion my shoulders were feeling. Barry and I were dumped in front of Judge Harper. In Paul Salstrom's account:

. . . the judge . . . launched into a narrative of the day's events as seen from his point of view. Gene and Barry made comments whenever they felt themselves misrepresented . . . The judge said the two should consider themselves still free to walk out the front door in spite of all they had done.
"Not without Russ," said Barry, who always says just the right thing.
"The same for me," said Gene.
Judge Harper commented that order must be maintained, and pronounced sentences of six months.

The pact was a success!

Now we were all in the St. Louis City Jail, but in different cell blocks. The first time he was there Russ had not been bothered by the other prisoners, but when he reappeared with all the publicity about our action, some of them beat him up patriotically.

I was left in a cell with a big guy who tried to rape me but who was content just to bash me around for a while instead. Luckily, Russ and I were transferred to another cell block with Barry, where there was no further trouble. City and county jails are rougher than federal prison.

That was to be our last time together for the next several years. One by one we were sent to different prisons: Barry to Chillicothe, Ohio; Russ to Springfield, Missouri; and I to El Reno, Oklahoma.

III

But Barry and I were not through with the struggle yet. On December 5, 1964, the two of us were to be released with a month off for good time, but Barry was delayed three more days because he started to grow a mustache. He was given a draft card on the way out, which he left crumpled in an ashtray. I had already been indicted three months earlier—for refusing to report for induction.

A marshal was waiting at the discharge room with handcuffs and chains. There was a lot of confusion and red tape at an Oklahoma City federal court that day before I was finally transferred back to Illinois. Meanwhile, my parents had arranged a property bond for me, so I got a Christmas furlough at home, which lasted three months, till all the legal formalities had run their course. There were joyful reunions with my family and with Joan Goddard, who showed me all the letters and articles and reports that had come in the wake of our demonstration. We phoned Barry, who was in New York, and compared prison experiences. Barry and I agreed we had already carried out the pact as it had been written. We had forced simultaneous arrest and prosecution and, having made that witness, we could now let the law take its own course in regard to our induction refusal, rather than risk again a diversionary charge such as contempt or disorderly conduct. If we had only been jailed a few days at first, we probably would have repeated the demonstration.

My arraignment was on January 5, 1965, at East St. Louis, Illinois. I entered a plea of *nolo contendere* (no contest). But

Judge William Juergens rejected the plea, so I let it be "guilty," and he ordered a pre-sentence investigation. I was not interested in stalling the court with a "not guilty" plea in this case.

Now a difficulty arose: suppose I was offered probation? I had learned from Joan that Russ had given in to strong pressure from her and a lawyer friend of theirs, and had agreed to let them file a memorandum asking Judge Harper to reduce the sentence to probation. (The motion had been denied, which was just as well, I thought, because the language of the brief tended to apologize for Russ's stand.) Moreover, my own girl friend had never been happy about the pact, which seemed to claim most of my attention. Worst of all was the subtle accusation that I just *wanted* to go to prison, enjoyed suffering, liked to be a self-made martyr, and all that. I wavered.

But when the parole officer interviewed me he was dumbfounded to learn that I wouldn't accept probation if Russ couldn't get it, and Russ wasn't about to get it.

The sentencing came nearly a month later, on February 2, and was a five-minute formality: three years. Barry was sentenced on November 18, 1965, to two years. Russ and I were paroled on March 24, 1966. Barry did not want parole restrictions and was released on June 9, 1967. Altogether, I had done eighteen months; Russ, twenty-one; Barry, twenty-three. But Barry had no strings attached to him; parole would ground me till February 1968 and Russ till July 1969.

Was the pact worth it? Obviously, being part of such a joint effort made prison that much more tolerable. Even so, the three of us by ourselves would have taken the same position against the draft. Did we need a pact besides?

I believe the most important thing about our pact was that we were translating a principle into action—not only draft resistance itself, but effective solidarity with a person who is prosecuted for acting in accord with conscience. I believe that any time anyone is arrested for any such cause, there should immediately be five or ten or a hundred or more who will say, "Set him free or take us too" and proceed to enter prison to show they are not merely talking or signing their names.

Resisting the draft should be everyone's business, not just that of young men. This kind of solidarity can involve *anyone* against the draft, of any age, including anyone exempted for any reason, including women.

And not just against the draft, but in any place where some human grit can be thrown in the war machine.

What about you?

Tom Cornell

NOT THE SMALLEST GRAIN
OF INCENSE

The early Christians refused to put a pinch of incense on the altar before Caesar's image, knowing that if they were to recognize the State in this way their lives might be spared.

> . . . The draft card was made a sacrament . . . The card itself does not facilitate the raising of an army in any substantial way. . . . But because it was given this sacramental character, I thought it should be desecrated.

In August 1965, the Selective Service law was amended to make it a crime to knowingly destroy or mutilate a draft card. Congressman Rivers of South Carolina described the purpose of the amendment:

> . . . It is a straightforward clear answer to those who would make a mockery of our efforts in South Vietnam by engaging in the mass destruction of draft cards. . . . If it can be proved that a person knowingly destroyed or mutilated his draft card, then . . . he can be sent to prison, where he belongs. This is the least we can do for our men in South Vietnam fighting to preserve freedom, while a vocal minority in this country thumb their noses at their own Government.

Whether this constitutes a rational legislative purpose or an unconstitutional attempt to suppress free speech was argued before the Supreme Court in the O'Brien case. Tom Cornell's own conviction and six-month sentence for draft card burning may be affected by the O'Brien decision.

This account was drawn from letters, statements, and articles published in the *Catholic Worker*.

I APPLIED for conscientious objection classification in 1956, shortly after graduation from Fairfield University. It had taken

me three years of study and prayer and counseling before I felt
ready to apply for I-O status. I had been trained by the Jesuits
for eight years; they are very strong on prudence, and are very
wary of "enthusiasms." I thought I owed it to myself to give myself enough time to make sure that I was doing the right thing.
It's wonderful to be able to have the luxury of time. The poor
guys that can't go to college and are drafted out of the ghetto at
age nineteen don't have the luxury of three years to mull over
their response to the call. I was sure that by the time I applied
I had weighed all the factors and that I was doing the right thing.
I was prepared to budge not an inch.

The Selective Service System took four years to classify me. I
don't know why the delay. One factor might have been the fact
that the Selective Service System asked the Catholic hierarchy
for judgment on conscientious objection, on the question "Can a
Catholic be a conscientious objector?" . . . The paper was never
made public, but one of our *Catholic Worker* representatives was
allowed to see it. It supported my propositions: one, that a
Catholic might be led by a stringent application of the Just War
theory (see p. 83*n*) to withhold his participation in a war which
he was convinced was unjust; and two, that on grounds of vocation, a Catholic may claim that the will of God for him, as he
has been able to discern it, forbids him to participate in war, following the example of Christ in this particular manner. There can
be an analogy made to the vocation of celibacy. A man has the
right to accept these paths to perfection, regarded as *counsels* of
perfection, rather than *precepts* or binding laws.

I was managing editor of the *Catholic Worker* from 1962 to
1964, having gotten involved in the Catholic Worker movement
back in college days, in 1953. . . . [After] I got my A.B., . . .
I came to New York, for six months worked as a part-time volunteer at the *Catholic Worker*, had a job of my own. Then I went
on a project that the *Catholic Worker* was interested in—re-
settling [in South Carolina] Italian refugees from the Po Valley
floods. I stayed with that for six months, until the project folded.
Then I took a master's degree in secondary education at the University of Bridgeport, and taught for three years, until I had

tenure and a permanent certificate. I felt that a man should have
the knowledge that he can "make it" in the "world," before he
throws himself into the Movement. I have known some people to
live off the Movement, not quite realizing that they were doing
so. I didn't want to have any doubt about myself. I think a man
has to have the internal security of knowing that, if he desires to
marry and raise a family, he can make it in the straight world;
and so, having proven this to myself, I resigned, upon attain-
ment of tenure, and came into the peace movement full time.
. . . It wasn't the first time I had experienced winter without
heat or hot water. When we were children, we went through
many a winter without heat and hot water. My father had tuber-
culosis for ten years before he died in 1948, and my mother
supported us all on $55 a week. The federal government then
gave us a widows' and orphans' pension, which came to about
$42 a month. So poverty was not something new to me.

As I said, it took four years to get my I-O. By that time I had
come into contact with CNVA [Committee for Nonviolent Ac-
tion]. I had participated in the first of the peace walks in 1958.
You might recall it was [a] three-pronged walk: from Philadelphia, New Haven, and some other point, to the United Nations.
I walked from New Haven. In 1960, I was involved in Polaris
Action from its earliest days. By that time I had become convinced
that noncooperation was the best course. I privately burned my
registration certificate and my classification certificate in New
London during that first summer of Polaris Action. I had a good
number of classification certificates left. I had changed status
many times and so had a I-A-O, a I-O, a I-S, a II-S; and because
I subsequently changed classifications (going in and out of
school) I think I had about ten cards. I burned them all at appropriate moments.

There have been many draft card burnings in recent American
history. An outstanding event is that which was led by Dwight
Macdonald here in New York (in 1947, I believe), when some
140 men burned their cards as a response to the beginning of the
Cold War. The federal government made no attempt to prosecute
anyone for this, although obviously, if men burn their cards, they

are no longer in possession of them and are therefore subject to prosecution. The same penalties can be applied to any violation of the Selective Service Act, that is five years and $10,000 for any violation, including nonpossession.

During the Second World-Wide General Strike for Peace, which involved about 150 unemployed or unemployable individuals under the leadership of Judith Malina and Julian Beck, a few of us burned our cards in Washington Square Park. NBC television was there, and asked us to repeat the show. Most of the guys didn't have extra cards. I did, so I burned one with Nelson Barr, and it was shown from coast to coast on NBC television. No one chose to take notice of this. Then, a year later, Christopher Kearns and I led a demonstration in Union Square. Dave McReynolds was the moderator of the meeting, but didn't want to become involved himself in civil disobedience at that time, and so gave the microphone to Chris and to me. We explained the penalties for nonpossession of draft cards, and invited all those who understood the penalties, and were willing to face them, to present their cards. About a dozen young men did. There were four FBI men in the audience (whom we could identify because they were wearing peace buttons, sunglasses, and drip-dry suits). They did not choose to move against us. My other cards went at various occasions. I think I hold the record, having burned ten.

Oddly enough, and very few people know this, we owe the draft card burning law to my good friend Christopher Kearns, mentioned above. . . . He wanted to burn his card at Whitehall Street in July 1965, when CNVA and Workshop in Nonviolence were having a demonstration against the draft. But Chris forgot to bring his draft card, and borrowed one from a member of WIN (Workshop in Nonviolence). It happened that a *Life* photographer was there and photographed Chris burning the card. The photograph appeared in *Life* magazine, opposite the photograph of Staughton Lynd and Dave Dellinger bespattered with red paint. Now this may indicate one of the reasons why we have such trouble with our Congress: the low reading level of our senators and representatives. If they subscribed to *Liberation*, to the *Catholic Worker*, or to any number of other journals, they would not have been so shocked by this photograph in *Life* magazine. But upon seeing it they went berserk. . . . The Congress passed a bill—without debate—making it a criminal offense to burn one's draft card, providing a five-year prison penalty and a $10,000 fine. Reading the *Congressional Record* for the day of the passage of the draft card burning law reveals a high state of hysteria, and an explicit will on the part of the Congress to suppress expressions of dissent.

. . . We knew we had to respond, to demonstrate the punitive repressiveness of this law. We wanted to expose it for what it is, an attempt to stifle protest and the expression of dissent in the United States. More than that, it made the draft card what it had never been before, something for which there had never been a place in American tradition, an internal passport, a license to breathe for every male between the ages of eighteen and thirty-five. The draft card became the symbol *par excellence* of involuntary servitude for the works of death, and the symbol of moral and intellectual suffocation. It deserved to be burned.

When the law was proposed, I spoke to Neil Haworth at CNVA, proposing that we burn draft cards publicly, down at Washington, in front of the White House itself, if we could determine the time when the President would sign the bill into law. We could not find out that information, however, and the CNVA did not seem to think the idea particularly valuable. A few of us persisted in thinking that a public draft card burning would have considerable impact. Among us were Dave Miller, Jim Wilson, and Chris Kearns, and, I think, Terry Sullivan. We proposed to sponsor such an event ourselves; but then Dave Miller, upon being asked to speak at the October 15 International Day of Protest against the war in Vietnam, decided that since he is not a dynamic speech-maker, he would burn his card instead. I advised him against it, thinking that it would be better to do it in a group, with A. J. Muste and Dorothy Day standing beside us, for protection and for greater visibility. But Dave was not impressed with what seemed to me very logical arguments, and in his unique way, did it, and proved that my logic was not sufficient.

. . . If the Holy Spirit had searched the face of this land for the best candidate to be the first to defy this law, he could not have done better. The nation saw in David Miller a normal, healthy young man, who could be their son or brother; a Catholic, evidently moved by the Gospel of Christ—admittedly a dangerous document, one from which immature minds should be shielded, as it seems in times past the Church well knew. He made a fantastic impression.

We then went to the Committee for Nonviolent Action and they decided to sponsor the draft card burning that we had earlier proposed. There was a wrinkle, however. After Dave's arrest, in New Hampshire, most of the people who had considered burning their cards withdrew. As a matter of fact, I was alone committed to burning my draft card in the CNVA-sponsored demonstration.

I felt an obligation to join the younger men burning their cards because I had made the first call for draft card burning in the pages of the *Catholic Worker* in the September 1965 issue. That is, the first call after the bill had been signed into law, on August 30. So I wrote to my local draft board this letter:

Gentlemen:
I am not in possession of my registration or classification certificates. I burned them years ago.
Please send me duplicates. Thank you.

. . . The new cards came in the mail just in time for our abortive attempt (I think it was October 29) in front of the Federal Courthouse. At a preparatory meeting at CNVA, it was found that the people who had been considering burning their draft cards had all withdrawn. I was alone. This upset me a little bit. I thought that perhaps if I had not possessed the damn cards, I would not have written that letter and gotten new ones. But I did have the things, and I knew I could not keep them. If I were to destroy them privately it would seem a waste, and not quite up to the standard of openness and truth which we try to set. So I determined that if I had to do it alone, so be it.

The draft card burning of November 6 . . . was more of a prayer meeting than a demonstration. The more than two thousand supporters maintained a most serious and intense, calm atmosphere. . . . We observed a minute of silence in memory of Norman Morrison, the thirty-two-year-old Quaker leader from Baltimore, who had immolated himself before the Pentagon four days before.

A. J. Muste and Dorothy Day set the tone with their presentations. They spoke from age and experience, with such depth of conviction and commitment that we were deeply moved.

Counter-demonstrators on the other side of 17th Street ranted and chanted "Moscow Mary! Moscow Mary!" as Dorothy spoke. "Give us joy, Bomb Hanoi!". . .

James Wilson, twenty-two years old, a former Maryknoll seminarian on the Christie Street staff of the CW; Roy Lisker, a twenty-seven-year-old mathematician; David McReynolds, thirty-seven-year-old field secretary of the War Resisters League; Marc Edelman, nineteen-year-old office manager for the Student Peace Union, and I delivered short statements explaining our actions. Part of mine follows:

> In the words of Karl Meyer of the *Catholic Worker* in Chicago (printed in the *Catholic Worker*, October 1965), explaining to his draft board why he destroyed his card, "If the penalty for damaging a paper card is so harsh, then the possession of the card becomes the universal act of fealty— incense on the altar of Caesar." The grave crime, we are told, is not the destruction of life but the destruction of a piece of paper.
>
> We cannot let this draconian law stand. Not only is the penalty provided outrageously disproportionate, but the very concept of the law indicates that the U.S. government, albeit accidentally and in a moment of frenzy, has taken upon itself the power to consecrate a piece of paper, invest it with a quality it cannot have, and then exact obeisance for that piece of paper. I can no longer carry that card.
>
> For a number of reasons, I am not eligible for the draft. I

am thirty-one years old, married, and the father of a young son. Selective Service examiners would not accept me. I could let the war in Vietnam pass me by. But I feel that I must associate myself with David Miller, Steven Smith, and Karl Meyer in the open act of destroying my draft card, not in the spirit of defiance of public authority, but as a plea to my government and my fellow citizens to turn away from the present course in Vietnam, to turn away from intimidation and the stifling of dissent and protest at home; and to call upon like-minded people to stand with David Miller and the others who have expressed so forcefully their dedication to the cause of peace on earth.

Many people have asked me how I can expose myself to such severe legal penalties when I have a wife and child to support. I can answer only in this way: fellow Americans, sincere and conscientious soldiers, leave their wives and families and go to Vietnam, subjecting themselves to the risk of their lives. We who have dedicated ourselves to the war upon war, to the development of nonviolence as an effective means to resist tyranny, cannot shrink from accepting the consequences of our conscientious acts. My family and I have faith that God will provide for us as long as we attempt to do His will.

The five of us stood together on the raised platform before the Union Square pavilion, presented our cards, ignited a cigarette lighter, and held our cards over it. Suddenly a stream of water doused us. There was no confusion, no panic, no hesitation. My cards were thoroughly drenched. I despaired of being able to ignite them, so I tore each in half and resubmitted the soggy pieces to the flame. They burned brightly, nonetheless.

I had hoped to try to remain calm, almost solemn, to communicate the better what we were trying to do. But suddenly, as the flames started to consume our cards and my drenched trousers warmed to my body heat, I heard a voice from the crowd, strong and joyful, singing, *This Little Light of Mine.*

The counter-demonstration across 17th Street went into a frenzy. "Treason!" "Burn yourselves, not your cards!" "Burn yourselves!" . . .

Public response was electric. All the media of mass communication gave heavy coverage to the event. Some of the reaction was extremely hostile. A polarization did occur. The reason for this is that the demonstration, along with David Miller's action, posed a question, or a series of questions, the kinds of questions people do not want to have to entertain lest the answers be uncomfortable. The answers threaten to change people's lives. Polarization is dangerous, but it is also necessary to focus the issues, to push the questions in the back of people's minds to the forefront of their consciousness. Reconciliation can then follow.

[*From statement before sentencing, November 1966:*] . . . The Justice Department took it all with unaccustomed gravity. The gods had been mocked.

It is characteristic of states to gather power unto themselves. With the accumulation of power they quickly forget the source and the purpose of that power. They tend to take on divine prerogatives. God alone has dominion over human life. Yet the state usurps that dominion by exacting capital punishment and by prosecuting war, always, mind you, in self-defense.

Throughout the Old Testament there is the recurring theme of idolatry. The early Christians were well aware of it too. Less so today. I submit, Your Honor, that the state today, the Government of the United States of America, is just as much a pagan god as Caesar was in imperial Rome, and that our society is just as guilty of idolatry as the worshipers at Caeser's pagan altars. This new Moloch demands the bodies of our young men in its service, the service of death rather than the service of life, and little by little it exacts the souls of all of us as well, so that in the name of anti-communism and anti-totalitarianism, we are moving toward universal conscription. As part of this process, the Congress took a small piece of paper, of no significant value to anyone but a bartender, and said over it, "Hoc est enim Corpus Meum." The sacrament of the state then had to be honored. So the act of burning the draft cards was for me an act of purposeful desecration and an act of purification. Let not any state have

such trappings, or arrogate to itself such prerogatives. It is
blasphemy! I suspect that the great public interest that was
generated by this symbolic act came from a dim awareness in
the public mind that a blasphemous profanation had been
made of the state religion. How else explain it, that burning
an insignificant piece of paper is a crime, but that burning
children in napalm is sacred duty?

. . . Dave [Miller] went to jail yesterday. It was the most
torturous and cruel court hearing I have ever witnessed. The
judge simply never got the idea. He seemed detached but anxious
to make it appear that he was willing to go as far out of his way
as conceivable to make an accommodation with Dave. He offered
deal after deal, offered time for Dave to talk it over with his
family. Dave very calmly and simply told him, at each point,
that he had examined the alternatives and that he was not going
to procure a new card, or seek I-O status. . . .

Marvin Karpatkin, our lawyer, pointed out the similarity of
Dave's situation with that of the Jehovah's Witnesses who were
convicted on the flag-salute thing. A term of probation for the
parents of the children was that they instruct their children to
salute the flag. Obviously they could not, and so were again
subject to punishment. Dave didn't burn the card to burn a card,
but to get rid of it and to disassociate himself from the Selective
Service System. To procure a new card would be to deny his
whole basis. They make you sentence yourself! "Render unto
Caesar," the judge said. I thought of Maximilian: "You must
render unto Caesar what Caesar needs." "I will never!" said
Dave, not with defiance, but simply as a statement of fact.

Not the smallest grain of incense on the altar. That's what that
card means to me. The smallest grain of incense. Fortunately
I didn't get any probation, just a six-month sentence. I'm really
grateful for such a light sentence, and feel all the worse, on the
other hand, for Jim [Wilson] and Dave. You don't really know
what a sentence like that is until you think of your kids. I had no
idea having a little boy would mean so much to me. And we'll
have another in August. Dave's girl and Jim's boy won't know

them till they're three years old! For me it will be over by next spring, probably. I don't think the government is fool enough to prosecute me for nonpossession of a card after that. At least I hope not. It seems too absurd.

On May 27, 1968, the Supreme Court ruled 7–1 to uphold the 1965 law which makes it a crime to burn or otherwise destroy a draft card; Tom Cornell began to serve his sentence in June 1968.

James Taylor Rowland

AGAINST THE SYSTEM

> . . . I speak of struggling against the system more than I
> mention Vietnam. You see, I feel the war is just a symptom
> of how sick our country is. Today the immorality (or per-
> haps, instead, a business-type ethics amorality, which works
> by expediency, and thus is capable of even the most vicious
> acts) inherent in this system festers as Vietnam; earlier it's
> been Cuba, the Dominican Republic—and tomorrow it will
> be someplace else. This is why we all must recognize, we
> who are doing battle against the war, that it's not just Viet-
> nam we are struggling against, but the very system which
> perpetuates Vietnams.

Much against the wishes of his family, Jim Rowland refused
his student deferment, dropped out of college, and made no
effort to avoid prosecution for draft delinquency. He pleaded
guilty and spoke for himself in court:

> I choose to break the law on the side of justice and man-
> kind.

Rowland was given an indeterminate sentence under the
Youth Corrections Act. If a person is under twenty-two years
of age when convicted,

> the court may, in lieu of the penalty of imprisonment other-
> wise provided by law, sentence the offender, to the custody
> of the Attorney General . . . until discharged. . . . [He]
> shall be released conditionally under supervision on or before
> the expiration of four years from the date of conviction and
> shall be discharged unconditionally on or before six years
> from the date of his conviction.

The intent is to provide flexibility in "correcting the antisocial
tendencies of youth offenders." When applied to acts of civil dis-

obedience based on conscience, there is an element of compulsion to abandon anti-war and anti-draft beliefs and associations.

Beginning some months prior to his arrest, Jim discussed his relation to the draft in a number of letters to a high school friend. The body of this account is extracted from these letters, which were written unguardedly and with no expectation that they would be made public. They reveal a progression of feelings as prison became imminent and then a fact.

I FIRST became acquainted with draft refusal through my cousin, Robert Anderson. Rob's dad mentioned that Rob had refused to be inducted, and was waiting for the U.S. to take the next step. (Rob eventually spent thirteen months on a two-year sentence here at Lompoc.) Thus, Rob showed me that people actually *did* just refuse.

Naturally, it took a long time for me to evaluate and analyze all of the positions possible concerning the draft. The decision to refuse to take the physical, and to be inducted, was a hard decision to make. I was under a lot of pressure to change my position, so I was constantly evaluating my stand—in fact, I did my hardest thinking during the last two months before I was imprisoned. I would suspect my actions here were typical of the actions of other draft refusers; after all, one would have to have an overdeveloped martyr complex to go to prison unaffected by the tremendous contradictions such action entails.

I refused the draft on two grounds, moral and political. Politically: The United States' policies in Latin America, in the Congo, and of course, Vietnam, are the result of imperialism—American imperialism. Such policies must be protested and organized against, and must be confronted directly. Draft refusal is a political act with great potential, and deserves to be given much wider support. As a political act, its effect is all out of proportion to the deed: that of one man going to jail. Morally: quite simply, taking part in the bestiality that is Vietnam would be unthinkable. Can the refusal to cooperate, in any way, with the butchery, the strafing, the napalming, ever be questioned? To be a man, with honor, means to say "no!" to the ugly, gnawing creature that is the U.S. foreign policy.

February 23, 1965: . . . Rob is a noncooperator with the draft. He won't acknowledge the government's right to ask, or rather to order him into the army. The judge said that Rob was in open rebellion with the government, and to sentence him to less than two years would be a disservice to all of the "boys" who are giving two years of their lives to the army. Rob considers the whole U.S. government to be immoral, and that is why he won't cooperate with it. When you look at what the sovereign government of the land of the Yahoos did in the Congo, in Guatemala, Syria, Cuba, and is doing now in South Vietnam, it becomes increasingly difficult to disagree with him. . . .

May 17, 1965: Many times I have wondered whether it might not be better to die now, rather than continue to live. But I have a curiosity about my fellowman; were I to die now, it would be like leaving one hell of a good play in the middle of the first act. The hero, mankind, may end by having all his hopes ruined, but I still want to see the end, even if the play makes me morose. Mankind has made some progress, and barring the destruction of it all, I think it just might make something of itself someday. We are now witnessing the key to the betterment of all the peoples of the world: the destruction of capitalism, and the rise of socialism. So long as one class exploits another, as long as profit is more important than the human being toiling to earn that profit, as long as governments continue to function for the benefit of the wealthy and/or privileged, then mankind cannot attain a true civilization, wherein no one need worry about the rent, food, medical bills, or old age. Yes, I think I'll stick around to see this little play. There's an interesting world outside our door—let's go and watch. . . .

You asked if I were motivated by anything. Yes, by a desire to know and learn, to experience new knowledge, to evaluate, to participate, to create and change, to better, and hopefully never worsen. That's it.

July 20, 1966: Well, it looks like things are going to be moving right along here. I awoke this morning to find that I had been reclassified I-A, and am to report to a San Francisco draft board on Monday, presumably to be drafted. I, as you know, intend to refuse to be drafted by this son-of-a-bitchin' system, so I guess before long I will be in prison for my independence. Frankly, I had no idea that it would come so soon, but I am rather glad it did, because it's pretty nerve-racking, having this hanging over my head. I have known that it would come someday for a long time, and now that it has come, I no longer have this dread.

. . . I frankly don't feel like writing much. I'm going to walk in the city for a while, until I regain my equilibrium.

July 26: . . . I probably didn't make myself clear in the last letter, as to the exact situation here, so I will now explain the exact process of draft refusing. First of all, what I had just received was a form to fill out, asking all sorts of questions, and also an order to report for my physical, which comes a couple of weeks before you are actually drafted. Since I am protesting the whole capitalistic, imperialistic setup, I naturally refused to fill out any of their goddamn forms, and I also refused to report for the pre-draft physical. This means I will be declared "delinquent" by my draft board, and they will send me a notice to report for immediate induction, which I of course will ignore—or at most, send them a letter back, explaining why I cannot be a part of the draft, and why I must protest against the U.S. government.

The only way to stop the aggressor is to physically confront him. To accept a conscientious objector status in the hope of registering some protest against the government is to engage in spurious reasoning. To become a CO is no protest at all, for one is neatly pigeonholed by the government, no confrontation having actually taken place; and without a confrontation, all propaganda value is lost. Therefore I find no alternative but to register an effective protest against the U.S. government by refusing to report for military service.

. . . It seems to me that if one categorically makes the assertion that there is free will, then one is an ass. It doesn't take the omnipotence and omniscience of a god to limit one's choice of action. For instance, I have a desire to go to school right now, to work a little, and to generally hang loose. But, that choice has been precluded. So, I can exercise my free will in one of several ways: I can allow myself to be inducted into the army; I can go to jail for my beliefs; or I can get the hell out of the country. Those are the only choices open to me. I was not able to use my will to pick the choices. I can exercise my will only after the preliminary selection of choices has been made for me. And, in my psychological background, I imagine one could discern the reason for my being unable to get out of the country, hence the choice is further limited by forces beyond my conscious control. Only two choices were left to me, and I chose the one which to me seemed most ethical. The puzzle is, did I really have free will regarding those last two choices, or did my ethical training and belief preclude even that? Hmmm. . . .

August 12, 1966: About this draft thing. Yes, I have looked at the pragmatic side of it. I, of course, have thought about getting a job in the future, but I don't really think that that matters. I intend to go back to school, if that is at all possible. If it turns out that an M.D. is out of the question, then I will go for a Ph.D. If I can't go back to school, because of my record, then tough shit, I just won't be able to go. I cannot let a thing like that hinder me at this time. The important thing is for a protest to be made against the criminal policies of our government. Whenever a person undertakes the task of *really* protesting his government, not just marching around with a goddamn picket sign, but really protesting, he has to be mature enough to realize just what the consequences are likely to be. When Goodman, Chaney, and Schwerner were working in Mississippi in 1964, they realized what they were up against, but they went ahead. As it turns out, they lost their lives in the bargain. And so it is with all people who see the choices, who are free to make the choices, whose histories are not yet determinate. But, for all that I have lost, there is one thing I have gained, which can now never be taken away from me, and that is my self-respect. Now that I have made this very important decision, in the future I need not worry whether or not I will do the right things according to my conscience—I know I shall. If I had failed here, the future would have been always in doubt, but now I have no fear. I think the worst kind of fear, of dread, is the fear that you yourself will fail to act according to your conscience. That fear is now gone. I am one of the freest men in this country. Can you understand that?

When Thoreau was jailed for refusing to pay his taxes for American imperialism, Emerson came along, looked at Thoreau in prison, and asked, "What are you doing in there?" Whereupon Thoreau answered, "What are *you* doing out *there?*" So, you see, I am not bothered by going to prison. What bothers me is that so many self-styled "radicals" are not going to prison. A radical should make of himself such a thorn in the side of the government that it has but one choice, and that is to imprison him.

August 20, 1966: Early in the week I received my "delinquency notice" from my draft board, and the day before yesterday, I received my order to report for induction. According to the order, I am to report to Local Board 33, at 106 East Roosevelt, the twenty-ninth of this month, at 8 A.M. Now, I'll have you know, I won't even be up at 8 A.M. I have already sent the board another letter telling it that I won't be there the twenty-ninth, or any other date. Now the waiting begins, and we shall see just what they intend to do. . . .

September 21, 1966: Still no word on when I am to be arrested. You can never tell when the ax will fall, only that it will, some day. I feel like one of the Franks, that I ought to be living in hiding.

October 31, 1966: When I wrote the last letter I was so much in the dumps. . . . I haven't been that depressed in years. Depression is not for me. . . . When I was younger I had periods of depression, deep, pit-like depression. I thought I had grown out of this, but I see I haven't. The whole draft thing has made me depressed, I guess. I think you understand this. In fact, I know you do. Prison is a break in my life, I'm burning my bridges behind me. Those left on the other shore are going to have to build their own bridges over to me if they want me. I'm no longer making the effort. The people in my past who hate me, who don't understand me, who patronize me, who tolerate me, and become puzzled by me, are gone. Friends, some good, some not so good, are probably lost. Does it matter? Well, beneath my iconoclastic exterior, I do care; but sometimes it is more important to make a stand, though your friends turn against you. Whether you turn against me or not is not a worry. I know you see the logic of my actions. And, it's easier to be hated than tolerated.

. . . It is easily imaginable that I will get four or five years. I don't feel like a martyr, and I haven't a martyr's desire to be pilloried so he will be admired. That is scant compensation. Besides, most people who question me don't have any feelings but a wonder that crazymen such as myself are allowed to run loose. Well, you just do what you have to do. I feel lonely. But what is my loneliness compared with the crying of burned children in Vietnam?

[*Arraigned, December 19, 1966*]

December 21, 1966: . . . I did spend a night in the city jail. Jesus, what a jail! The worst in all creation, I am convinced. The feds don't accredit it for federal prisoners—they can be held only overnight. I was all set to be taken to Tucson (actually Florence), when my parents got me out on my own recognizance. . . . It's better than being in prison, generally.

[*Tried, February 6, 1967*]

Federal Prison, Lompoc, California, March 19, 1967: I got here February 23rd, so I'll be moving out of here into another unit (cell block) this week. All new prisoners stay in A & O unit a month or so for tests, exams, lectures, etc. But I won't be in the other unit long, because I am here on a sixty-day observation only. My number, YE-253, stands for Youth Evaluation, which means they doubt my sanity (or at least the judge feels he needs more information before sentencing me). So, I'll be back in Florence in late April, for holding until my court date. Then I get my final sentence, which will probably be the Youth Corrections Act, a splendid piece of misfortune which will keep me here up to four years. Cheers. They have to release me January 23rd, 1971, no matter what, though, and it looks like I will be here a while, as paroles for draft refusers are scarce now. To have a radical's conscience, one has to pay a radical's price, and it's worth it.

. . . Stay cool, and don't worry, I'm fine. I look ahead confidently. My convictions haven't changed—rather, I am positive, I am unshakable, in the belief that a better world can come about through radical socialism. We must remain radical, and live radically, without compromise.

March 19, and 24, 1967: . . . I really have apreciated the letters; you are the only one, outside the family, who has written me. Perhaps other letters have been turned back, and if so, I'll feel better; but I doubt it. In prison you certainly find out who has been so busy with their lives that they can't spare a few minutes a month to pen a letter. I'm glad I have so many busy friends. . . . The list is certainly restricted, but beggars can't be choosers here, now, can they?

March 24, 1967: . . . I can't conceive of myself fitting into the American Dream . . . I have too much to do, to fit into any pigeonhole. Prison has given me a chance to solidify, as no other experience could, my politics. I know why Joseph Vissarionovich Dzhugashvili chose the name Stalin—steel; I, too, feel like steel. I'm not bitter, just determined. I know how to live, how to make a living, within the system, and yet at the same time work to destroy the system, and replace it with a system built for men, not for profit. That is my perspective. And that is why the prison doesn't get to me very often. Actually, this place has only gotten to me once since I've been here, and that was because I did not maintain my perspective. I can take most of the nonsense here with equanimity. Actually, I'm able to maintain my composure more easily here than on the streets, because I don't have the radio or TV news to irritate me constantly. I haven't subscribed to a newspaper yet, as I'm to be here only a few more weeks, anyway. When I get back, I'll then subscribe to the papers and magazines. I'll be in Phoenix a month from now; it will take no more than three weeks to sentence me and ship me back here, so I'll take my magazines and papers about two months from now, and get them in June.

You see, by little devices, such as waiting for magazines that won't be delivered until June, I make the time go quickly.

[*Indeterminate sentence under Youth Corrections Act, four years maximum, March 25, 1967.*]

July 18, 1967: . . . I'm not in a cell any more; I'm in a dorm, and it is easier to move about now. I just sally down the way to get a drink, or take a shower, or leave the unit. The next time I'm in a cell will be in C unit—semi-honor, with the doors open all of the time. That is what I call having the best of both, mobility and privacy.

July 23, 1967: . . . The time goes quickly, but the end seems nowhere in sight. . . . There is no such thing as "easy" time, really. It's all relative, making some time "easy" and some "hard." There is an expression here (we all use it): "I'm doin' hard time." It means you want to be free; or, that you're worried or nervous; or . . . just about anything to anybody, but basically, it expresses a desire to do something coupled with the inability to do so. . . . I am depressed as hell. I'm listening to a couple of guys singing "500 Miles," and that makes me even more depressed. . . .

July 31, 1967: In the library, I'm there an average of five and a half hours a day, Tuesday through Saturday. That takes up enough of my time so I'm busy, yet still leaves me enough time to do what I want to do; I read and sit in the yard quite a bit.

Ah, yes, at least a thousand times I've gone over my college times, and high school, and thought, "Who'd ever thought just four years ago . . ." It's a game all convicts play. Four years ago I was just out of high school, and waiting to enter college. Brother, it went so quickly, and now I'm in a federal prison. But, I would not change the steps that led me here.

Hopefully, more men will refuse. Thousands have gotten out of the draft through various means: II-S deferments, admitted drug addiction, feigned homosexuality, and the like. But the question is—is merely saving one's own self enough? Or does a stand, a moral and political stand, need to be made? Obviously, I feel men should refuse to cooperate, not in the pitifully small numbers of today, but by the hundreds. The way to point out the illegitimacy of the system is not by taking draft physicals, trying for deferments, etc., for every act of this type furthers the aims and control of the system, and lends it greater legitimacy. Only by standing up and saying, shouting, "We won't go!", is it possible to begin to build a cohesive movement in the struggle against the system.

Jayne Switzer and Judy Galt

WIVES OF IMPRISONED OBJECTORS

"Hard time" may be served outside prison as well as in. Marion Brown, the wife of a soldier whose refusal of orders and efforts to win conscientious objector status dragged out for more than a year before a terminal sentence was imposed, wrote as follows:

> . . . I must admit that I am constantly up and down. Having things with Dave finally somewhat settled and determined has helped a lot, but I miss him more than ever, and as I begin to feel like doing things more with other people, I am constantly reminded of how I would like things to be and how they are not. To feel married and always be lacking a husband is not easy. And though it is nothing new, I still resent being identified as Mrs. Conscientious Objector. This has really messed up my sense of my own identity. I must admit that I long for the normal life.
>
> . . . The thing that was hardest during his confinement, and really through this whole thing, has been that, well, people seem to lose sight of the fact that we are more than one big court case, and indeed we lose sight of this ourselves sometimes. People are always asking me, "How is Dave?" "What is the situation with Dave now?" One day in December someone asked me, "Marion, how do you like student teaching?" I was so touched that someone thought to ask, and people know this is something I am really involved in and love to talk about, that I actually got all broken up.

Jayne Switzer

Jayne Switzer, whose first child was born while her husband was in prison for noncooperation, felt that what sustained them was that "we did it together."

BOB AND I knew from the beginning of our relationship that separation was imminent. Bob was under indictment for two violations of the Selective Service System when we decided to marry and then, to conceive a child.

We met in Albany, Georgia, early in 1964, when we were both participants on a peace walk, and again in Chicago, when each of us returned home for the summer. Together we picketed, leafleted, and on July 31, stood and burned Bob's draft card on the federal courthouse steps. Draft card burning was relatively unheard of at the time and our act provoked more curiosity than hostility from the crowd that gathered.

The decision to direct our efforts towards protesting the Selective Service System was difficult for both of us. I had planned to spend the summer working with the civil rights movement in Americus, Georgia, and Bob had planned to work in Selma, Alabama. We both felt, though, that radicals had to devote more attention to the draft, particularly with the escalating war in Vietnam.

In the weeks that followed, we decided to marry, despite the obvious difficulties we faced. We felt that together we could accept the consequences of our actions, and we realized that prison would be a threat throughout our lives if we continued to work for the movement. And so, on September 20, 1964, we became joined in a simple ceremony among friends.

For the next six weeks we endured trial continuances and the fear of momentary imprisonment. At night we held hands tightly, expecting each day to be our last. We decided that, despite the selfishness of having a child, we wanted to have as much as we could to hold us together during our separation. Shortly before Bob's trial began in mid-November, we learned that I was pregnant and then, during his trial, I began to miscarry. While I was home resting, I received the news that he had been found guilty of two violations of the Selective Service Act: refusal to carry a draft card and refusal to be inducted into the military. He was denied bond and dragged from the courtroom by a handcuff.

The two weeks that followed were the most difficult we faced. I sublet our apartment, moved in with my family, who were sympathetic with Bob's position, and found a secretarial job. The greatest difficulty was not being able to communicate with Bob in any way. Visiting was not permitted for two weeks, and Bob had refused to sign censorship papers, so we couldn't write.

The full impact of prison struck me on our first visit at Cook County Jail. I had to wait on a long narrow row of steps leading to the main door until I was admitted with two other visitors. Inside the huge door I waited, gave my name, identification, and relationship with the prisoner, underwent frisking and was relieved of shoes, purse, and chewing gum. At this point I was admitted to another long hall where I waited until I was led into a small cell and locked in with three other visitors. Inside the cell were four small glass windows with grating beneath them to talk through. After a brief wait, Bob appeared in front of the window, pale and thin from his two-week fast. To talk, we had to bend down and shout through the grating, which meant that we couldn't talk and look at each other at the same time. I shouted to him that I hadn't lost our baby and that he was going to be a father. Happily he rushed forward and kissed me, five inches on the other side of the glass window.

On November 20, Bob was brought before Judge Julius Hoffman for sentencing. The courtroom was packed with sympathizers on one side and the army and veterans on the other. Several Episcopal clergymen came as character witnesses for Bob and attempted to point out to the judge the moral law that compelled Bob to act as he had. Judge Hoffman refused to hear their arguments and allowed only Bob to speak. Bob read a prepared statement in which he explained his actions; it was sincere and had an obvious emotional impact on the spectators. The court was silent when he finished and we all waited tensely until the judge pronounced sentence—two three-year terms, to run concurrently. I cried with relief after hearing the sentence, because it was shorter than we had expected, and because at last we knew how long our separation would be. Bob and I were permitted to visit briefly on the opposite sides of the courthouse bars; then he was returned to the county jail.

Three days before Christmas I received notice from the federal authorities that Bob had been transferred to Sandstone, Minnesota. I was relieved to have him out of the county jail and happy he had not been sent to Chillicothe, a prison known for its violence, where several other noncooperators with the draft were imprisoned.

On Christmas day, Bob's family and I drove through blinding snow to Sandstone, fifty miles south of the Canadian border. The temperature was 40° below zero as we approached the desolate town, consisting of two rundown hotels, three restaurants, and a small chain of stores, standing on opposite sides of the railroad station.

As we reached the pale yellow brick institution, encircled by the houses of the prison personnel, I was surprised to find that it looked like a rural elementary school. Inside we waited in a comfortable waiting room and were admitted together to see Bob. In a few minutes he was sitting next to me and, for the first time since his imprisonment, we could touch. The unexpected joy of his nearness made me cry our entire visit.

For the next seventeen months, Bob and I were able to write often, sometimes two or three letters a day. We were able to visit frequently, as the visiting privileges were flexible and generous. The first several months, we visited once every four weeks. I would arrive early in the morning by train and stay at the prison from 9 A.M. until 4 P.M., Saturday and Sunday. Saturday night I would stay at the hotel in Sandstone and suffer the stares of the townspeople and the mercenary attitude of the woman who ran the hotel. I was annoyed by the nine-dollar charge for a room with no bath and, seemingly, no heat. The restaurant closed before visiting hours at the prison were over, so, after not eating on our first visit, I brought fruit with me. The woman who ran the hotel provided a shuttle service to the prison, which cost $2.50. When the weather was not too unbearable, I would plod through the snow the four miles to the prison. In April, when I was seven months pregnant, I walked to the prison and arrived slightly blue from the cold. A secretary drove me home.

During our visits, the rules allowed us to embrace on arrival and departure, and to hold hands. For fifty cents I was able to buy a box lunch and we would eat together. I was also permitted to buy cigarettes and Coke in the waiting room and bring them to Bob.

Occasionally, on our visits, Bob's parole officer would come to try to convince me to have Bob join the Army as a means of release. On our first encounter he said, "I know Bob is probably a better Christian than I am, but we do have to obey the law." I asked him whose law he considered more important, the law of God or man, and he left the room.

We had adjusted to the routine of daily letter-writing and monthly visits when our daughter, Karen, arrived prematurely, early in May. Having been promised a call to Bob after the baby's birth, I eagerly called the prison. The officials refused to let me speak with Bob, even after I explained that the baby was having difficulty breathing and was in danger of death. "If she dies, call back," the guard told me, and hung up.

During the first anxious days following Karen's arrival, my only comfort was a tradition Bob and I began early in our separation. At exactly 10 P.M., we would stop whatever we were doing and think of each other. At least I knew that he was with us in spirit.

Following Karen's birth, our visits became less frequent. The little money I had saved was spent quickly on her incubator care, and it was weeks before she was able to make the long trip to Sandstone. For the first time, I had to rely on the peace organizations for financial assistance. I was relieved to find that Peacemakers [see p. 328], a Cincinnati-based organization, could send me the $65 a month I requested. The cost of traveling, however, was approximately $125 per visit, so until Bob's release, we saw each other about once every three or four months.

When Karen was two months old, my family moved to Pennsylvania and I began living with my brother and three other graduate students in Madison, Wisconsin. Aside from the letters to Joan Goddard, Michele Nyysolla, and Darlene Hoffman, all women with husbands in prison, I had little social contacts.

In November 1965, Bob went before the parole board and we both counted the days until their reply. We were crushed when we learned that he had been denied. Karen and I flew to Minnesota to be with Bob shortly after receiving the news and arrived at the prison an hour before closing time. After a tearful visit, we learned we would not be permitted to see each other again for two days, as the visiting hours had been changed without notice. Angry and depressed, I returned to Madison.

In the months between Bob's parole denial and his final release, I felt the first bitterness towards the officers at Sandstone. Instead of engaging them in friendly conversations as I had previously done, I was cold and withdrawn. All feelings of dislike vanished when we received news of Bob's release date.

I was visiting my family in Pittsburgh, trying to accept the fact that Bob might be away another year, when I saw the air mail letter from Sandstone. After reading the first line, telling me of his impending release, I called Bob's parents in Chicago and together we laughed, cried, and made hurried plans for the future.

On May 18, 1966, Bob came home. Walking off the plane, he picked Karen up and the three of us began life as a family.

Friends ask us if we would do the same thing again, and our answer is "yes." Prison was painful and yet it was beautiful in many ways. Through prison we learned that we could still say "no" to an injustice, and that only by saying "no" could we be free. The iron bars of prison were temporary, and now we have free minds. When our children ask us what we did to stop the killing, we can answer them.

Judy Galt

This account was written in February 1968 at "a particularly tense and impossible time—between parole hearing and parole decision." Parole was granted.

I AM NOT a political theorist, nor could I be described, by any stretch of the imagination, as an activist. My one qualification for writing about draft resistance is that my husband is serving a four-year prison sentence for refusing induction. I do not pretend to understand what must be done to abolish the draft and bring about the basic social change our society so desperately needs; I have few "Roman thoughts." I do not have the revolutionist's commitment to die for a better future for someone else. I want to be happy and have babies and love my husband. If I do not ignore the world's ugliness, it is not because I wouldn't if I could—I would, gladly—it is because that ugliness threatens even the simple things I want from life. I will not presume to argue that going to prison to fight the draft is wrong —although that is my impulse—but I will try to describe Fran's and my experience, hoping that in so doing I may dissuade those who would make the choice too lightly and, perhaps, help prepare those who go ahead anyway.

Each case is, of course, unique, no matter how much all have in common. In Fran's case, there would have been no hassle obtaining a I-O classification if he had applied: he grew up in a pacifist household, the son of a minister who went to jail rather than accept a clergy deferment during World War II. But the alternative of cooperating to get legal status as a conscientious objector had been ruled out before I met Fran. I knew what his position was when I fell in love with him, and when I married him. We felt our love was strong enough, and each of us was tough enough, that we would be able to sustain our marriage while he was in prison without the nourishment of living together and lying together. So far we have succeeded, but we did not know how hard it was going to be. Had we known, Fran would not have gone ahead. Not knowing, he did what he then felt he must do.

[*Francis Galt wrote the following letter to Lee W. Smith, July 1967:*] . . . Any person whose mind and senses are open to the world will naturally devise many . . . principles, of greater and lesser importance to him. These principles may, at times, clash, as mine did when it came time for me actually to go to prison. A principle against contributing to an injust, rapacious, and murderous institution led me to the brink of prison. A principle (and more than that, a profound, controlling feeling) of love for my wife and concern for her happiness led me away. The dilemma was acute, and nothing in my experience had equipped me to deal with such a sharp clash of principles. Having no principle on principle-conflict to guide me, I chose what seemed at the time of greater significance and came to prison. (Not really that my love for Judy ever seemed less significant—it merely seemed somehow tied up in it and dependent on it: I could not perfectly love Judy if I became a party to injustice and hatred.)

Now, though the conflict is still present, I would choose the other. . . . It should have become evident to me that, given the particular structure, attitude, and inaccessibility of our government, my noncooperation would have no practical effect whatsoever, and that even this would not serve totally to divorce me from the roots of the circumstances I deplored. . . . I became not even a bee in a block-headed bonnet; means of disposing of me and "my type" had been fully integrated and institutionalized into the system, to preserve our silence and their sanctity.

If going to prison could be effective politically, if it could be meaningful in terms of the first causes of principles, then it would be excusable and even admirable. But if one suffers —and causes others to suffer—for a principle which will have no beneficial effect on anyone, and whose breakage would have no deleterious effects on anyone, he is suffering only for pride in a hollow principle.

It is highly possible—though impossible to determine comparatively—that while I am locked up, Judy is less free even than I. This is my sadness, my regret, my guilt, and yet I can't resolve it until I too am free, for I love her not only abstractly and reverentially, but personally, passionately, selfishly, and I do not want to grant her her freedom from me even if she would—which I neither think nor hope she would—take it.

Fran found it was impossible to cope with prison in terms of "why he was there," soon after arriving. Life in prison is lonely, painful, and trying; it must be met day by day on the level of just getting along with where you are, and that uses up your energy well enough. Both of us came very quickly to the belief that prisons, as they exist, are unjust whatever the offense may be. Maintaining some small sense of your own dignity in an institution where there is no privacy, where every moment is regulated, where hundreds of degrading humiliations are the daily routine, hanging onto your manhood in such a place is hard work.

Prison, like the mystic vision, is impossible to prepare for and to verbalize as one lives it. I thought I would have certain problems while Fran was gone, for instance, the problem of finding work and the problem of solitude. Instead of these external difficulties, I find my whole self-concept and love being subtly undermined. I am part of the total plan to emasculate Fran because I am intensely close to him, and yet I am free. During Fran's imprisonment we have tried to sustain an intense and fulfilling marriage. It is nearly impossible. We love each other very much, and, alone, much of what I do seems dry and sterile—for instance, my scholarship. My ideas need to fire his mind if they are to grow or even seem significant. We have some of this relationship, of course, even now; we both write every day and I visit every month. This does not begin to replace living together. It cannot. Our letters are as free and open as possible, but we cannot forget that someone else must read our most intimate and frightened feelings. Once even, a letter, in which I told Fran of a dream I'd had, was returned to me marked "obscene." Also, we now face a terrifying abyss. We have worn out the medium of paper and pen. We need more total communication. We've done what we can with words, and the frustration becomes more and more intense. I feel the separation blighting what is beautiful and productive in our love. I must admit to Fran that the ecstatic love is becoming impossible to maintain in this situation. I am worried about our marriage.

Fran expresses better our belief that it is more important to "be a poem" than to sacrifice our hopes for an abstract principle. He says in one letter:

My love for you caught up in a terrible eli eli lamma lamma sabacthani threnody of moan. I sit disconsolate and woebegone while your heart races on encompassing me, but still I cannot quell this passionate insistence of who's-reading-verses-to-her-now beside the still or mighty waters. This hell, this hard-time Pandemonium rages on (Whatsforchow? Leavinginthemorningseeyou. Wannaplaycards? Ohmygod.) and you are a distant dream of a future Elysium. And you lost and lonely too take a drink, sublimate, write a letter, grow in your sorrow and ask—why. Once there were answers, once solutions. Or maybe those lost days are only dreams of a dusty youth and never were—when the questions were simple and we were too. Nothing. No hope. Only and over-ridingly my love for you. My need. My fears of what would I do if suddenly you weren't there. Oh Love Love Love Love. What is more natural or simple in magic than you and me together—and we cannot be. And our lives are caught on Asian shores where ignorant armies—over and over with their new adhesive napalm, their more effective antipersonnel bombs, their politicians, their lies, their contrived assassinations, their propaganda of the land of the free. . . But I am not free. But you are not free. But WE. . . And again and again and again I need your magic calmness, your fantastic smallness beside me. To cry new tears, to dance new dreams, to make new and various love in excitement and tranquility. No hope but you. Nothing but to love you. . . . Dreams. Visions. Mystic prayers. Crazymad dreams. Together. Quiet. Or not. Walking in the wild rainstorm with leaves blowing at our feet. The epiphany of the shower. Tomorrow. Always and ever tomorrow. We define ourselves by each other. But so many others want to push their definitions onto us. So long, so very long till I hold you again.

Once I had a dream of a magic country of liberty and justice and ideals. She tore my dream from my head and showed me her dungeons. Now I want only to be left alone, to wander strangely with my weirdly wonderful wife down distant paths which lead to rivers and perhaps to fall, jump, or be pushed into the completeness of the water. To climb laughing from the wet and ascend a tree where we own all we see because we have made a forever bond with life.

Why *is* all this? . . .

Oh Love I miss you so *much*. These interminable weeks between visits are so hard.

Please love me. And forgive my wallowings.

"Once the judge says, 'The prisoner is remanded to the custody of the Attorney General,'" according to Fran, the gesture of protest is over, the role in the movement is done for the duration of the sentence. And as one is ground between the massive mill wheels of the United States Department of Justice, one of the first things to be crushed is the belief that his action had made any difference in the imperial polity. You sense almost immediately that the system is designed to handle you; the only problems you have caused, you have caused yourself and those you love.

It is a terrible and frightening thing when you try to remember what it was like before your husband was in prison and these memories grow less real than the letters and the visits you have become to each other. It is an awful thing to be able to see each other for only sixteen hours every month, to have a guard tap your husband on the shoulder if you kiss too long when he comes in or just before he leaves, to sit across from each other unable to touch in any way but holding hands. It is castrating for the man and it emasculates the woman too.

Sometimes, when I read about Regis Debray or Che Guevara or the valiant resistance of the Vietnamese people to U.S. genocide, I wonder if I am too petty and selfish, if I am somehow immoral for feeling that I suffer, but I don't believe that, really. Julius Lester has pointed out that the romantic images of revolution are not at all romantic when you have to live them; and that "have to" should not be slighted. Because that is when sacrifices are made: when they have to be, when men no longer have a choice, or when the range of choice is so narrow that the victim of the situation says, "What the hell; I've got nothing more to lose!" That time may be coming, even for those of us who don't live in the ghetto, but until it does we do have something to lose—relationships with each other we ought to try to hang onto. I don't believe it is counterrevolutionary to live close to those you love and try to keep your family together, and if it is, then I have little hope that what is wrought by a revolution threatened by these things will be any better than the antihuman society which holds us captive today. I am afraid there will be more than enough who will have to go to prison and even die, but I hope that will be something done to us, against which we resist; we do not need, I think, any more who choose to do it to themselves.

David Gearey

THE DOWNPOUR OF ABSURDITIES

David Gearey applied for status as a conscientious objector after receiving an induction order. The draft board refused to reopen his classification or allow any appeal rights at such a late point. Gearey refused induction in July 1965. He was sentenced to two years in prison in April 1966, by the United States District Court. The United States Court of Appeals for the Second Circuit ordered a new trial because they said it was not clear that the draft board had denied the CO classification. They also ruled that if a man becomes a conscientious objector after an induction order is issued, his claim must be fully considered by Selective Service. "The realization that induction is pending and that he may soon be asked to take another's life, may cause a young man finally to crystallize and articulate his once vague sentiments." (If the objection existed but was not claimed before the induction order was issued, the classification could not be reopened.) The "Gearey principle" has helped other late-maturing conscientious objectors within and even outside the Federal Courts in the Second Circuit. Most other Circuits still maintain that an application for conscientious objection need not be considered after an order to report for induction has been issued.

Gearey's own case was tried again by the District Court in April 1967 and Gearey was not permitted to testify at the hearing to determine whether the draft board had denied the CO classification without "any rational basis in fact." The court upheld the draft board's opinion that the claim was not genuine. This time the Court of Appeals agreed with the District Court. The Supreme Court has refused to hear the case and Gearey's conviction stands.

ONE DAY I became eighteen years old. My recollections center primarily around anticipations of celebrating the occasion by making a ritual visit to the nearest tavern. Society was accepting me as a paying member with a license to drink alcohol, and I had every hope of satisfying their trust in me. There was another factor however, which effectively helped to annoy the day, since it required me to move my lazy body to a local Selective Service center in order that they could welcome me as a possible source of fire power. The day was brisk and overcast, and I found I wasn't thirsty after all, but I succumbed to the comfortable challenge offered by a glass of beer. I also meekly gave in to the magnetism and authority of the local draft board. The offense to my personal freedom was less threatening than the fear of unbelieving bartenders when I showed up without the magic card.

My feelings about the draft were so vague that one could say I had none. The ominous, bureaucratic structure which was sitting like a great mother hen over me and all the other eighteen-year-olds, warming us till we could be properly hatched, sat so subtly and softly that neither I nor my companions had the notion to pinch its bottom, or in any way disturb its well-supported perch. It was to be respected and obeyed, as was all authority; it was there and apparently necessary, guiding the behavioral reins and making officious pronouncements. All we could do was abide, sometimes avoiding petty responsibilities for the lure of loafing in a corner or in a movie somewhere. On the edges of my imagination, I knew that I didn't like the draft. It was so ignoble. We never talked about it, although it was something we all could feel, the division between us and Them: Them with the power to manipulate our lives, and us who were trying to figure what all the ruckus was about.

I spent four and a half years getting my bachelor's degree. I read books, engaged in local school mini-politics, and went to frat parties. At some point, I discovered that there was something else to living besides this triumvirate, and it had something to do with "reality." It was also a little bit more complicated; it seemed that not everyone saw the situation as I did, and I wasn't exactly sure what I saw, and what I saw I couldn't articulate. In this somewhat unconscious state, I passed most of my time in Academia.

Like all good American boys, there was a time when I wanted to be a Marine. I was attracted by their big chests and rugged, ragged look. In all the movies, they played like I did in sand lots —tumbling down dirt mounds, falling out of trees, running stooped over rocks, shooting with precision aim, dying with suitable passion, and falling into heroic heaps on the ground. Man against death—the bullfighter, the trapeze artist, the soldier; that thin line of tension between breathing fresh gulps of air and a last black and empty gasp. The moments which can make a man. . . . As I grew up to be a little more abstract, I chose the Navy. Big guns, submarines—you don't see the men you're killing. It's only steel hulks, easier that way to salve one's conscience. . . . I then changed my mind to the Coast Guard. I was learning that when older men fell into heaps on the floor, they weren't laughing. Adults play their games for keeps. Visions of polar expeditions, scientific explorations, and rescues at sea, filled my kindhearted reveries, since by then I was more concerned with an objective scientific principle here, or a colorful sunset there, than I was in demonstrating my manhood over the lifeless bodies of men from foreign nations.

However, I was a college student, and one should not put a book down until it's finished. So I picked up and put down books in dutiful order. Being reluctant to break this secure and comfortable habit, I decided not to join the Coast Guard until after graduation.

As a dark mass of clouds loom, threaten rain, and pass away quietly over the dry earth, I came to the conclusion that war was abhorable. Glossy pictures of men lying dead in muddy ditches, donkeys sprawled grotesquely by tanks in Belgium cities, children sitting, skinny by the ruins of saturation bombs: these were the real but detached images of man's cruelty to men. Somewhere I must have read a poet and the *Charge of the Light Brigade* became an inane but glorious absurdity. Thou shalt not kill, and love thy neighbor. If someone strike thee on the right cheek, turn to him the other also. Blessed are the peacemakers. Etc. So I was opposed to war. Around this time, I also learned that I wasn't a god. My will wasn't the reality of the rest of mankind. Other men had designs, and they were actively drawing them out. And war was often painfully real.

I was opposed to war—but I had learned well the schizophrenia of Academia; theory and practice, dream and reality, and the draft was a practical issue, far removed from the problem of war.

Because of an error, I was required to spend more time getting my degree from St. Francis College than anticipated. I was supposed to graduate in June 1964. I spent that summer in Peru and Mexico, working in an orphanage and traveling, and when I returned, I started to take the additional credits. Through their extraordinary kindness and consideration, the draft board gave me special permission to complete the course. I had had enough of school, so graduate studies would only have been a prolongation of the masochism which held me in the institution. However, having graduated, I became aware of cinema and chose to make it my work. Having spent most of my life in schools, by force of inertia I was again taking courses, this time in film-making. My local board gratified me with a special deferment as a student, from September to that following June, 1965.

During this time, my opposition to war was becoming more defined, my aversion to the draft more totally obvious, and my position more precarious. I discovered that there really were conscientious objectors, people who were refusing to be drafted. In other words, there were alternatives to the tyranny of Selective Service. I knew at least, that I did not want to be drafted, but in this I was no different from anyone else who does not voluntarily enlist, those who want to put it off till the final order comes, those who are not dodging, but waiting.

In my typically impractical way, my reaction was "they won't get me," rather than the more forceful "I won't go." At the time, I hadn't been drafted and so was still involved with the whole panorama of alternatives, and unless the government considers their established alternative classifications to be illegal, searching for them can in no way be incriminating. I was a student. I wasn't in the Army. Dodging? No. Simply not being in. But there were other alternatives, and all they involved was opening up a few credible possibilities. With little tension on the string of sanity, a mild neurotic can become a raving psychotic; normal friendships with the male sex can become "homosexual"; a small thievery can make one a criminal; association with subversives can make one dangerous to the state. Or, one can join the Army and then act like a free human being—resulting either in your hasty discharge, or in a stay in prison. Being aware that most of these possibilities could with time become actualities, I centered my energies around my studies and ignored the soldierly monster that was breathing down my back.

Then, in ten rapid days in March 1965, my student status was revoked, and I was notified of my induction. In trying to clear up the mess through the telephone, I gathered the story. In their records, the board thought I wanted to go to "Graduate School," which they thought was St. Francis, an undergraduate college. But I was going to film school. They had received notice that I was no longer attending St. Francis: I had in fact graduated in January 1965. They couldn't understand then, why I was on a student deferment, and when I reminded them of my film studies, they asked me to prove my attendance there. Within the time these reports were being arranged, I received notice for induction in March.

I did not want to go, not least of all because I was still going to school. I was also pretty sure that I objected strongly enough to be a CO, but knew that my feelings and their classifications might be far apart. I also thought that CO classifications were stigmas of sorts, and was afraid it would endanger some far off and future berth. The position of objectors seemed to be theoretical, and I wasn't sure that I could really be one in practice. In this dilemma, I hurried to the War Resisters League for some advice, and they suggested that I request a postponement of the induction order so as to have some breathing space, or I would find myself marching to Fort Dix, trying to convince a bulldog sergeant that I really shouldn't be there. They also suggested that I request an application for conscientious objector classification, although they weren't sure the board would send me one since the induction order had already been sent.

"There is small choice in rotten apples" as Bill S. says, and the problem of choice becomes an even more absurd game when you have to do it within five minutes, or ten days, or whenever the "bureauminds" press the buzzer. A man is not allowed to make up his mind unless he can do it to their time and tune, and if they do not like his choice, they will force him into its opposite.

It seems that a man becomes something else once he's been slipped an induction order—some sort of a puppet of the Department of Defense, or a brainwashed loser from the Selective Service System, since at the point he receives his notice, he can no longer exercise his natural rights to conscience. He forfeits the right to examine what is happening to him, and must submit meekly to the manipulations of military no-minds. If he begins to think, and then decides that he wants nothing of what is happening to him, he is accused by the government of playing falsely, of trying to evade the trap they have set for the likes of him. If he decides to act on his objections, if he decides that he will not allow the government to intimidate him into voluntarily taking the final involuntary step, he becomes a criminal and is accused of the vilest and unpatriotic deeds, despite the fact that he has performed no action. He becomes guilty because he acts like a free agent, and refuses to perform what he considers to be a criminal act.

In requesting the CO form, I tried to explain my indecision and my half made up mind, my reluctance and my confusion, but it came out all wrong. They interpreted the imprecision of my letter as expressing the fact that I had long ago made up my mind. Actually, I don't think the local board determined this; in the court they said that they felt I had just made up my mind. It was the judge who resorted to this at the last moment, when he had nothing else in fact to lay on me. The government and the courts have been trying to convince me that in asking for the form, I had already been for a long time, a CO. Part of the difficulty is that neither the government nor the court wants me to testify on my position, and so I can't explain to them that I didn't consider myself to be a CO until I put the application into the mail box. At that point it passed beyond me and became a public and legal application. The government doesn't want to believe this: they seem to prefer their interpretation, and naturally don't want to be contradicted. If you have to deal with them, make sure your language is simple and precise; keep one jump ahead of their narrow formulas, and be sure to tell them nothing more than the absolute minimum.

After receiving the form, it took me three weeks to complete. Reading the damn thing is one issue: it reads like an entrance exam to the theology department of the Pentagon, and answering it honestly is like making a dissertational confession to the Pope. Each time I sat down to answer it, the confusions of theorizing on pacificism and "what would I do if attacked on First Street?" struck me as absurd. The narrow hairlines of religious belief seemed posed for Cardinal Spellman; and finally, the assininity of having to justify not wanting to kill somebody, exasperated me beyond measure.

At any point during this time I could have changed my mind and been inducted in June, and several times I almost went that way. I could have gone to the induction station wearing a suit of armor, waving a bloody dirk in one hand and a copy of *Batman* comics in the other, a far away look in my eyes and patriotic obscenities in my mouth. A pocketful of hash and a sixpence of pot would also have done a trick. But I'm more drawn to philosifying than dramatics. With small twists in my personality, I would have had no compunction about using imagination at Whitehall Street. The government is continuously dealing with the youth of this nation in a dishonest fashion, so I can find no rational reason for the youth not dealing in some reciprocal way with them. Someone is cheating in a game where all the rules are not above the table, or where one member is playing with different rules. But I have a liberal's trust in both reason and government, at least I did when this whole mess started, so I tangled with the problem of being a CO.

Since the Constitution has proclaimed that the government can make no law respecting the establishment of religion, the Selective Service law respects the establishment of religion. Only those who have beliefs against war which are related to religious beliefs can be exempt. Blessed are the peacemakers—as long as they make peace along the lines we uphold and propose. Let us have no dissent when it comes to peace, for God is on our side and we cannot be too liberal with such a radical issue.

So many of the problems we face in human affairs, are the eternal gaps in communication, and one big hole exists in linguistics. How do you define your reality? What terms do you use and what do you mean by them? What is religious? Its meaning has changed, in CO cases, from referring only to long-established pacifist groups, to indicating a belief in some force or energy to which man owes his allegiance. To me, this energy is the life and simple existence of man. Man exists, he lives, and the pattern of this process is that he sustain life as well and as long as possible. The forces which attempt to destroy him in his struggle either to live well or to live long, are the evils which civilization has tried to combat. I do not see it depending on God, but rather on man. I do not accept the interference of God in the affairs of men because such claimed involvement has always been arbitrary, and I will have no truck with arbitrary and false gods. But a Supreme Being seemed to be a special character (at least he rated a special box on the CO form); and I wasn't sure of my relationship to him, especially since I wasn't sure that he existed at all. A belief in a Supreme Being has scientific overtones, and in these times where surety is lost in personal interpretations, the question is an unfair one. To make belief in this demanding force in the universe a prerequisite for being allowed to practice peace, is to allow the government to legislate in favor of theism. And this, of course, is a violation of the freedom of religion. I suspect this is easy enough to overcome; call man "god" and we make a small linguistic leap into understanding. Also, according to Webster, "religion" is any object of conscientious regard and pursuit. With very little stretching, an ethical system can become a religious one. Just make sure you use the correct words, for when the government prosecutes you for idiomatic or grammatical errors, they use the same maniacal tactics and will put you in jail whether you refuse to kill because you messed up the definition of "religious," or because they simply prefer not to believe you in the first place.

Since I didn't know about this Supreme Being, I answered the question about belief in it, by explaining my doubts: the position of a skeptic. At first, I denied existence in any religious sect, but later I accepted that I was born a Catholic and did engage in some of the rites of that Church. If I was an unorthodox Catholic, that was my business. It is in no way up to the draft board to decide the complications of religious affiliations; it is, first of all, none of their business, and secondly, they are not properly qualified. Many of them are not even qualified to do the job they are doing, but so is the way of political appointees. They may be patriotic and prestigious citizens, but they are neither trained as judges nor as arbiters of consciences. The members of my board demonstrated in court that they were not even competent in knowing or understanding the basic laws of Selective Service.

In filling out the CO form, I was continually struck by the complete absurdity of the entire thing. First of all, as I mentioned before, it is a sad point in history when men have to justify their intentions to be peaceful citizens. Secondly, the problem in dealing with the local board is that if one doesn't have a history of being an active pacifist, they are likely to disbelieve him. A man living a quiet and peaceful life doesn't always make noise, and in a country where demonstrations and exhibitions serve as a primary way of defining a man's personality, the absence of publicity may mark him as being one who has something to hide. A man cannot all of a sudden become a legal pacifist, although he may have lived a pacifist's life.

Another problem is that a pacifist position may be thoroughly theoretical from the draft board's point of view. If a man has never been violently attacked, or even witnessed such an attack, he can only assume how he would act. He may be able to preserve a reasonable amount of control—although there are points of irritation which when scratched, send a man into a fit of surprised passion. In spite of this, I believe that a man has the right to assume, the right to suppose how he might act in a given situation.

There are two further questions which arise out of this, however, and they seem well worth considering. A man who acts violently may be filled with disgust for the way he has acted, or at least be disgusted with the effects of his action, and decide that he wants nothing more to do with such situations. He should be allowed out of the Army.

The other question is one of rights: does a man have the right to choose the type of environments or situations he wants to be involved in? My own belief is that no one has the right to force another man to do anything against his will, or to become involved in any situation against his will. The basic but oversimplified principle is that no man has the right to violate the rights of another.

My final decision to complete the form and send it in came as I was walking home one afternoon. There was nothing special that happened. I just became very tired of the whole thing, and decided that I felt strongly about certain things. It was silly to continue the dialogue with myself, weighing contradictions and measuring possibilities, especially since there were no answers for my questions, only solutions of a personal nature. Also, in spite of some of my own questions, I felt strongly against war and any participation in it, and before it was too late altogether, I had to decide what involvement I would permit with the Army. So, despite some lingering doubts, I got a hold of the fact that I was a free man, and decided to confront the Selective Service bureau with who I was at that moment in time—and be damned to futures and mutabilities. Allowing myself to be drawn into the Army, and then deciding that I wasn't the sort who can play ball in a war game, would leave me confronting the military conception of justice, which is a little more brutal and barbaric than the civilian kind.

A question may occur: why did I choose this method when I obviously approve of other methods of finding alternatives to the military service? I suppose it might be a hang-up on integrity.

I like to say what I'm thinking without beating too much around the bush. Expression is a vital force, and it is most forceful for me when it can come right from what a man is feeling, and I was feeling more like presenting my views to the local board than flipping out before them.

They granted me an interview during which I was interrogated with all the subtlety of pigs running to their stys for dinner. They did not understand why I would not serve as a medic. Telling them that medics were as much a part of the Army and of the force which did the killing, as the front line soldier, was to no avail. (One of the duties of the medics is to clear the field of wounded so that fighting troops are not hampered by the cries and bodies of their buddies.) Saying that I would help a wounded man if I could, but would not do it as part of the Army, seemed to confuse them. In overhearing their brief argumentation in voting, one board member bellowed that I was only trying to avoid the draft. When I returned to them for the decision, I told him that he was absolutely right: I was trying to avoid the draft because I did not believe in going in the Army. I think I asked him if he thought I was lying. He replied that I was. I lost.

I was arrested the next day when I refused to take the final ceremonial step. The lieutenant at the induction station couldn't understand how a Catholic could be a CO. He obviously didn't know about the early Christians. Nor did he understand that my beliefs passed beyond any one religious sect, toward a universal belief in the sacredness of man. He also seemed sad that I was screwing up my life. He couldn't see his part in contributing to my situation, nor did he seem to understand that my life was important so long as I was able to freely live my beliefs. He was at least confused.

Spending one night in jail was an experience I will not forget. Besides all of the social and personal discoveries which can pop up in such a place, I was struck most by a paradox. While I was waiting to be released on bail, I was in a cage like what we call animals. I paced—have you ever been to the zoo? But it struck me however, that I was free. I was free because I had made a choice; a decision which uncovered a little bit of soul. The guards working in the jails, the bullish sheriffs, or marshals, whatever they call themselves, the business-like FBI, were all on the other side of the bars, and I became aware of their dilemma—they were as much behind bars as was I, perhaps even more so.

That was for one day: I am sure that a few years would play on, and with, my mind. It is curious that the government would put men in cages when they offer like I did, to work in alternative service. I suppose it is a habit of thinking for the petty bureaucrats—they probably spank their children. It would be much more productive and advantageous for the state to use the energies of young men in creating roads, or growing crops, or building experimental cities, or dealing with poverty, or planning alternatives to war, or painting pictures. This would be tyranny of a more creative sort. I would fight against it, but probably be much more likely to serve. I would rather see men allowed to choose freely the type of work or life they want to live. If the government created the situation where men could work in such projects for a period of time, with no intimidation, I suspect that many would be willing to volunteer, as long as such projects allowed for the men to be creative.

Since the arrest, about two years have passed. I have been convicted, unconvicted, and convicted again. My lawyer, Marvin Karpatkin, is doing an excellent job of dealing with the "nice sharp quillets of the law," and as well, sparking me with some life when I become washed out in the downpour of absurdities. If any of you want to know of the trial, read Kafka.

Stephen Fortunato, Jr., and Others

THOU SHALT NOT KILL

Stephen Fortunato served in the Marine Corps Reserve from 1960 to 1965. The war in Vietnam aggravated the experience which he describes. Prior to discharge, he stopped carrying a weapon and refused to attend classes oriented to preparation for combat. He rejected the implication that there must be something wrong with you if you do not want to kill, and sought to convey that the terms the military uses must be viewed on one's own terms and not theirs.

> *The government is free to call me anything they wish—"reservist," "rifleman," "private," "killer." But these brands do not change the fact of my conscientious objection and opposition to war.*

The account was extracted almost entirely from a paper written for a political science course at Providence College.

Following the discussion of the Just War theory which Fortunato introduces are added comments by three Jewish conscientious objectors.

I CAME to conscientious objection over a somewhat circuitous route—via the Marine Corps. At the age of eighteen I freely enlisted in the Marine Corps Reserve, more out of a spirit of adolescent adventure than anything else, and certainly not because I thought freedom would be better preserved if the government stuck an M-1 in my hands.

With all the passion and exuberance of youth I became a trained killer. I went to classes where I learned how to rip a man's jugular vein out with my teeth. I growled like a tiger when I was told to growl like a tiger. (It would indeed be edifying for religious and educational leaders to see their flocks brandishing bayonets and yelping and grunting on command, like well-trained jungle beasts—all for the preservation of Western civilization!)

I was told that the Ten Commandments, however worthy they might be in civilian life, had to be suspended in the name of national interest. I was greatly impressed to see that an act perpetrated by the enemy was *ipso facto* vicious and deceitful, whereas the self-same act perpetrated by the United States was just and praiseworthy.

For two years I did my reserve duty without questioning the purposes or the means of the armed forces. It remained for one of the cruder excesses of military training to wrench me from the spiritual doldrums.

At a summer camp, three hundred of us reservists filed into an air-conditioned auditorium for a lecture on guerrilla warfare. A crew-cut captain greeted us with these words: "What does k-i-l-l spell?"

"Kill," was the obvious, though not too loud, reply of most of the three hundred voices.

"What does k-i-l-l spell?" repeated the man with silver bars on his shoulder.

"Kill!" This time, louder.

"What?"

"Kill!"

"I can't hear you!"

"Kill!" A deafening chant began: "Kill! Kill! Kill! . . ."

I looked around me. Clerks, mechanics, teachers, college students, a few professional men, all were screaming, "Kill!" Who cares who? Just kill. Kill anyone that the President, the Congress, and the generals brand as "evil," "aggressors," "the enemy."

But who is my enemy? Thou shalt not kill.

After two years of mute acquiescence I was now painfully awake. The screaming shades of a Bund meeting—this was the rancid fruit of power politics, something the textbook theoreticians and congressional "realists" never see, or else ignore.

As I look back, I cannot condemn these men, or those who went before or now follow them. Very few of these men are inherently cruel, depraved, or deranged. But fear, power, and hatred are the order of the day, and it is to these forces, so constantly presented to us both by demagogues and by those who should know better, that men submit without question. Good men do bad things because they are too benumbed to ask "Why?" or say, "No!"

Our society, but particularly the military, demands men who will follow without thinking. From the day I witnessed the mass blood-thirst of my fellow Marines, I began to think. I viewed the military as ludicrous as it was tragic. The lectures, the manuals, all seemed inane, but in a sick and frightening way; for I knew the large sphere of influence martial doctrine has.

The line the military instructors spoke with the greatest urgency was: "There is no place for an individual in the Marine Corps." Read any service manual on leadership. You will see that the whole function of military training is to destroy the individual will and substitute for it the will of the functionary who happens to be one step higher on the chain of command.

The military has an almost metaphysical concept of its power and righteousness; the military demands that the individual abandon his reason and his conscience in a supreme and "patriotic" act of self-abnegation in order that he might proudly assume his niche in an invincible mass of manpower and machinery that will—to use military terms—"close with the enemy and destroy him."

My first break with the ways of the military was emotional and intuitive. The contradictions of war and war preparations became clear and self-evident. It did not become a rational creature to permit himself to be led in cries for the destruction of human life; a truly free man would not support a totalitarian system to defend freedom; one cannot bring about peace by threatening to incinerate mankind. No, I came to believe that a free man preserves his freedom by acting freely and not by following those who would herd men into regiments or send people scurrying like moles into bomb shelters. Most important of all, the free man must remain free *not* to kill or to support killing.

Following my sentiments, I began to read and talk often and long about war and war resistance. I can remember especially my enthusiasm upon encountering the *Catholic Worker,* a radical newspaper advocating, among other things, conscientious objection. I pored through Tolstoy's heady tract on nonviolence, *The Kingdom of God Is Within You.* As a Christian, I was encouraged to see that many Christians are—and always have been—in the vanguard of war resistance.

Though perhaps few realize it—or if they do, are unwilling to take note—Christianity has at its core a long and vital tradition of resistance to martial preparations and adventures (or misadventures). True, the parroting of government praises by most religious leaders has obscured this tradition, but it has not erased the fact. The New Testament is replete with injunctions urging men to abandon the use of violence to resolve disputes (Matthew 5:43-44; 19:17-18; 26:52; Thessalonians 5:15). The New Testament, particularly in such statements as the Sermon on the Mount, is pacific in spirit and merits reading by the Christian before he decides to enter the armed forces.

I read . . . works by both Christians and non-Christians opposed to the war system—A. J. Muste, Bertrand Russell, Erich Fromm, Dorothy Day. I talked with people who had committed their lives to the pursuit of peace—Tom Cornell, associate editor of the *Catholic Worker* [see pages 33–43], Bradford Lyttle, leader of the San Francisco-Moscow and the Quebec-Guantanamo peace walks, Bob and Marj Swann, leaders in the Committee for Nonviolent Action. Their ideas helped me to sift and develop my own. I thought: if we accept the premise that we pass our days on earth as a part of the "brotherhood of man" under the "fatherhood of God," if we pursue to its logical conclusion the notion of the Mystical Body and Christ's dying for all men, then it becomes apparent that war—all war—is fratricidal; all war is civil war; all war is blasphemous.

I knew I had arrived at conscientious objection. I was opposed in body and soul to the organized, budgeted, and officially sanctified use of violence called war. I was opposed to the compulsory and regimented aberration from the laws of God and reason, called conscription. I could no longer, in conscience, bear arms.

What course of action was I to take? I had freely enlisted in the reserves. But how free was I? Our society conspires in favor of the armed camp set-up we now live in. At the age of eighteen, I had not once considered military service as confronting me with a moral decision. It is one of the more gruesome paradoxes of our time that in a free—or supposedly so—society the atmosphere of choice on such a crucial issue has been so stifled. . . . As a member of the armed forces . . . I had to remove myself from an institution I viewed as pernicious.

After much soul-searching—and always haunted by the searing doubt that I would not be able to follow my convictions—I submitted a letter to the commanding officer of my reserve unit stating that I would no longer bear arms or attend classes oriented to the preparation of men for combat.

The Marine Corps denied my petition for discharge as a conscientious objector. Military policy in such matters is: "No vested right exists for any individual to be discharged from military service at his own request before the expiration of his term of service whether he is serving voluntarily or involuntarily." (MCO 1306.16A) This statement is not inconsistent with the government's attitude toward conscientious objectors. Conscientious objectors have no "vested rights"; "the fact of conscientious objection does not exempt men from the draft," says the government. Any consideration shown conscientious objectors is regarded by the government as a judicious favor that happens to be consonant with national interest. We are born with inalienable rights, freedom of speech, assembly, worship. Do we not also have the inalienable right not to kill? The government does not think so.

At this point, I was ordered to have a psychiatric examination. I first thought of refusing to go through with this, but then said to myself that I should confront each and every one of the military's officials who wanted to get into the show. After the psychiatric examination, I wrote to the Commandant of the Marine Corps and the Director of the Selective Service System restating my case:

> . . . I ask that the Marine Corps discharge me, not on nebulous medico-legal grounds, but as a conscientious objector to war.

. . . I am asking for a review of my case and for discharge as a conscientious objector. It does not require a psychiatrist to see that a man who has traveled the torturous philosophical and theological path to the commitment to the ideal of nonviolence is, *ipso facto,* psychologically unqualified for military service. The point I wish to stress is that this particular psychological disposition flows from a prior act which is essentially volitional.

Purely and simply, my position is this: I freely choose not to bear arms or to serve, either as a combatant or noncombatant, a policy which I consider to be immoral, barbaric, and reckless. I will answer no call to arms. For all practical purposes, I no longer consider myself to be under the aegis of the Selective Service System or the Marine Corps. I pray that God give me the grace and strength to hold to my beliefs.

Two months after I sent this letter, I received a manila envelope from the Department of the Navy. I expected it would contain a list of the laws and policies I was violating, but to my great surprise I withdrew a discharge, a General Discharge under Honorable Conditions.

The Catholic conscientious objector is frequently queried regarding his position *vis-à-vis* the Just War.* My answer is this: Christ said, "Thou shalt not kill," and, "Render, therefore, to

* The Just War theory to which Fortunato refers came, through Catholic tradition, from St. Augustine. A "Just War" must meet all of these tests:

The war must be the last resort after all peaceful means of solving the conflict have been exhausted.

The war must be an act of defense against unjust demands backed by aggressive force.

The war must be declared by the legally constituted authority of the nation concerned.

There must be a reasonable possibility of victory.

The harm caused by the war must not outweigh the good hoped for.

The military tactics and objectives of the war must discriminate between soldiers and civilians.

The classical theory of Just War allows no recognition of the justice of revolution until or unless the revolution becomes the established govern-

Caesar the things that are Caesar's." He did not say, "Thou shalt not kill—except in Just Wars," or "Surrender to Caesar your soul and your conscience."

There is good scholastic logic behind the Just War theory. But did there ever live a ruler or foot soldier who did not believe his cause was just—that in marching to war he was *defending* a *right* by means *proportionate* to the peril that threatened him, only after having exhausted *all* other means of resolving the conflict? And where can there be justice amidst the blood and screams of the battlefield? Perhaps at some time in the distant past, all the conditions for the Just War were satisfied. But these conditions were defined by men, and whatever speculations they engage in, they cannot command anyone to act contrary to his conscience.

Even if one grants the "rules" defined in the Just War theory, these rules cannot in any way be satisfied by the total warfare of the twentieth century. . . . Though today theologians and philosophers still wrangle over the morality of war, the Church has remained unswervingly and majestically committed to the principle of the primacy of conscience.

Christ told us to make an effort to live with one another as brothers. Some men tell us to submit to—and even pray for—a system that threatens to incinerate mankind. Wars cannot be blamed solely on the Napoleons, the imperialists, the munitions makers, the Hitlers—someone had to follow. The Germans claim they did not know that Hitler and his followers would lead them on such a barbarous course. Will we say some day that we could not see our nation surrendering more and more control to the military? Will we say that we did not know our arsenals were filled with the most calamitous instruments of murder? Will we say we never thought our leaders would use the weapons they

---

ment. Because war must be under the auspices of legitimate authority, guerrilla warfare is by definition unjust, regardless of whether it seeks to resist oppression, to rectify injustice, or whatever the cause. Some modern efforts are being made to develop a Just War theory which can encompass warfare to resist oppression, to rectify justice, on the part of people who do not have legally constituted authority.

spend so much money for and talk so much about? Will we wish we had said "No!"?

Carl Sandburg tells of the ingenious question once posed him by a child: What if they had a war and nobody showed up? The child deserves more than an awkward grimace and condescending pat on the head for an answer.

Jewish conscientious objectors deal similarly with the commandment "Thou shalt not kill" and the problem of discriminating under what circumstances violence may be used. Here are three:

. . . The seventh commandment is brief and to the point. It does not say "Thou shalt not kill, except in wartime," or "except in defense of freedom," or even, "except for freedom of worship." It says, "Thou shalt not kill." Thus, to my mind, the Bible is here expressing a deep-rooted horror of killing in any form. This fundamental regard for the sanctity of life is felt in the legal sections of the pentateuch as well: they stress premeditation and violence as the criteria for distinguishing murder from excusable homicide (e.g., Numbers 35). . . . The commandments must always be obeyed so as to preserve life—even if this means temporarily disobeying—since God is he who sanctifies life.

—Raphael Zahler

[The] dual obligation, to God and man, is compounded in the familiar axiom that man is made in the image of God. In Judaism this notion takes on a literal meaning, as I interpret it; that man is God-like—that he knows the difference between good and evil and that he is capable of conducting himself in a just and merciful manner . . .

. . . Judaism is explicit on this point: life is good. Life is man's opportunity to manifest his divinity and evoke it from others. To strike another is to strike at another's divinity, and, in the same blow, destroy the God-ness resident in oneself.

—Martin Weis

[*Paul Denison refused shipment to Vietnam in May 1967, after his first application for discharge as a conscientious objector was denied. Attorney Francis Heisler pointed out that this soldier was charged with disobeying the verbal order of his commanding officer when he should have been charged with failure to comply with the written order of the Commanding General of Fort Ord. The charge against Denison was dismissed. Denison reapplied for discharge as a conscientious objector. His claim was recognized and he was granted an honorable discharge in February 1968— almost the only discharge on grounds of conscientious objection since May 1966. Consequences for refusals in the service are usually more severe than those encountered by Fortunato and Denison.*]

In closing, I add excerpts from the Sabbath service which a Jewish friend and I read in the Union Prayerbook this morning in the stockade chapel. The nature of my religious incentive, my present state of mind, and my spiritual aspiration, are reflected by these words:

Loving Father, hear us as we call unto Thee from the depths of our being. Dark is the world without Thee. Our ways are often confused; the good seems evil and the evil good. Material pursuits deaden us to the needs of the spirit. Swayed by the impulses of our senses, we frequently stifle the voice of conscience which speaks of Thee and Thy eternal laws. We exchange our glory for things of naught. O God of truth and light, help us to find our way unto Thee. Open up within the desert of our souls the living fountain of Thy love that our lives may be brought to flower in the beauty of Thy goodness.

—**Paul Denison**

John Otis Sumrall

FREEDOM AT HOME

> . . . *We can write and ask our sons if they know what they are fighting for. If he answers "Freedom," tell him that's what we are fighting for here in Mississippi. And if he says "Democracy" tell him the truth—we don't know anything about Communism, Socialism, and all that, but we do know that Negroes have caught hell here under this American Democracy.*

This concludes a statement written by several Negro youths in McComb, Mississippi, in August 1965, after a friend who had been active in civil rights was killed in Vietnam.

John Otis Sumrall was one of the first Negroes to bring a suit challenging segregated draft boards (1966). The court was asked to forbid induction or classification of Negroes until the number of Negroes on draft boards was proportional to the local population. The suit also charged that the Mississippi State Director of Selective Service had personally intervened to have three criminal charges against Sumrall dismissed, and that Sumrall was called out of turn for induction "so as to terminate his civil rights activities." In August 1967, he was sentenced to five years in prison and a $2,500 fine for refusing induction.

This account was edited from a tape recording of a speech given at the "We Won't Go" Conference, December 4, 1966, in Chicago, Illinois. Supplementary notes were written for this book.

WHAT I am going to talk about is the reasons that have been given to me by a lot of Mississippi Negro people or guys that are of draft age as to why they do not want to go and fight in the U.S. military in Vietnam.

The fight for justice and equality and equal economic opportunity is very limited in the U.S. Scores of black people have been evicted from their plantation homes for trying to register and vote. These people only wanted what was rightfully theirs, and to gain a little self-respect, and for this, they were kicked off the land where they lived, and had to live in tents. The American government made no attempt to help these people.

In every state in the Union there are some people who do not work—black people, who are citizens of the United States—and this is reason enough why black people feel that they should not fight in the war in Vietnam. And that's one of the main reasons why I asked some lawyers for me to file a draft suit against the local draft board for trying to induct me into the army three times this year.

When I went down to be inducted the last time I was in Jackson, I was talking to the lady there and she said, "Why you don't want to go, do you?" I said, "Well, not necessarily." (I was so scared I was going to be, I didn't know what to do. I started talking out of turn to her.) I told her that if I am inducted I am going to try to organize all the inductees, the draftees, and the volunteers and anybody else against the war. And she said, "You're going to try to overthrow the military government, aren't you?" . . . I went on to try to explain to her why I didn't want to go and why I am going to get a lot of other fellows around my community not to go.

And the reasons are simply because in 1964, when the Mississippi Freedom Democratic Party was denied the seats to rightfully represent the whole people of Mississippi, not just a group of white folks, it was made clear to me that I am not a citizen of the United States. I don't have a country, so I don't know of any reason to go over in Vietnam and fight. Then it was simply said that we do not recognize you as citizens of the United States. And now when the United States is in a time of crisis they want to save face, so they want to get everybody they can, especially black folk. And I don't go along with that, because if they didn't recognize me as a citizen then, then I'm not a citizen now. And I'm going to remain that way. And I'm going to try to get a lot of other people, guys of draft age, to remain that way. . . . A lot of guys have come up to me who have heard about my draft case, and say like, "Man, how can I get out of it, because I'm like you." And also because I feel that the United States itself has a lot of problems inside the country— for instance, ghettoes and slum areas. And also because of the segregation that's all over the country, because of the un-represented people, and because of a lot more problems that rapidly are depreciating the United States.

If I am not looked upon as an equal citizen in everyday life, why am I looked upon as an equal citizen when it comes time for me to report for induction? The local draft board there in Clarke County, . . . where I'm working for the Congress of Racial Equality, are the same people that are so down on Negroes now. They are especially down on me and some of the people that work with me. They are the same people that beat people while they are trying to demonstrate or exercise their constitutional rights. They are the same people who are behind the burning and killing of local black people around the state that try to participate in activities that advance the black move-ment or the civil rights movement.

There are more black people now being inducted in the armed services in the South simply because they are now starting to take hold, to look up and fight for what is rightfully theirs. The white people there are afraid of this. They have several different ways to put an end to this. First of all they use their old method—the lynch rope. And secondly, they try to scare them out, and if they can't scare them, if they can't shoot them or do something like that, then they use the legal way and draft them into the army. And because of this, Negroes feel that they should stay in Mississippi and fight—not only in Mississippi—stay in the South, or stay home and fight for freedom. Because, I guess most of you might know, or if you don't, I'll tell you, there is less freedom here now than there is anywhere else. At least people in any country I know of usually are not bombed, are not lynched for trying to exercise their constitutional right.

The Negroes here now, black people here now, are all so

frightened or scared or intimidated to the point where they are risking their lives to even go down to the courthouse to register to vote. And now the local draft board, which is composed all over the State of Mississippi of nothing but local white folks, are asking them to go out of their country, to go out of their states and leave their homes, to leave their loved ones, and go fight in a war where they don't know what they'll be dying for. The guys over there now don't know what they're fighting for. They just know, "my country right or wrong."

I picketed an induction center in the North once, and one of the white enlistees asked me why? He said, "I see what color your skin is fellow. Why?" I said, "That's why, man, because of the color of my skin. I'm going to stay here and fight the *real* battle for freedom." I have no freedom here, and the more Americans go over there make that country that much farther from freedom.

The rich, sick people who support this hypocritical war care only about getting richer. Every time a G.I. is killed, someone over here gets richer. And I'm not going to make Coca-Cola a million dollars by going to Vietnam and getting killed. . . . People here, poor blacks and poor whites, are still suffering because of the racial strife here. The rich gets richer and poor gets poorer. How can we turn our attention away from our own problems and make more elsewhere.

. . . I don't feel that I should go because, one reason—when I do get there I'll have to be 200 per cent better than the white guys over there, simply because I'm black. . . . I got information that the Ku Klux Klan is in operation over there also. Like they got segregated restaurants and segregated bars over there also, you know. Negroes walk into a place and then get kicked out, the same as it is over here.

This is a special note for those optimistic guys who say, "Well, I might as well go and get it over with, ain't nothing I can do about it." Well, if you guys are really serious about not going, if you are serious about wanting to stay out of the military, then don't go.

I'd much rather chance a jail sentence here than a possible

death sentence, or even more important being a part of a machine that stamps out people's lives—innocent people's lives. For me personally, I would feel just like the KKK over there. Denying those people freedom of choice, just like black people are denied freedom of choice in the U.S.

So that's why I want to stay here and fight for freedom in the United States and not go outside and murder innocent men, women, and kids, and burn homes, like what is happening now. . . . That's also happening here. And I think that more people should stay here and try to put a stop to that, than go outside the United States and do the same thing. . . . That's my whole point. Stay here at home and establish freedom and equality—and then I think the U.S. will have done its job.

David Mitchell

WHAT IS CRIMINAL?

David Mitchell believed that if your conscience tells you something is wrong, you don't seek to protect your conscience, you attack the wrong. Mitchell is best known for raising the Nuremberg principles as a defense for draft refusal. (See Appendix C, pages 318–324.) He pointed out the unwillingness of the courts to be bound by international law or morality when in conflict with the basic trend of political decisions in this country.

He fought the draft not only as an individual through legal channels but also as an anti-draft organizer. Four years before "We Won't Go" groups were springing up throughout the country, Mitchell was a member of the Initiating Committee of a group called "End the Draft," abbreviated etd. Etd sought to unite and broaden anti-draft resistance beyond pacifist opposition by focusing thinking on the draft as a blatant preparation for war and instrument of war. Their publication, *downdraft*, gave comprehensive coverage to Mitchell and other war resisters.

The body of this account was taken from a speech at the "We Won't Go" Conference in Chicago, December 4, 1966, two months before Mitchell went to prison. Additional selections from *downdraft*, legal documents, and personal letters have been added. Nicholas Salvatore and Ellen Schneider assisted in providing the information.

IN JANUARY 1961, I came of age in terms of eligibility as cannon fodder for the military machine of the United States. I was in my freshman year at Brown University and, although questions were starting to arise in my mind concerning the justice and sense of America's policies, I registered with the Selective Service. Thereafter, though, I became continually more aware of the aggressive and dangerous nature of America's policies. My examination of such policies was first sparked by

Cuba and the attempts by the United States to turn back the Cuban Revolution and regain an economic and political stranglehold over the Cuban nation. It soon became obvious to me that the United States had, for years, acted with a similar arrogance of attempted or actual domination toward large areas of the globe. And it became obvious that, besides the criminality of such a course itself, it was threatening to bring on World War III and the destruction of the world.

In April of 1961, the United States launched its trained and financed invasion against Cuba, and Adlai Stevenson stood in the United Nations and repeatedly denied the United States' role. I wrote Stevenson on April 19, 1961, and expressed my disillusionment in him, saying to him, in part, "You have been a cog in an evil machine in this case. You avoid the issues of self-determination, of sovereignty, of anti-Castro bases on our soil, of our supplies to rebels, of troop movements in this country, etc. You ignore charters which we have adhered to and encouraged through the OAS or the U.N. You ignore the laws of the U.S." . . . I said he would be guilty of helping to destroy hope.

A few days later, as I had announced in my letter to Stevenson, I left Brown University. To me, Brown was a treadmill which threatened to conform and doom me, and also, I wanted to act on the issues that were starting to concern me, rather than die after a life that put off living. . . . My main concern seems to have been the rather individual and personal one— that I withdraw and not lend myself to the crimes of my country. I was then at a stage where I simply wanted to "save my soul" by withdrawing from the "dirty mess" going on around me, and my position had no development or any concept of application to affecting the world beyond that. If anything, my only "political" concept was the rather utopian one that, by personal example, individuals could be "touched" and "converted" and thereby chip away support from the evil around them.

In the summer of 1961, I was involved in swimming out to protest against and symbolically block the launching and deployment of a nuclear-armed Polaris submarine. I was jailed, and after being released from jail in New London, Connecticut, I found classification forms from the draft board awaiting me. I refused to fill out these forms, and in a letter to my draft board, October 8, 1961, I raised my objection to the "military preparation for nuclear war" and stated that "To cooperate with conscription law would be to acquiesce to evil." When this letter was ignored and when my draft board urged me to seek an exemption, classified me, and declared me delinquent for not filling out forms, I again wrote my local board on December 3, 1961, restating my position. That letter read in part:

> Let me repeat: I will not play any part in the conscription system. I will not even play a part in seeking or serving alternative service, for then I would be contributing to an immoral system and hardening all men's acceptance of this system without dissent. . . . My dissociation and my non-cooperation is not complete if I cooperate with the crime being prepared by being silent, so I pledge that my resistence to militarism shall be heard.

After that, I heard nothing further from my local board for over two years, and the delinquency notice—by which arrest was threatened for refusing to fill out forms in October of 1961—was never acted on. During this two-year silence, I did, though, hear from other agents of the government. . . . The FBI visited my place of work, my apartment house, and called my family. . . . The intimidation failed, and, in fact, the two-year lapse provided me with the opportunity to see the need for going beyond simply a personal refusal—to a direct challenge of the government in order to attempt to stop the criminality which they were pursuing.

In grasping and developing the potential in my position for such a direct challenge, I was aided by becoming aware of the case of Fyke Farmer, a Nashville lawyer who had refused to pay taxes during the Korean war and, who, in his lonely battle, had been the first to invoke the principles of Nuremberg Law and International Law generally as his justification and defense— a defense that goes beyond the civil liberties issue of accommodating the rights and demands of one's conscience to refuse to cooperate with what one thinks is wrong, and thereby gain one's exemption on grounds of conscience. This defense instead demands the application and enforcement of law to justify and demand a refusal to participate in what *is* wrong and, thereby, a condemnation of that wrong itself. The vindication of such a defense would not just free one from participating in the crimes of the United States government, but would condemn the crimes and the criminals. In Fyke Farmer's case, the courts had refused to apply morality and law when it came to issues involving their own government in a parallel to the Nazi courts which had become pawns and instruments of national power and policy. I decided to try again to raise the standards and judgments applied at Nuremberg that were first raised in United States courts by Fyke Farmer.

During the two years of silence from my draft board, I also aided in the formation of the End the Draft Committee, which stated:

> In the tradition of Thoreau and the principles of INDI-VIDUAL GUILT and INDIVIDUAL RESPONSIBILITY established in the Nuremberg trials and in the first session of the United Nations, we assert the right and obligation of the individual to protest and dissociate himself from these criminal preparations.

End the Draft was formed at the end of 1962 to oppose the draft for its use as a tool for immoral and criminal policies, and to support dissociation from such policies.

[When the Selective Service law came up for renewal in 1963, End the Draft issued the following flier. See page 96.]

In February of 1964, I again heard from my local board by way of a "Current Information Questionnaire." I wrote back saying, "I certainly haven't changed my mind since my refusal to fill out classification forms in 1961 and my letter to you about same of December 3, 1961." I also said in part:

> I realize that I could employ means to gain exemption from induction, but this does not interest me. My purpose is not to be classified quietly within the draft system, but rather

how to beat the draft...

IF YOU'RE FOR IT

Can't get a job with that 1A? ENLIST -- the "preferred" way to beat the draft hang-up and get away from it all.

Fed up with sweating it out? Press that panic button and take it like a man --HAVE YOUR NAME PUSHED UP on their lists.

Don't be a sucker.Do it the easy way.SIGN UP FOR THE 6-MONTH DEAL. Only 6 months down --the rest payable in small weekly installments.

Do it in style. JOIN ROTC: avoid nasty sergeants, KP; get higher pay and officer's privileges; have others salute YOU.

Where do YOU stand?

IF YOU'RE BUGGED BY IT

Scared out of your wits by the prospect of losing two years of your life? ACT NUTS at your physical...

or ACT HOMOSEXUAL -- at the risk of your hard-earned reputation.

GET JOB DEFERMENTS -- it is hard not to be essential defense manpower if your field is engineering, science or math.

MARRY SOMEBODY WITH KIDS.

KEEP YOUR BOARD'S QUOTA FILLED by getting others to enlist.

Get draft-immunization --SPEND A FEW DAYS IN JAIL every six months (try sit-ins,peace actions,etc.).

BECOME A PERENNIAL STUDENT.

EMIGRATE.

DEVELOP FLAT-FEET,A HEART MURMUR OR A PUNCTURED EAR-DRUM --do not risk cancer, leukemia or any of those sure 4-Fs.

Put it off--JOIN THE PEACE CORPS.

IF YOU'RE AGAINST IT

To Beat The Draft...
END THE DRAFT.

To a certain extent, our government has recognized that the draft is repugnant to certain religious principles. Why the special consideration for religious ethics as against ethics generally? And if the draft is repugnant to ethics generally, let us get rid of it, not simply in specific cases,but altogether. ** We see the draft as an integral part of our country's domination or threatened domination of small nations. We oppose this as being arrogant and criminal, both in terms of a people's right to self-determination (e.g. Cuba, South Vietnam) and in terms of the possibility of guerrilla aggression escalating into nuclear war.**In allowing our government to place youth in military subjugation,we accept the insanity of nuclear war and the criminality of the so-called "limited wars." ** The power to draft allows government manipulation of world tensions by allowing arbitrary increases in the size of the draft. ** It dismisses our rights and responsibilities by disrupting our lives and channeling us (deferments, enlistments) into military roles. ** The draft is used as an easy out (both dangerous and artificial) for economic ills by turning unemployed youth into grist for the war preparations mill. ** We support all who have and will boycott the draft.The rushed passage of the draft extension bill has not ended our efforts. HELP US TRANSFORM CONCERN INTO ACTION TO END THE DRAFT.
e.t.d. c/o Mitchell, 1010 President St., Brooklyn 25,N.Y.

to oppose the draft. While classification might suit some sort of individual "convenience," my acceptance of classification would be a negation of my social responsibility.

I oppose the draft, not as something wrong for just me or wrong for only certain people, but as something wrong for the peace and survival of the world. Selective Service is the criminal in this case, as can be judged by American militarism throughout the world—from Cuba to Panama to South Vietnam and by our basing of policies on nuclear war. I refuse to cooperate in any way which would support the continuance of such activities. I certainly wouldn't have worked in a Nazi concentration camp just because I would not have to tend the ovens or the gas but could be a guard or a clerk.

The next move from the local board was an order to report for a physical examination dated April 2, 1964, a resulting delinquency notice for my refusal to report, and then an order to report on June 10, 1964, for induction. Instead of reporting as ordered, I wrote an article for the "occasion" which was printed in *downdraft* [May 1964], the publication of End the Draft, and sent [the article] to the draft board, to arrive, instead of me, on June 10. . . . I consider my article to be expressing the attitude of ETD, in the sense of saying that we must go beyond refusal to *challenging*.

CHALLENGE THE DRAFT!

After nearly three years of numerous forms, threats and FBI visits, I have been ordered to report for induction on June 10, 1964, because of my refusal to cooperate with the draft. The purpose of this article is not to rehash my position on draft refusal. . . This article will discuss the failure of draft refusers to focus on the issues and some means by which I plan to raise the issues.

The problem with the anti-draft movement isn't that the government has been too strong, but rather that the movement has been too weak and emasculated by individualistic abstraction. Instead of analyzing the militarism which the draft upholds, the movement tends to withdraw from those issues and talks instead about non-violence and love or retreats into other such philosophical ivory towers. We must get down to the job of fighting the draft and changing the world, not by getting stuck on the *you* involved in the draft, but by getting involved with fighting the draft as a threat to the world.

In my own case, my draft refusal rests, not on an abstract philosophy, but on the political situation as it exists. I non-cooperate with my government, not because I am a pacifist or occupy a position somehow uninvolved with the world, but on the contrary because I am very involved and specifically condemn the United States for crimes against peace and humanity. I refuse to cooperate with any Koreas, Cuban invasions or blockades, Vietnams, or with the nuclear arrogance with which we threaten to blow up the world.

Arrest and trial should not be a time when we—with a limited number of friends—react by meditation and philosophical backslapping. Rather, attacks and threats by the "powers-that-be" should be exploited as opportunities to focus on the issues. Let's remember why we're involved in the fight against the draft, not simply to communicate with our souls, but to speak to the world in order to change it. The government helps increase the interest in the issues by prosecuting draft refusers. Our job is to utilize every threat, FBI visit, court fight, or jailing as a means of following through on our prosecution of militarism and the real criminals. When the government acts and creates publicity on the issue, we must utilize every means to make sure that they end up with burnt fingers and a kick in the behind.

Many draft refusers fail to get down to the political issues in their cases; many refuse to contest their own "legal guilt" in court. Yet an effective way of challenging our government's policies and morality is by maintaining a *not guilty* plea in the courts. The position of individual guilt and individual responsibility, and therefore one's obligation to dissociate himself from war crimes, is established—not only philosophically, as by Thoreau, etc.—but historically and legally by Nuremberg International Law which is part of the law of every country. Under International Law the United States is guilty of Crimes Against Peace and is also in violation of the Kellogg-Briand Pact, other international agreements, and Article 2, Section 4 of the United Nations Charter, which prohibits a policy of force and threats of force. [See Appendix C, pages 318–324.] Only if we served as accomplices in these activities would we be guilty morally or legally.

If I am brought to trial, I plan to use my trial as a forum in which to try the United States Government before the world. . . .

We should never allow ourselves to be salted away, either in court entanglements or in jail. We should wage the battle on as many fronts as possible in the realization that the draft and militarism cannot be disconnected from the general insanity of our country. Besides the work of lawyers and defense committees, we should be prepared to cause people to focus and refocus *even* when we end up in jail.

. . . The main point is that the protest must not end when there is a change in the proceedings. Only our means should change in order to use government actions and proceedings as opportunities to focus against the government. . . .

In response to the arrival of my article instead of my person, another silence ensued from my draft board. Then, over two months after my refusal to report for induction, the local board wrote, on August 18, 1964, that my delinquency status was removed and the induction canceled. Again their processes had been forced to a halt.

But the local board began a new cycle when they ordered me to report on October 21, 1964, for another physical examination, and then, on November 10, 1964, declared me delinquent again for my refusal to report. Thereafter, I was ordered to report for another induction on January 11, 1965. Again I refused. After nearly half a year, during which time there was a major step-up in the war in Vietnam, including the beginning of bombings in the North, I heard further. This time it was by way of the FBI which I learned had been scurrying up ladders into the window of my second floor apartment. On June 1, 1965, I called the FBI, met them in my lawyer's office, and there surrendered to a warrant for my arrest that two agents had, while three other agents "surrounded" the office building.

. . . On June 14, 1965, I pled not guilty in a New Haven, Connecticut, United States District Court, and asked for a jury trial. Then with my attorney, Conrad J. Lynn, a thirty-seven-page brief was prepared for a pre-trial motion to dismiss the case against me. The brief spelled out the violations of Nuremberg, international, and constitutional law committed by the United States by its intervention and conduct in places such as the Dominican Republic and Vietnam. . . .

[From Appellant's Reply Brief:] The question which this court is called upon to decide in this case is:

WHETHER A DRAFTEE, ORDERED TO REPORT FOR INDUCTION IN THE ARMED FORCES OF THE UNITED STATES MAY LAWFULLY REFUSE TO OBEY THE ORDER UPON THE GROUNDS THAT THE GOVERNMENT IS ENGAGED IN THE COMMISSION OF CRIMES AGAINST PEACE, WAR CRIMES, AND CRIMES AGAINST HUMANITY AS DEFINED BY INTERNATIONAL LAW RECOGNIZED BY THE CHARTER AND JUDGMENT OF THE NUREMBERG TRIBUNAL AND AFFIRMED BY THE UNITED NATIONS GENERAL ASSEMBLY; AND, THEREFORE, THAT OBEDIENCE TO THE ORDER WOULD RENDER HIM GUILTY OF COMPLICITY IN THESE CRIMES.

[Affidavit by defendant:] My position is clear. I have stated it over and over for the past four years as I have challenged, obstructed, and pursued the United States government in an attempt to bring *it* to justice. My draft board's response has been a complete avoidance of the issues. . . . Their actions have been those of harassment and intimidation by means of forms, orders, and FBI visits, but never did they face the position or my charges against the United States.

Yet, now with the United States in the process of compounding its aggression and slaughter around the world by a massive use of bombs and troops to "pacify" and occupy Vietnam, they have summoned the legal machinery to take me in tow—to get me out of the way. Obviously with the United States pursuing such criminal and dangerous acts against justice and peace, the United States cannot let stand my refusal to take part for fear of it mobilizing an opposition.

But the United States is mistaken. My case is not my prosecution, but rather the prosecution of America for its oppression and slaughter at home and abroad. America's guilt cannot be scared away or locked up. It is there to be seen and to be broadcast by every attempt to silence it. The Germans claimed they submitted unaware of Nazi crimes. With American crimes staring us in the face, are we to goose-step down the same path of domination and genocide to the final holocaust?

America is long overdue for its Nuremberg. There is no one who can remain untouched in my case—not the judge, not the United States attorneys, not the public; for everyone is on trial who takes part in America's crimes!

On September 8, 1965, the brief was argued before Judge Timbers of the U.S. District Court in Connecticut. The oral argument had been set for later in the month, but, at the last minute, the judge moved the date up in an apparent effort to get the case over before the return of students to Yale University. Supporters of my position picketed outside the court and held a rally; the courtroom was jammed with spectators. After argument, the judge reserved decision, but set the trial for the next day.

Meanwhile, due to conflicts with my attorney on how to conduct my defense, and in the interests of maintaining my fundamental indictment against U.S. policy as criminal before morality and law, I was forced to dismiss my original counsel. Judge Timbers, though, refused to give me proper time to exercise my right of counsel of my choice and to prepare for trial, and instead attempted to impose a former U.S. attorney as court-appointed counsel. I refused to accept such a violation of my rights and refused to participate in the trial, except to protest its unfairness and reassert my need for counsel to raise my defense. I protested that the judge was rendering me incapable of presenting my defense by subverting my rights to a fair trial.

On September 16, 1965, I was convicted and immediately sentenced to five years and $5,000 fine. Judge Timbers had ruled my defense out as "irrelevant" and therefore ruled "futile" my right of counsel and my right to have a jury hear my defense.

I then appealed my case to the Second Circuit Court of Appeals in New York. The American Civil Liberties Committee entered a separate brief in my behalf on the counsel issue; the End the Draft Committee retained Fyke Farmer as my attorney on appeal. Fyke Farmer argued before the Court, in January, 1966, that the defense I raised was valid and that the first trial court excluded it, and, on learning what my defense would be, rushed me to trial in violation of my rights.

On January 13, 1966, the Court of Appeals reversed my first conviction and sent my case back for a new trial with a new judge, saying, in part:

> Of basic importance is the fact that appellant, for the four previous years . . . had taken the position before the Draft Board and in the District Court that his refusal to comply with Selective Service requirements was not because he was a pacifist but because, if he submitted to the draft, the "Nuremberg Law" would render him "guilty of complicity in crimes defined by the Charter of the International Military Tribunal," specifically wars of aggression and acts of inhumanity. Apparently it was his plan of defense to attempt to prove in one way or another that the United States had been guilty of such wars of aggression and acts of inhumanity in Vietnam, Cuba, Panama, Santo Domingo and elsewhere. . . . In essence, what the trial judge failed to take into consideration is that this is not "a very simple case."

The ruling of the Court of Appeals was a unanimous one among the three judges that heard the case.

My retrial took place in March 1966, with Mark Lane as my attorney. But again the trial court refused to apply international law to judge the validity of the war and thereby the draft, and refused to admit evidence from reporters who had been to Vietnam, ex- and current servicemen, visitors to Vietnam, . . . and the presence and testimony of Vietnamese victims of U.S. presence and conduct in Vietnam, which we were ready to present.

I was reconvicted and resentenced to five years in prison.

On November 7, 1966, I was again before the courts in an attempt to have the U.S. courts invoke international law and bring the U.S. government to justice. Mark Lane, my attorney, argued before the Court of Appeals at Foley Square, New York City, that the trial court that convicted me and sentenced me to five years was wrong in refusing me the right to present my defense that the draft is now invalid and criminal because it is being applied in conflict with international law and morality.

[*On December 6, 1966, the Federal Court of Appeals upheld the lower courts and ruled that "we need not consider whether the substantive issues raised by appellant can ever be appropriate for judicial determination." Mitchell filed a petition on January 28, 1967, requesting the Supreme Court to hear his case, but before this could be decided, he was ordered to surrender. David Mitchell began to serve his sentence on February 6, 1967. On March 20, 1967, the petition for a writ of certiorari was denied. Justice William O. Douglas wrote a Dissent on Denial of Writ of Certiorari, which follows.*]

Petitioner did not report for induction as ordered, was indicted, convicted, and sentenced to five years imprisonment and his conviction was affirmed. 369 F. 2d 323. His defense was that the "war" in Vietnam was being conducted in violation of various treaties to which we were a signatory, especially the Treaty of London of August 8, 1945, 59 Stat. 1544, which in Article 6 (a) declares that "waging of a war of aggression" is a "crime against peace," imposing "individual responsibility." Article 8 provides: "The fact that the Defendant acted pursuant to order of his Government or of a superior shall not free him from responsibility, but may be considered in mitigation of punishment if the Tribunal determines that justice so requires."

Petitioner claimed that the "war" in Vietnam was a "war

*of aggression" within the meaning of the Treaty of London
and that Article 8 makes him responsible for participating
in it even though he is ordered to do so.**

*Mr. Justice Jackson, the United States prosecutor at Nurem-
berg, stated: "If certain acts in violation of treaties are crimes,
they are crimes whether the United States does them or
whether Germany does them, and we are not prepared to
lay down a rule of criminal conduct against others which we
would not be willing to have invoked against us." (International Conference on Military Trials, Dept. State Pub. No.
3880, p. 330.)*

*Article VI, cl. 2, of the Constitution states that "treaties"
are a part of "the supreme law of the land; and the Judges
in every State shall be bound thereby."*

*There is a considerable body of opinion that our actions in
Vietnam constitute the waging of an aggressive "war."*

This case presents the questions:

*(1) whether the Treaty of London is a treaty within the
meaning of Art. VI, cl. 2;*

*(2) whether the question as to the waging of an aggressive
"war" is in the context of this criminal prosecution a justiciable question;*

*(3) whether the Vietnam episode is a "war" in the sense
of the Treaty;*

(4) whether petitioner has standing to raise the question;

*(5) whether, if he has, it may be tendered as a defense
in this criminal case or in amelioration of the punishment.*

*These are extremely sensitive and delicate questions. But
they should, I think, be answered. Even those who think
that the Nuremberg judgments were unconstitutional by
our guarantee relating to ex post facto laws would have to
take a different view of the Treaty of London that purports to
lay down a standard of future conduct for all the signatories.*

I intimate no opinion on the merits. But I think the

---

* [Note in original] *The trial court charged the jury that the Treaty
of London did not interfere "in any manner in respect to this defendant
fulfilling his duty under this order."*

petition for certiorari should be granted. We have here a recurring question in present-day Selective Service cases.

[*After going to prison, David Mitchell wrote the following in a Petition for Rehearing of Denial of Writ of Certiorari:*]

The effect of the Supreme Court's decision to deny certiorari is to close off legal channels for challenging the present actions of the U.S. in Vietnam. The government in its brief in opposition to the petition urged the Court to refuse to review because it would interfere with "the ability of the Chief Executive to conduct foreign affairs." It is for this reason particularly that the Court should review this case. The Courts have a responsibility to stop an illegal use of Presidential power—not to place the President above the law and beyond the judicial check of the Courts. In Germany, Hitler could only be stopped by war. Today the American Courts have the power and responsibility to stop what may be adjudged to be illegal use of Presidential power by giving a fair hearing to the petitioner, who is willing in a court of law to test the actions of the government according to its own laws. By its silence the Court becomes an accomplice to the actions of the government and a mere instrument of national policy.

I am only one among other individuals who in various ways and with various positions are refusing and challenging the draft and thereby raising a challenge to U.S. policy. So far, we have remained only individuals, for no coherent and organized program has been forthcoming to deal with the issues and effect the challenge that we raise. In some quarters we have been martyred, called heroes, or whatever, but to my mind such a response only isolates our acts as impossible and therefore closets [them] into "irrelevance."

[*Mitchell wrote in 1965:*] . . . Individuals, good as they may be, will never be enough to carry the fight through *alone*. It is not for us to glory in their sacrifice—or to put it aside, but rather to build on it—to make it more meaningful, more

effective than it already is. . . . Their protests can never be
wasted or meaningless sacrifices, *even* if we do nothing to
build on them, because they did what they had to do, they
attempted to fight what has to be fought. Right cannot be
judged by success or failure, *but* we do a disservice to what
is right and those who fight for it if we don't try our
damnedest to succeed.

My purpose is to contribute to building a movement to challenge and end policies of aggression and inhumanity. My purpose
(if not to win a legal victory to end the Vietnam war in the courts,
which is near impossible) is to raise, and focus on, the issues and
help to elicit the response of organizing *power* that can effectively deal with them. If such power was forthcoming, then the
legal victory would come forth as an aspect of the implementation of *change*.

In terms of building a response to the Viet draft, let me conclude by noting a few points:

(1) Not everyone who refuses induction has the same position
entirely, or the same philosophy in terms of any draft, any time,
nonviolence or whatever, but everyone refusing the draft is concerned with the draft *now* as an instrument of present U.S. policy,
and can unite and provide mutual support on that basis.

(2) Not everyone concerned with the draft feels they can refuse the draft *outright*—but regardless of the various devices a
given individual uses to deal with the situation, that individual
can join a movement to support and build into political relevance
the challenge of those who refuse, or exile themselves, because
of the draft; and that individual can join a movement that cam-
paigns on the general issue of ending the current draft by such
means as draft board sit-ins and disruptions, . . . campus activity building towards possible student strikes on the draft or
whatever.

(3) And third and lastly, we must remember our main concern at the moment: the aggression and slaughter in Vietnam
and our main enemy in that regard—the U.S. government. That
concern will not be resolved by battles over draft reforms . . .
which people propagate as effective because it "hits people

where they are at." It's time we dealt with the situation with its mounting deaths and danger where it's at—by supporting and building on the fundamental challenges to the draft that already exist and educating and acting about the draft as an instrument of murder!

[*Letters from prison, summer 1967:*]

. . . I know what I did and why, and if there are regrets, they are the same I had before prison and not the kind that affect what I did—I did what I did not joyfully or without regrets, but rather because I felt I *had* to. . . . I was not cut out for silence, because to me that always meant acquiescence to and contributing to the wrong. I would lose my own self-respect if I did that, as I believe that to *be* me . . .

How would I deal with "price . . . paid"? Heck, I'm not sure if the "price" should be paid. I don't mean by that that one should not risk paying it—I believe firmly in that. I wonder though— I have an old philosophy: One should fight the battle but duck the bullets. Maybe the "price" was a bullet to be ducked. . . . Being here (for me) involves a great deal of feelings of guilt and frustration as a result of isolation and inaction. But that's a big question really, because, as there is no practical way or meaningful way to continue resisting in the country while on the run. Perhaps (and I don't really know the answer) there is more "resistance" or whatever accomplished by me in jail than safely in another country, where perhaps I would be more isolated and ineffective. . . .

. . . I don't want to write anything to or for Alice Lynd about my feeling about being here. What the hell can I say? That it's a very painful experience is about it. That one feels one is wasting time (life), and perhaps, even personally deteriorating at times —in terms of ability to think, etc. That one becomes very much aware, suddenly, of age and has a tremendous fear of aging in a situation of non-living and waste. That one feels the "bit" is endless and every day fights to reassure himself that he'll make it and that life somewhat will remain intact. That one finds oneself besieged with insecurities and fears. Also, that one's life, hopes, dreams, loves, or just plain stamina, will be shattered. That one is often depressed and touches on moods of despair because of feeling isolated, and therefore completely powerless. It's a state wherein one is made somewhat alienated and very much emasculated and fearful of his insignificance to people and activity outside. Yet one is jailed—and therefore life and individual self-assertion is held in a suspended animation (a limbo). One therefore lives on the "remembrance of things past" and the hopes and dreams for the future, which, because they are so removed from concrete here and now contact, become such frightful insecurities themselves at times.

I have nothing to write for her. You can tell her it is hell. Maybe I should write for her but I can't! I never pretended it was "otherwise" before coming and, as then, I would still do what I did on the basis of my own integrity and in a striving and with a hope for effect and change. I would probably, though, reconsider the "jail" question, but then I always had that question as an open one in my mind to the last and still do. But also, now I question even more whether jail adds any mileage to the position or struggle, and other alternatives leaving me active although possibly removed, could. And then—as I said—jail is hell.

[Permission to use the prison letters was granted with the qualification that perhaps they paint a more discouraging picture than David Mitchell feels after a year in prison. A letter from Ellen Schneider explains:]

Not that it isn't difficult but he does not see the difficulty as a factor to discourage taking the position—fighting the fight to the end—even if the end is jail. He sees the need for the movement to provide a means by which men can make the fight—resist the draft—and if possible remain in the country —out of jail to continue resisting. But at the present time such an alternative does not exist, and for David, in reality, after the courts jail was the only way he could remain to fight another day. The point he would most want to get across is that the fight has to be made and that he feels as strongly about that point now as ever.

Richard Paterak, David Taube, and Petrokovsky

EMIGRANTS TO CANADA

This section contains brief accounts from three men who emigrated to Canada to avoid the draft in the United States. Two of them describe not only their personal reasons for emigrating to Canada, but their view of what the experience is for some others.

The following appeared as an advertisement by the Vancouver Committee to Aid American War Objectors in the *National Guardian*, April 1967:

AID DRAFT RESISTANCE

During the past two years several thousand Americans have evaded the draft by coming to Canada. Many more who would have evaded the draft in this way are now in the army because they didn't have accurate information about how to get legal status in Canada. Anti-war groups in the U.S. have up to now done very little to distribute information about immigration to Canada. We find that deplorable because:

1. Those who oppose this war should not only be trying to change the policies of the American government, but should also do whatever possible to obstruct the prosecution of the war. We hold that large-scale draft evasion is at least a minor obstruction.

2. Anti-war groups have a special responsibility to young men whom they have convinced that the war in Vietnam is unjust. While we encourage and expect these young men to refuse military service, we must at the same time assist by providing them with information on all ways of avoiding induction into the army. EVERY act of non-compliance with the military should be welcomed as an obstruction of the war effort. . . .

Anyone considering emigration or renunciation of American citizenship should have up-to-date information and advice appropriate to his own situation. (Contact the Central Committee for Conscientious Objectors or another reliable counseling service. See pp. 325 and 329.) Countries which have similar laws return lawbreakers to the authorities for punishment. Canada does not have a draft and American draft offenses are no bar to Canadian citizenship. However, in most cases men who flee the draft can never expect to return to the United States without facing immediate induction or prosecution.

Richard Paterak

IN the following notes, I will try to do two things: (1) a brief background sketch of myself and my motivation for coming to Canada; (2) since I have had close contact with a number of draft-resisters in Canada and have been working to help more to come, I feel a necessity to present a short review of this whole situation.

(1) As I proceeded through life my background was middle-class, and as I went to college, it swung to upper-middle, through the grace of American upward mobility, i.e., the rat race. I was a Roman Catholic in a suburban Roman Catholic town. My political leanings were always ill-defined, but always tending toward some evolutionary (Kautshuts) socialism—although highly anti-communist.

It was with that background that I tramped off to college—Marquette University—in Milwaukee. Seventeen years old, 1,000 miles from my New England suburb. I soon learned that Marquette was home for the Catholic *nouveau riche*. Their folks had just made it, and not the "niggers" or nobody else was going to interfere with their enjoying it.

Thus I began an isolated existence, where encountering a palatable, non-Ivy-League-looking Democrat was an occasion to remember. I proceeded, realizing the absurdity of competing for high grades with my classmates who were interested in high grades for rewards only. Strangely enough, I had gone to the university with an idea that education was becoming a fuller human being (I was later to learn that Plato defined education as a process whereby one becomes more human). With this in mind, I became quite introspective, spending a good part of my time just thinking and/or relating my classwork to myself and self-understanding. I majored in sociology and minored in psychology with that in mind.

I guess I was nothing more than a liberal's dupe until just before I graduated in the spring of 1965. The bombing of North Vietnam didn't quite sit right with me, so I investigated the situation as best I could. My unavoidable conclusion was that we were being politically impractical, internationally as well as domestically, and, at the same time, immoral.

I graduated [from the] university and still being a starry-eyed liberal do-gooder, I joined VISTA. I must say that the war was the first major crack I saw in the System, but that crack allowed me to see in deeper and see that the war wasn't the problem, but a manifestation of it. The problem was the System. As I trained for VISTA (six weeks at Temple University) I became what I thought was more radical. I must point out that our training was radical in content. (It is still trying to be forgotten in Washington—"too negative an approach.")

I went on to live a year and then some out in projects in Louisville and Chicago. I accomplished nothing in the first instance, due to the nature of the project and in the second instance due to the nature of me (no matter how hard a white tries, he is still not black).

During my VISTA service, I became resigned to the fact that I was going to have some jail time to look forward to. I slowly came to the conclusion that this would accomplish nothing, and possibly, I could maintain my integrity and my radical self-respect some other way. Canada was my solution. I had always felt more a citizen of the world than an American. Also, my belief was that a radical could find a constituency wherever there were people. With these beliefs, my wife and I packed up and resettled in Canada. I have been active in the anti-draft movement here ever since.

(2) SUPA's [Student Union for Peace Action*] anti-draft program, Vancouver Committee to Aid American War Objectors, the Montreal Council to Aid War Resisters, etc., all are undertaking the same task: informing the American man that the age-old alternative to fighting a war is still available—that being emigration.

After being involved in this for six months I find it very strange that such work is being done, but a brief glance at the present state of the U.S.A. brings me back to reality. Men have

* Dissolved in 1967; replaced by Toronto Anti-Draft Programme.

been fleeing conscription unaided for centuries; why now do there have to be groups to show men how? To my mind, it seems clear that the reason lies in the nature of American life: America has indoctrinated its young so well that the thought of emigration is extraordinary (actually emigration is only considered when a better job offer—more money—is found elsewhere).

We have only seen a minority of the draft-resisters who have come to Toronto. Some others have used our literature but not our counselling service. And still others, after reading about us or other groups in Canada, have taken the cue and proceeded unaided. All of which is fine. Most of the fellows are traditional conscription fleers, i.e., the war doesn't relate to them in a meaningful way, therefore they are unwilling to kill or be killed. Others (this is an increasingly common reason) are actually opposed to the war itself. Very few are radicals as such.

The act of draft resistance, as I have witnessed it in Americans in Canada, is an extremely personal thing. The majority of those we have (which are a minority) do not want any prolonged contact with us—just want to blend in with the woodwork. This of course is good for Canada, but not for those interested in radical politics, etc.

In the end, what is the effect of all of this? Men who would normally reluctantly fight are being removed from the war machine—this is not to say that some of us wouldn't have gone to prison—thus making our work legitimate anti-war work, as well as material for good propaganda.

As to why more radicals don't come to Canada, I don't know. There is plenty of room for them and plenty of work. I can't see wasting a good portion of my life in jail due to commitment to revolution in the U.S., for I believe revolution in the U.S. will be provoked as much from without as from within. It is my hope that more radicals will agree and move north rather than waste their precious radicalism in prison.

David Taube

I PROTESTED the war, but did nothing to avoid the draft until it was too late to act in the U.S. I honestly felt that I could rationalize a noncombatant position in the service, and since I didn't base my objection to the Vietnamese war on a belief in a supreme being, I did not bother to apply for CO status.

I enlisted in the Army Reserve on a three-month delayed enlistment in Des Moines, Iowa, on November 10, 1966. My army recruiter indicated that I could have my choice, in writing, of schooling or a substitute suitable to me should my first choice be full. I went to Des Moines to enlist and signed a paper saying that I would go on active duty for twenty-four months. I later found out that in order to get my choice of schooling, I would have to reenlist for thirty-six months, and that if I merely went for twenty-four, I might have to kill people. The fact that I would have to reenlist had not been explained to me prior to enlistment. Then, the army was not able to give me my first choice of schooling or either of two alternates. This developed over the next two months and I decided I would not go at all. I even investigated the possibility of stopping my income tax payments and applied for admission to Canada. . . .

I was to report to the service on March 9, and I entered Canada on March 6. . . . I received orders and travel vouchers to report to Fort Campbell, Ky. When I didn't show (I told them I wouldn't) the FBI harassed my family and a RCMP [Royal Canadian Mounted Police] man was sent to talk with me. He asked if I was going to stay in Canada and after I said "yes" we had a nice talk about the YMCA camp I was working for at the time. . . . I am definitely a deserter . . . but legal authorities tell me that now I am landed . . . I am in no danger of extradition. The Army even wrote my mother to tell her I should come back "because I was losing all pay and other benefits."

I had briefly studied German resistance to Hitler and came to the conclusion that the present U.S. regime should be resisted in much the same way. I was too chicken and was going to go peacefully to jail instead. . . . I concluded that if I were to kill innocent Vietnamese, I could not live with myself. Since living with myself is important to me (who else can I live with?), I was about to go to jail. Although this wouldn't be as good as active rebellion for the anti-war cause, it would have at least made the U.S. feed and clothe me for five years. . . . Canada seemed to be nicer than a jail, however, so I chose to opt out of the struggle. This makes me feel guilty at times.

I sometimes think I should have stayed and fought, but could see no way to really do anything meaningful anyway. I would condone violent as well as nonviolent attempts to overthrow the present U.S. regime because it is unconstitutional (Art. I, Sec. 8). Thomas Jefferson said, "God forbid that we should ever go twenty years without such a rebellion (Whiskey). The tree of liberty must constantly be watered with the blood of patriots." . . . I don't frankly know that I am doing anything meaningful here to fight the U.S. Nearly all the natives I meet are also against the war, so I am not convincing anyone new about anything. Canada has permitted me to stay out of jail and live with myself. In the U.S., I would have had to choose between the two. If this is a jail, it sure is a big, beautiful one.

Petrokovsky

I AM a British subject who was in the States for ten years. . . . I did not have to leave to avoid the war. I could have gone to graduate school, got myself arrested, or, however unesthetic, faked the physical. I did not want to continue in school, however, and felt the need for a clean break with the past. I was moderately successful in the university but in my last year I was finding it increasingly difficult to satisfy, within the academic structure, my interest in thought and words. I felt a continual tension between what I wanted to do and what I was supposed to do, that no doubt was exacerbated by my discomfort with being supported by my parents. I was finding the crisis atmosphere in the United States and the incessant propaganda from the mass media increasingly uncongenial. I wanted to live some of Kerouac's adventures (I am doing so), but in the United States it would have been too easy for me, once out of school, to join the hippie community. Also, in the United States I felt a duty to be political but I did not feel comfortable with myself as a political animal. Socially, too, I was uncomfortable. I was beginning to fit too much into a groove. . . . In a strange way I was losing my ability to feel.

Certainly the draft and the Vietnam war were reasons for my leaving. Under present circumstances I will not fight in Vietnam. I am not a pacifist, but I do not like violence or killing. There would have to be strong reasons for me to participate in a war. I think the strong reasons existed in World War II— violence was a necessary last resort to defend a qualitatively better society—and I think that without hesitation I would have fought in that war. I do not find the strong reasons in Vietnam. Whether the South is better than the North I think is unclear, and not mine (or the United States government's) to decide. I think the "today Vietnam, tomorrow X" argument is pure baloney that was concocted up after the fact to justify the American military involvement. It is not necessary to fight in Vietnam to defend a better world somewhere else.

My view of the Vietnam war is that it came about through the failure to make a decision rather than through the manipulations of crafty men or through the needs of a capitalist economy. A commitment was made in Vietnam over a decade ago when the commitment seemed relatively free of risk, and in terms of Dulles' foreign policy, small, measured against the likely gains. This commitment was never seriously reevaluated despite a change in circumstances and a change in the goals of American foreign policy; rather, in order to make the commitment meaningful, it was increased in a series of small increments. By the time the elites realized the size of the commitment that had been made and the weakness of the government the U.S. was supporting, it was too late to admit failure because that would be an admission of the elite's own failure and the failure of American power.

. . . It was not a "we" decision that made me come here. I was acting for myself alone, and I am rather proud of the fact that I did act—that I did something radical about my situation. Suggesting that I took the decision in consort with others somehow degrades the act. A suggestion that, in a narrow sense, I acted for the sake of others is a false suggestion. My draft board has a quota of men. If I don't go, someone else is made to take my place. If I had really wanted to try to do something about the Vietnam war for the sake of some "we," I would have stayed in the States and fought the warriors there, or even have enlisted and tried to cause dissension in the army. . . .

. . . The individual's sensitivity to himself and to his being part of a community has to be increased at the expense of a concern for what other people think of him and for his standard of living. This I think can be done more by art and by example than by politics. And it is really part of a larger issue—the issue of alternatives to the kind of lives most Americans are leading.

I think that if there is one thing I would like to say to people, all people, not just young Americans facing the draft, it is that it is possible to act independently, that it feels good if you are strong enough to follow through on your act and, I think as more people do, it will be a better world. Certainly I have been better for myself, better for other people, since my major independent act of the last few years—leaving for Canada.

. . . For most of the draft evaders it was not an easy thing to leave the United States. A condition of shock is characteristic of the first few months after arrival; the draft evader spends most of his time in his room reading, and the event of the day is the arrival or non-arrival of mail from home. Very few, if any, however, regret their decision to leave. Eventually they return to school or get jobs, often attaching themselves to a university. A few are attracted to the frontier life of Canada and get jobs in construction, logging, or mining. . . .

Compared with the States, most of the draft evaders find Canada a simpler, quieter, saner society. The difference stems from political and social structure, history and world-role. Canada is ten provinces and two territories joined not so much by a common history or even by a common langauge as by a disinclination to become American. It is the country of the loyalist, the country of people who are content with their private traditions. It is a country of immigrants, even more so than the United States. (Ten percent of the labor force immigrated since World War II.) . . . There is more cultural differentiation in Canada than in the States, and at the same time, less pressure to conform, more tolerance, more sanity, and in some ways, more freedom.

Perhaps, above all, Canada, particularly western Canada, is the country of the frontier. Canada is a vast country, the second largest in the world, but has a population of only 20 million; and 50 percent of the 20 million live within seventy-five miles of the U.S. border. Off the main communication routes, access is always an issue, often *the* political issue. The economy is not yet primarily manufacturing or service-oriented but, in a broad sense, extractive.

. . . It isn't just in terms of geography and economy that Canada is a frontier country; it's the men and their experience. . . . Hitch-hiking in Canada, one is picked up by men who have worked in, and who talk of, the mines, the railroad, the sawmills, the oil fields, and the forest. . . . Unfortunately, Cana-

dian tolerance does not extend in all its force to the hippies. . . .
Still, the lines have not solidified to the extent that they have in
the States. . . .

As for me, the writer, the draft evader, the laborer making
$1,000 a month on a dam off the Alaska highway, I am glad I
came. It is a time to try new ways of living, to try new faces, to
think, to remember. I am not committed to remain. I might move
on to Montreal, or Toronto, Paris, or the Orient, but now it's
where I want to be. Things are building. It's a good country for
young men.

Due to the large number of young men going to Canada, the
employment situation, at least in the major cities, has become
difficult. Those planning to go are urged to make arrangements
ahead of time and check for latest information through one of
the groups listed on page 329.

The following excerpts are from a letter from Phil Mullins to
former associates in the Southern Student Organizing Committee, written in March 1968:

. . . If the employment scene is as bad as we see it now we'd
like to let the kids in the states know so they wouldn't come up
here in such numbers. Keep those boys home on the farm and let
them make revolution. . . .

Some guys are giving up and going back to the states. Fortunately lots of the guys aren't in trouble with the law yet so this
option is open. For some of us it's either sink or swim . . . and I
guess eventually we'll all swim.

Jack Boykin, Jr.

POOR PEOPLE HERE AND
POOR PEOPLE ELSEWHERE

Commonly known as "Junebug," Jack Boykin, Jr., is a full-time staff member of the Chicago Goodfellows. This local group started in the summer of 1966, "when a couple of hillbilly guys had an idea and got together. And the idea was that something had to be done about police brutality." In the winter they opened "a place for young guys to hang out. A place where we could talk to guys and try to get through to them and be friends with them. . . . Not only on police brutality, but bad housing and food co-op and everything that is wrong with this . . . society."

Junebug is also on the Organizing Committee for JOIN (Jobs Or Income Now), a community organization in the poor white neighborhood of Chicago where he lives.

The account was transcribed from an interview which Richard Rothstein tape recorded for this book in May 1967, seven months after Junebug's eighteenth birthday. The quotations are from an article, "Goodfellows Find Place," by Junebug Boykin, in *The Movement*, June 1967.

Interviewer: What did you do to resist the draft or military service?

Junebug: Well, first thing when they sent me my [Form 100, Classification] Questionnaire, I applied for CO, which is just a question they ask you and you're supposed to sign your name to. So that went back. Maybe a few weeks later I received the application [for Conscientious Objector, Form 150] which I had a counselor, which helped me fill it out, in which the stuff I give was the truth. I mean, at first I thought I might try to weasel out of it, tell some lies, you know, just to get out of the army. And that wasn't it. It came out that I just was completely honest in what I said. And in doing this, I found out myself—like, I didn't believe in organized killing. Then [I] just didn't leave it at that. . . . I looked at that and see what that meant. And there was a whole number of things. I mean like, organized killing is something that you're supposed to go out there and kill people by orders as been carried down through somebody, a human being just like you are. And why should you kill somebody just because this other man says so. And this person you're killing, he's just the same as you are. And in my situation, I'm a poor person, and the people that I would be fighting over there would be poor people, poor farmers like some of my grandparents were. And that's one of the best reasons I have.

Interviewer: How did you come to your decision to be a CO . . . and what kind of pressures were on you?

Junebug: Well, one of the pressures that was on me is that I didn't know . . . much about CO and like, very little time for me to decide whether if I should or not, because I was at the age of eighteen, or getting there, and I hadn't decided if I was going to apply for CO to keep from going into the army. And I thought about it, and I thought maybe it would be like, if I didn't go into the army, I'd go into like a VISTA thing. Not a VISTA thing exactly, but you know—like doing stuff around the country, which I wouldn't like to do too much. I'd like to work where I'm at, where I'm good at, where I think I'm the best at, and that's right in my own community. And the ways I used to try to talk to them was just . . . like telling them that I was trying to, in a way, reform young guys like myself from around the neighborhood, to give them jobs, give them a place in society where they won't be just et up by all the people.

Interviewer: But how did you come to your decision to be a CO?

Junebug: It was partly because of my work, what I was doing. It had a great affect on it. And, like I said before, the people that we're fighting over there is not people with big machinery. . . . This is people that farms their land and grow their own food, just like my people do. And I can't see going over and killing people that live the life that my grandparents or myself have lived.

Interviewer: Was there anybody in particular that you talked to about being a CO, that influenced you?

Junebug: Well, it wasn't as much as being influenced as much as trying to learn. . . . I would try to work my own thing out and the thing I believe in most and how it was working and so I did that. I went about it that way, just trying to learn what people had to say, not getting influence from them. . . .

Interviewer: Do you remember any particular conversation you had . . . about CO that affected you a lot?

Junebug: Well, the most part that affected me I found out on my own. [I] was looking through books, that kids getting et up by that napalm, and stuff like that—which had a great affect on me, I guess. And I looked around the streets and I see kids that are dirty, don't have much clothes, and people with large number of kids in a family, doesn't have enough to eat, and stuff like that. And why should this be? If we're going to fight with people like ourselves—I mean—who started the fight? It's not these poor people over here, because they ain't never been outside, they don't know what other people—what languages people talk. And it had to be somebody other than the poor people that started it, and that leaves only one person—the Big Man. . . .

Enough of it was that it was poor people we was fighting, and that a lot of people do disagree on it. And at first I had the feeling that seemed like pretty much putting myself down as a coward, or something like that. But that's not the case now, I know. Because, the guys over there dying could, if he had a chance to go through what I went through, to try to help people out like I try to do—seeing what kind of people they really are over there. They're farmers. . . . I think if these other guys had a chance to find out, they wouldn't be the way they are. . . .

Interviewer: How do you feel now about what you've been through?

Junebug: Well, I feel pretty good about it that I got the CO. And that one of my jobs will be as an organizer is to talk to guys and help them to try to get it. But not only to just to get out of the army routine, but the thing is of learning what I've learned—through going through these—changes, you could call them.

Interviewer: What do you want your action to make people think about?

Junebug: About poor people here and poor people elsewhere. The one basic thing is poor people. And who are we fighting is poor people. That's the most important thing.

Interviewer: Is there anything you would say to other young men who are trying to decide what they should do about the draft or military service? . . . This book is aimed primarily at young guys who are puzzled.

Junebug: I'd say, think! About the poor people of the United States, and having to go out and kill them because they're poor. And then think about the people over there, of how they're poor, and you're doing the same thing over there that you would be doing here. I mean, it's that they're people, they're human beings just like we are. I mean, they might talk a different language, but that's no big thing.

Interviewer: I remember when we were talking about your CO form, a number of things came up which you haven't mentioned. I wonder if they are now less important to you, or what. You had a very interesting way of answering the Supreme Being thing. Is that less important to you now?

Junebug: No, it's not. I think that, well, a lot of people believes in people, I mean, just in good out of people. And I think that this good, . . . what you call love, is the thing that is over the people. It's not that you go worship this love, it's not that kind of a thing. I mean it's a thing that happens to you every day when you meet a friend, shaking hands with, you know. And that's the sort of thing I believe in. And that's what I think people should be. . . .

If some were saying . . . like the President . . . well, you got to go and fight . . . well I say, I ain't listening to you, Man. You're nothing to me. I do what I believe in. And say he gets ten or fifteen cops to carry me off, or a hundred cops, and puts me over there. I mean, they *put* me over there but they ain't made me

kill anyone. . . . I wouldn't follow one man, I wouldn't follow a
hundred men. . . . They couldn't make me do something I didn't
want to. They can't prop me up and put a gun in my hand and
tell me to kill this person. That's something I just don't believe in
and something I won't even lift a finger to try to do.

Interviewer: When you first applied for CO they turned you
down. They gave you I-A, and then you wrote in and said you
wanted a personal hearing. Do you want to tell . . . a little bit
about what went on at that personal hearing?

Junebug: Well, there wasn't much. There was these two guys.
When we walked in there I had my suit on and you had yours on.
. . . And they looked at me and they asked me a question, "What
you have against the Selective Service System?" . . . [I told
them] the main things of what my belief was, and what I believed
in. And they asked me what the name of my organization I work
in, and am I fully employed there, and what type of work do I do,
and who's the boss at the work—and I had to go through a thing
of telling them that it wasn't run by the boss, it was run by the
people, . . . the community people and other people, which
seemed to have a good effect on them. . . . I run down about
what I believed in, and then, any kind of work I was doing,
trying to help them guys. I ran down in a way that I was just
getting the guys jobs, you know, trying to get them off the
streets. You know—like I was doing *them* a favor instead of doing
the guys a favor.

Interviewer: Why do you think you're different from most other
guys? Why don't most other guys agree with you that they're
just fighting their own kind in Vietnam?

Junebug: Now that's a hard question. Well, other guys, they
got a shield . . . like . . . some guys think it's silly and just
won't do. Because they've been taught to not like it, it's silly.
Just like two billy cats are taught to hate Negroes. It's the thing
of how the society . . . brought them up. That's the whole thing
about it. And some break out. Some wants to learn about it. And
some do and some break out, and a lot don't.

Interviewer: You have no idea, though, what makes those who break out break out? What is in your life that makes you want to break out and other guys don't want to?

Junebug: Well, I think one of the things is like curiosity. I want to know what stuff is about. I just don't want to look at it and walk away from it. I want to look inside of it and see what makes it tick. And which a lot of guys try to avoid, and try to put it out of their minds. Which I don't. I think that's one of the differences. But there could be others, too.

Interviewer: How does a guy like you, who is against violence, how can you get on in a neighborhood like this where most guys are always fighting, and how can you hope to organize guys— most of whose life is violent—if you go around saying you are nonviolent and you are against war?

Junebug: I can't say I'm nonviolent now. . . . [When] I raised up, I was fighting. And I did stuff like this, which stuff society forgives, stuff that you was expected to do. But I finally answered that I wasn't supposed to do that because I'm just making a fool out of myself and doing what the Big Man wants me to do.

There is something I want to say, and that is when guys like myself keep popping up with ideas, they might just fit together and be the answer to our problems—though it might take a lifetime. This is my life now, and what I just wrote gives me and people like me faith.

James M. Taylor

THE SPIRIT OF THE ARMY

The spirit Jim Taylor found in the Army conflicted with his primary allegiance as a Christian. What was most important for the purposes of this book—his refusal to train—was of secondary importance to Taylor.

The account was extracted from hundreds of pages of journal and letters which he wrote between July 1965 and January 1967, enough to comprise a book in itself. These selections are not representative of the bulk of material. Several inserts were taken from the Record of Trial of Pvt. Taylor's General Court-Martial at Fort Ord, December 22, 1966, thanks to the assistance of attorney Francis Heisler.

Taylor knew when he registered that he "never intended to participate in war in any form" and he signed Series VIII on the Classification Questionnaire, claiming conscientious objection. Two years later the draft board sent him a Form 150 for conscientious objectors which he completed and returned. After several years in college preparing for the ministry, he reduced his course load below that of a full-time student in order to earn money for tuition, and thereby was reclassified from IV-D (pre-theological student) to I-A. After his physical examination he enlisted for four years in the Regular Army, on the advice of a retired Army officer who told him that if he were assigned to the Army Security Agency he could go to language school and avoid combat.

Had Taylor been adequately counseled, at this point he could have requested consideration of his Form 150, a personal appearance, possible appeals, and determination of his noncombatant status, before entering the Armed Forces. However, what Taylor experienced could have occurred even if he had been counseled and had gone in as a noncombatant.

Because he had indicated his conscientious objection *before* entering the service, it was ruled that he disqualified himself under the *military* regulations for discharge as a conscientious objector. He had recommendations from several superior officers that his application for discharge be approved, and his defense lawyer argued that Selective Service had failed to record any decision on his original claim.

The following instruction to the court indicates the manner in which the law may be expected to be applied to the facts in cases such as Taylor's:

> *Now, gentlemen, you are instructed that members of the military are required to obey lawful orders which require the performance of a military duty, despite the fact that such orders may involve a violation of their religious or moral scruples. In other words, the fact that obedience to a lawful order involves violation of the religious or moral scruples of an individual is no defense to a charge of willful disobedience of a lawful military order.*

On January 10, 1967, Taylor was released when his sentence was cut from three to two years (he had accumulated sufficient good-time) and his discharge was changed from dishonorable to undesirable.

July 15, 1965: Arrived at [Fort Ord] last night—learned that Sergeant hates only two things—both of which are recruits!

July 17: There is really not enough time to formulate thoughts into words around here. . . . We have to memorize the chain of command which starts at President Johnson and comes in twelve steps down to us. . . . So many things are new that one has little occasion to develop a train of thought along any line other than military. . . . So few people are happy or confident.

July 22: I will not carry a gun—I am in for a hard time. Will not kill for my country, I will not kill for myself. I will not kill any man, *nor will I harden my heart by pretending.* I could be a medic or a chaplain's assistant but I cannot do anything which will harm anyone.

July 24: . . . I am not free. Combat boots bind my feet and my head is covered and my back wrapped in three layers of olive drab denim.

I listen for nature's voice and I hear

". . . You are here to prepare to destroy the enemy . . . our freedoms are being challenged . . . Your lives are being challenged" . . . "You may some day in the near future find yourself in combat" . . . "we will turn out the product"

—and I say, "what enemy?" Does a gun kill an enemy? Is the enemy a man? Is the enemy a man on the battlefield, a power plant, a stray child . . . what enemy—?

and I ask, "what freedoms." Have I any freedoms today?

and I ask, "what life?" I find none of that here . . .

and I say, "what combat?"—are you so foolish as to miss the ever-present struggle of this world . . . ?

and I ask, "what product" is it that you seek to produce? An animated conditioned response, a heartless soul that cries "I hate mother," and "we love blood," "just for fun."

This world is a giant killer and a fool-nourisher—the battlefield and the morgue.

I made a mistake—I joined the Army. I did not know the spirit of this thing. I thought of it as a job and a chance for a free education.

July 26: Right now I do not know what is in store for me. Anything from indefinite jail to discharge have been suggested. It has been said that I might be sent to the front lines with no weapon. The Lt. spoke of beating some sense into me but realized that such a thing would be of no avail in bringing about a reconsideration on my part. . . .

I have filled out forms that will be considered as those above view the situation and come to a conclusion—and decide on what steps are to be taken in dealing with me. . . .

The Lt. said that I was a quitter and that this was just another demonstration of my gutless nature. I have quit many things, but since the time I truly realized that the only thing of any importance was "seeking the Kingdom" I have used this as the factor by which I determine whether a thing should be pursued or not. . . .

I am not afraid. I do not like the sort of treatment that one is subject to here, and I realize that the mind whose aim is trained toward the things that a soldier's is trained toward, can operate only in this manner.

I have considered the most extreme possible result of my present actions—being shot—and I find no fear, though I do not look forward to this sort of thing. Imprisonment does not frighten me, but it will be much less than pleasant if I am not allowed to read and write.

I will do nothing as a part of the U.S. Armed Forces. . . .

July 28: [*Refused to train on this date.*] My eyes have been opened to many things since coming here—

Slowly and almost unnoticeably they deaden your senses. First of all, they cut your hair all off and put you all in the same clothes. This is sufficient to erase most distinctions—class, educational and taste.

Fear is used widely, and anger aroused whenever possible. Any fear or anger they can draw from you they channel as they choose at the alleged enemy. Also by keeping one constantly angry, they effect deadened senses. . . .

. . . When Dad was a kid he wanted to join the Army. It was a privilege. But today it is different. Then the people loved America and [it was] worth dying for. No one had to be "lied to" in order to make him serve. But today there is so much distrust of our state officials and apathy is so much a part of our way of life that there is no real need felt in the people as a whole. We no longer "fight for freedom" in a tangible way. We seek to maintain face by pretending to defend a tiny country half way around the world.

We are told one thing and then another, and I cannot feel that we are being trained to do what they say we are being trained to do.

Actions that do not spring from faith demonstrating itself in love are sin!

I have no faith in this whole business!

July 29: They were shown a movie yesterday and were given instructions on how to use the bayonet. Some of the boys felt

sick. Soon they will be able to talk about and see these things
without emotion.

August 5: The Army is not as I expected. But, as I have realized, I had no expectation. I was thinking that anything would
be better than selling men's dress-wear at Penney's. But as it is
that I am awaiting a special court-martial, you must realize that
I do not find myself at peace with the U.S. Army.

U.S. Army = United States *Armed Forces*—Army Branch. I
am now at Fort Ord Basic *Combat* Training Station. Combat is
killing people, and training is learning how. I am mentally prepared for the six months of jail that I will probably get for refusing to train.

I have been forced to do some relevant thinking lately. Unfortunately, I started the thinking too late to keep Hell from burst-
ing out in places. . . .

On three occasions Jesus faced a decision of a specific nature
and on all three reacted in the same way. First, at the tempta-
tions—Jesus was offered the kingdoms of this earth. If this had
not been a credible offer there would have been no real tempta-
tion—or, perhaps I should say, a chance at physical control over
the kingdoms of the earth, a chance to bring about reforms, a
chance to make of this world a Utopia. But he chose not to
accept this position. Why? Perhaps because he realized the im-
possibility of bringing about such in this physical world. The
point being: HE REFUSED!

Second: After feeding the multitude he was again offered a
position of earthly power. He could have posed a real threat on
the established order— HE REFUSED.

Third: Upon his entrance into Jerusalem, he again had enough
support to threaten the established order—or at least exerted a
considerable pressure on those in power—BUT—HE DIDN'T.

This is not to mention the fact that he had these opportunities
without exerting any effort in this direction—

"My kingdom is not of this world"

"Resist not evil"—

If "Christ is the Answer"—I am of the opinion that THE
Armed Forces ISN'T!

August 6: When Christ was asked the question, "Shall we pay taxes?" he asked for a coin. Upon that coin was Caesar's sign. He then said, "Render unto Caesar that which is Caesar's and unto God that which is God's"— . . . But show me the man upon which is stamped the image of Uncle Sam, or show me the human life that has upon it the likeness of any material establishment! . . .

I would probably never have wrestled with these problems had it not been for the present circumstances.

For the past week I have been confined almost to this room. Any day now I am to be transferred to the stockade for pre-trial confinement, and as I mentioned, I may get six months. The charge is failure to obey a direct command. I will plead guilty and go from there on the grounds that I was unable to conscientiously execute the order. I have no idea what my chances are or what awaits me. I am not afraid for I know that God is aware of me and cares.

I have my banjo here with me and have improved much in confinement. Also, I have learned how to juggle and am working rewardedly on my hand-balancing. One of the boys who is a squad leader in the platoon that I am now a part of, has performed all over the world as a juggler and hand-balancer. He and I have become good friends. . . .

I have not been mistrusted by any of the boys in the platoon— in fact I have established several close friendships.

August 16: Again tonight I am imprisoned by my aloneness. There are many people in many places, and they all are good people who would help anyone. But no one can help me. My need surpasses a momentary consultation. What I need is a mate. Someone who trusts fully in God. . . . One who loves Jesus and lives freely.

I cannot be subdued. . . . I will not be smothered—as I feel I am being. I must read, I must sit down, I must write, I must think—I need to know a physical intimacy—I need someone to cry on—to love, to speak softly to, and to treat tenderly. There is no tenderness here and my whole system convulses—I feel a need to throw up—to cry, to run and to sit down, to write and to sleep, to talk with someone, to go walking—

Perhaps this is why I revolt within—my feet have no place to go but up the stairs and down the stairs and up the hall and down the hall. Never getting anywhere, never going anyplace, never anything fresh—and no one to share the commonplace of what must be withstood in here.

I love someone somewhere—

August 18: [*Refused noncombatant duty.*]

"To *Me or not* to Me."

Yesterday I had to go out to the range. Some of the noncombatant work that I had to do was stapling targets on the cardboard backings.

Questions:

Would you be a cook in the Russian army?

Would you take care of the KKK firing range?

Would you prepare targets for a Nazi training squad?

Tonight is lonely. I have been moved out of D Company into the Headquarters Company Barracks. They moved me out today with no word to any of the guys in my platoon. I'm sure that they all think that I am in jail. I tried every way I could to rationalize and do the things I was told to do but I just got sick. Today I told them that I would do nothing more in the Army.

. . . I realized that a noncombatant area in the U.S. Army was nonexistent. So when I was told to continue to train in noncombatant areas and do details while not in training, I refused—because I could not see the distinction between combatant and noncombatant as it was drawn by the orders.

. . . My dad came down to try to drive some sense into my head but found that I wasn't deliberately causing trouble, as he had been prone to think before. . . . I talked at length with Dad and as he left I told him that I would continue to attend training sessions, though I would not train. As I saw it then, I would not be contributing or hindering that which I opposed. I told my platoon sergeant that I would comply and attend training in "noncombatant" areas. That seemed to cool things for a while.

Then it came my day for KP. . . . I didn't refuse KP because the other boys had been doing my dishes and it was my turn to do theirs. But when I got off that night I was told that I was to report for KP . . . for the next two weeks. If I had done this I would have been taking another boy's place; this would mean that by my taking his place, he would be getting trained in that which I opposed. For this reason I refused to go on KP. The next afternoon I was taken to the shooting range and told to plant and trim ice plant. I did this. Then I was told to staple targets on cardboard backings for the rifle training. I did this but felt no peace within myself about it. . . .

Now my defense told me that I would need to explain why I had begun training again after refusing in the first place. As I tried to find a valid reason, I found myself with none—except the fact that Dad had told me to.

[*August 24: Special court-martial; sentenced to thirty days' hard labor, confinement in stockade, fined two-thirds pay.*]

August 25: At last I have found the noncombatant branch of the U.S. Army. . . . *September 2:* —— said that God must have some big things *in store* for me. Tell her that I think He is keeping nothing in *storage* right now.

September 1: I can understand why some kids try to escape from here. It is the feeling of futility that overcomes them. They are, because of the confinement, cut off from their past, and because of a lack of eternal hope they lose hope for the future. As a result, the present is the thing of importance and "right now" becomes very important. Also, many of the illusions that they have grown up with are ruptured. Counting today, I have seventeen more days. . . .

I have become personally involved with several people here and because of this much of the confinement's potence has no effect. Today, though low physically, I have felt real cheerful and I feel no suffocation as I have felt in past days. . . .

Tonight I saw 2 WWI movies and became more intensely aware of my inability to accept the premise that war is the answer.

September 10: . . . We have to display everything we have every day on our beds: our pillow and pillowcase, our toothpaste and brush, our razor, comb, blades, soap, shoe polish, brushless shaving cream, jacket, handkerchiefs, shirts, pants, underwear, towel and boots—also our stockade rule book, our record of trial, and our Bible, and laundry bag and sox. That is all we have except pencil, pad, and envelopes. They all have a specific place.

We have breakfast about 6, then PT which is physical training. Then we go out on our details until 11:00. We return for lunch, then go out on another detail. After this (4:00) we return, have roll call and eat dinner. Then DD which is dismounted drill and training—which is in 2 places—one for nonrestorable men and one for restorable men. [*Taylor was "nonrestorable."*] We usually see a war movie. . . . Then we have to polish our boots, shower, shave, and pass boot inspection. Then to bed. We have 3 roll calls that I didn't mention.

September 11: In here you learn to anticipate the joy of sitting in a chair, or at a desk, or looking at a mirror or at a clock, walking alone across a field or down a street with civilian houses and yards—a glass of ice water or to squeeze your own lemon, a bed to lay down on in the afternoon, or a trip across town to see someone, a telephone call or a strange new face, a clean conversation, a suggestion uttered softly, an expression of tender regard for someone else, a rug on the floor, reaching in your pockets and finding a penny, . . . having 2 tubes of toothpaste or leaving your razor assembled, hanging a shirt up, going outside without a hat; an art book or a song—any song, to compose at length; to turn one's mind loose and ramble on paper—drawing a picture, hearing a newscast, or seeing the 3 stooges—seeing a movie without war; taking off your T shirt or going barefooted, skateboarding or bicycling, going to church, reading late at night, talking to someone about ideas, planning simple things, playing my guitar and banjo, whistling, shaving with a sharp blade, having hair enough to comb, a radio or a record player, going anywhere, running, goofing around, wrestling, staying somewhere because you want to, writing letters to anyone anywhere and saying anything, wearing a watch, looking at a calendar, climbing on something, getting up from the table without permission, and getting mail—I got none today. . . .

September 18: [Released from stockade (five days good-time).] I, in my failure, ache for a response, a real repent response, a real sight of a new-born soul, a time in the sight of one who grasps hope and that joy Jesus offers us . . .

The greatest lesson in gratefulness is taught by Sadness and her sister Loneliness.

How can one taste his freedom if he has never known captivity?

September 20: [The stockade] was an enlightening experience and I will not regret it. . . . I've realized the value of the prison type punishment. It changes no one. It does not deter those that are put there from committing the same offense upon release. One becomes accustomed to the routine and does not mind a return trip. . . .

There is much about prison that one misses when one gets out. There is security in knowing exactly how to do everything every minute, to know exactly what is going to happen every hour of every day. . . . One learns to spend one hour per night on a pair of boots that will be scuffed by 6:30 the next morning. But it isn't important. One can think and talk or pray or sing as one polishes boots. . . .

One gets much more personal attention than he would normally. . . . A gun on one makes that one important, puts him in the spotlight. It makes him somebody. . . . One makes friends and he hates to leave them. . . . I understand why some of the boys just keep going back—and don't really mind. . . . I would not feel at all bad if I were to get a 30 day sentence again some day. . . .

September 23: . . . I am less free today than I was last week. Then there were bars and restrictions and hate and fear and hopelessness; but the death there was the experience, and much more easily borne than the hypocrisy and training in death that characterize the techniques and purposes of the First Brigade. Until my release from the stockade I could look myself in the

face and say, "I have done according to my conscience's dictates." But now I do what I refused to do in the first place. I play
the game. My first thought is not, "Is it right?" I must suppress
my every thought—or at least divorce my actions from my convictions. Today I have been making a reenlistment poster. I either
do what they say or go back to the stockade. My discharge could
come any day and I will be a drone until such time as it comes or
I no longer can push my heart back down.

I have failed!

September 27: . . . I feel a need to be alone but that can
not be done under the circumstances in which I am living. To
go somewhere quiet and just sit or read or cry—or sing or pray,
somewhere peaceful.

. . . Today was to be my wedding day—so much can come
between a man and his plans—Jesus told us not to think of tomorrow. This has been one of my greatest sins in life. Much of my
sadness has been because I have laid my treasures up in plans
for the future. Much loneliness has been mine when I found that
what was never mine at all was not mine in the day that I had
thought it would be mine.

It was plans that put me here. I got so busy planning an easy
future that I got myself into a real fix. Many heavy things are
pressing on me.

October 10: . . . Today I was told that my discharge has been
refused and that I will be ordered to begin training in the morning. I do not understand why my discharge was refused. . . .

If, in truth, a conscientious objector has any rights under our
laws I have yet to see any of them in reality.

God, . . . Help me accept prayerfully and with joy all that
you have planned for me, if you plan for us. Help me see . . .
No! Help me have more faith. I am too anxious to walk by sight!
Help me see! Help me see! That's all I say. Help me love. This
is the thing. Help me realize that if I give all that I have, or
have all knowledge or wisdom I am nothing if I don't love— . . .

Guide me tonight in my search for the answer of what I do
tomorrow—guide me then.

I confess my lack of faith, my lack of love . . .

I've been stripped naked. . . . I've been thrashed and thrashed
—and still there must be much deeply hidden chaff, for God
leaves me here. He doesn't explain and he doesn't lift the veil
from my eyes—it may be that he is lowering yet another veil so
that I can walk only by faith if I am to walk at all.

If it were not for Job I don't know what I would do—

October 13: AR 635–20 states:

b. Requests for discharge will not be entertained when
based solely on conscientious objection which existed, but
which was not claimed prior to induction, enlistment, or
entry on active duty, or active duty for training. Similarly,
requests for discharge will not be entertained when based
solely on conscientious objection claimed and denied by the
Selective Service prior to induction.

*[From Taylor's testimony:] . . . On about the thirteenth of
October I was told by the battalion commander that I was being
recycled, my discharge had been turned down and I would be
expected to begin training the next morning. I told him I would
do as he said until I could get legal advice, and that evening I
wrote my commanding officer, telling him that I was not training.
My reason for not training was the same as before—conscientious
objection. My commanding officer talked with me three days
later and told me that if I was to get out of the Army it would
be through Leavenworth.*

Got my first taste of bayonet training and it doesn't agree with
my system. Didn't eat much lunch. Not too hungry. Cadre is
patient, kind and understanding but have orders—

To the Company Comm-C-3-1 Fort Ord   Oct. 13, 1965
Sir,

I am not preparing myself to defend myself—I am not training. I am doing, perhaps, an exercise in self-discipline or what
could be an attempt to separate the body from the soul—until
such time as I can get legal help which will relieve the Army of
me and me of the Army—

Dear ——————

Tell me what you believe about the conscientious objector question. I am, in a way, very vulnerable, alone right now and very vulnerable to the influence of those I love. I took up the weapon today.

God Help me! Please spare me this—please! I beg, using all the strength of Jesus name—spare me this.

[October 16: Refused orders.]

Charges . . . allege that the accused, in violation of the Uniform Code of Military Justice, Article 91, having received a lawful order from . . . his superior noncommissioned officer, to get into a Class A Uniform, break his rifle into three (3) main groups, open his wall locker and footlocker for inspection, did . . . willfully disobey the same (Charge I), and that the accused, in violation of the Uniform Code of Military Justice, Article 90, having received a lawful command from . . . , his superior officer, to report to the Mess Sergeant for detail in the mess hall, did . . . on or about 16 October 1965, willfully disobey the same (Charge II).

[Taylor was confined in the company area until October 25 when he was returned to the stockade.]

October 29: I can not improve on Paul's way of saying what he said in Phil. 4—nor do I feel that I can say anything by way of interpretation, other than I hope to grow more and more as he was—*content.* There is no doubt in my mind that I am doing the right thing or that I can do it with God's help and your prayers— it is being *content* that I must grow in. "Handicapped but never frustrated, puzzled but never despairing"—I know the meaning of these now— "We may be knocked down but never out." This too makes me smile with recognition.

November 1: Mom—You can't let your concern for me darken your life or weaken your awareness of life— There is nothing that can happen to deter me in my mission in life. The only thing that this can bring to me is the lack of a choice in where I am to serve. As long as I'm not in "solitary" and sealed off from everybody, I am not being slowed down. As is apparent, I personally would prefer to work and live under different circumstances. But I have no great hope for getting out soon. I am neither fearful or hopeful to any great degree—what God wants will come to pass— People look to you to see how much you really believe that God cares and is in charge— Don't fail them.

December 6: I just had to mop out the latrine for doing a handspring at the wrong time.

December 8: I can't see that confinement changes my attitude toward life or my reaction to other people much. I think I am now as content as I could be anywhere. I never look forward to tomorrow with fear or hope. Yesterday blends into today and I feel very much alive and useful in my present position. Isn't that what life is for?

December 18: As I cut new boys' hair [in the barber shop] and listen to the thoughts of the boys concerning their hair I realize more acutely the significance of the role one uses his hair to play in his expression of his reaction to today's world. . . . It is a better, louder speech than can be yelled on a street corner or in a park. It quietly angers those who think they know the meaning of genteel. It says, "I have blood and glands and a body and an animal inside that refuses to be chained." It says I'm free and I'm lonely. It says "I don't believe everything can be trimmed down and parted and beveled and greased." It means that hell could freeze over before you will yield to someone else's lies. It says I don't see your reasoning.

[*December 20: Reapplied for discharge as a conscientious objector.*]

[*December 22: General Court-Martial:*]

LAW OFFICER: . . . *This court is not here today to determine whether or not Private Taylor is, or is not, a conscientious objector. We are here to determine whether or not he received orders, legal orders, and whether or not he disobeyed them* . . .

TRIAL COUNSEL: *In the area of military type offenses, the offenses of which the accused is guilty today are just about the most serious type of offenses one can commit. Why are they? Because what is the Army? The Army is an organization within society which is founded and based upon discipline and obedience to orders. Without obedience to orders we would have chaos, no Army, and possibly no society as a result thereof.*

[*Taylor was sentenced to three years confinement at hard labor, forfeiture of all pay and allowances, and a dishonorable discharge.*]

December 30: Fox and a Navy Commander came to see me today to try to convince me that I am wrong and should reconsider and that I am hurting the Church and that the reports, though distorted by reporters and hearers, are hurting the cause of Christ and that someone saw Dad on TV say that The Church of Christ was opposed to service in the Armed Forces.

I would just as soon they stay away. They take up my education time and only come to the conclusion that I am an impractical idealist—which I could tell them simply in a brief note. . . .

January 4, 1966: Today has been hard. Inspection this morning and all the short tempers that go with it. DD [dismounted drill] for two hours tonight and more harassment than usual. Days like this I come close to getting put in the box.

January 8: Nietzsche once said, "It's not so much that you lied to me, it's just that I can't trust you anymore." So far I have had this bit of truth come to my mind many times in the present environment. . . .

Things haven't been going too smooth here lately. I've been "on the bars" four times in the past three days, each time getting off without any disciplinary action—but nonetheless, it isn't good.

January 23: I'll be leaving here Saturday for the Big L. Emotions are mixed.

[*January 31: Arrived at United States Disciplinary Barracks,*

Fort Leavenworth, Kansas, after three days' travel by train, hand-cuffed to another prisoner.]

February 10: The loneliness that I have felt in the past seven months is no unique loneliness. It is the same loneliness I have lived with since [I] first realized the scarcity of love in this world. It would have been easy to think that it was the U.S. govt. that has caused me any unhappiness that has been mine lately, but I know better. The fact is that the most enjoyable things that have come to me in the past seven months have been specifically because of the Govt. The realizations that have come to me have been gifts forced upon me.

. . . I am becoming more gentle, more aware of my own narrowness and more aware of the vastness in God's grace . . .

Though I have knocked a lot of the idealism off of my scheme for life, I still find no way to rationalize participation in war.

February 11: . . . after wasting three years paying room and board and tuition I've finally found an institution that makes an education accessible. Where else do you work a day and study a day—no dates to worry about, no status-seekers to try and keep up with. I knocked ten lessons out in one month for American Literature and find myself with a 93 average. In college we are bored to death with daily class and it would have taken me thirteen weeks to do that much and even have a 70 average. Here it isn't agreeing with the teacher that counts. It's gaining an understanding of the material. The correspondence course is my way of school. I am a stop-and-go learner, and schools just aren't made for me. My energy comes in bursts and my interest the same. . . .

February 23: It seems that, though a thought of how God will take care of tomorrow is fine, that we should not be looking always to his final arrival and helping hand in the nick of time. Why not cultivate an awareness of his presence—which makes me so excited about what he is doing right now, today, at this moment, through me—that I have no words for tomorrow.

. . . I would rather be criticized than encouraged in a feeble tone of voice—to me this is no encouragement. To me *life* is encouragement, and I am spurred on by seeing it anywhere—though it be in spotting my decaying spots. . . .

February 28: This "agony when perception evades" has been mine—but only when I tried to reconcile truth with lies. When I tried to see that if I did what I had to do I would face five years in jail—well—so what? My faith just wasn't too high at the moment, so again we see agony as the monster who preys on our weaknesses. Seek truth—it will speak to you simply and there is no agony then—it is sweet, the voice of truth, it is exciting and it is a flood sometimes, sometimes a trickle.

. . . "I asked the grass why it was green—and it did not answer because God had made it both green and mute." . . . Be a child of truth, cultivate in the love of Jesus a passion for the meat of life, for reality. Then things become obvious. . . .

March 15: . . . Most of the guys accept their fate, adjust to it and live on, content for the time being to live on lies about the past and imagined exploits of the future.

Anything we do in life will impose upon lines that we can not safely cross. If we live always resisting these boundaries, we are miserable. Try thinking of your body as a prison. You can not escape it. If you try to you only destroy yourself. . . . One has no other choice. We are prisoners of earth, but how many people have ever lost any sleep just because he had to live life on earth— . . .

Every time you dot an "i" or put a period at the end of a sentence, you are accepting a law. Every time you place yourself before the eyes of others, you are being shaken down.

One reason it seems so unbearable to you is because it all is only a possibility—determined perhaps by choice—you can stay out or do something to get in. . . . This is how our faith works in us. It limits us in the same way. . . . We can make a burden of our physical limitations or accept them and build with the materials at hand . . .

Titles and labels aren't always worth much. Am I a dishonorable person just because I am getting a dishonorable discharge? Does a conviction always prove guilt?

March 29: I was . . . told that if I were to stack up all my mental blocks, I could go right over the wall and never be found —Ho! Ho!

April 24: . . . one boy was upset because his clemency, parole, and restoration were turned down—that means he has almost two more years to serve. The guy next to him had "life," but has gotten that cut to seventeen years, and in the several years he has already been here has found a very simple solution. It's called the "laugh-it-off" cure and it goes something like this. Ho. Ho ho, he he ha ha ha ha ha ha ha ha hoo hoo yuk yuk yuk, chuckle chuckle chuckle, tee hee, tee hee, hummm hum, ho hum . . . hody hody hum, haw haw, gurgle gurgle gook, spit sputter sputter . . . pickle puckle pockel, pinkel ponkel pankel, redel, rodel, rudel, orange L, blackel, blue L, fuel, fool, pool, food, rule, ruler, yardstick, measuring tape, inches, feet, miles, yards, grass, dandylions, clover up! ops, aps, taps, saps, maps, roads, towns, cities, standies, walkies, runnies, bunnies, bonnies, bannies, bennies, red devils, yellow jackets, hornets, bees, bumble bees, queen bees, honey bees, wasps, flies, cries, trys, tried, is trying, has tried but have now given up, pup, sup, cup, coffee, tea, milk, malk, muck, mock, tick tock, clock, Grandfather clock, grandmother clock, niece sock, ant sock, ant hill, ant mountain, person mountin', person ridin', hidin', sidin', fridin', diden', living, giving, taking, shaking, breaking, making, snaking, faking, bacon— Oh ho ho— bacon—ha ha ha—*bacon*—ah ha ha—he he he he he he, haa haa haa haa—hug—yes *hug*—

Late April or May: I think fear is the basic motivation for men submitting to the dictates of the Army. There were a few men that I met while at basic training that were "gung ho," but even they were so because of their family tradition—it was all because they wanted to be like dad—or a few who were so anxious to prove themselves men that they saw nothing clearly. Most of the guys were against the whole thing, but too weak of character to act on what little feeling they did have on the subject.

I think the Army does make an effort to deaden—to kill a man's sensitivities and make of him a conditioned-response. Identity is destroyed effectively at basic training and patterns are drilled in hour after hour. No mind is called for, no thought process cultivated. Just do, do, do—to learn to do without thought —and, as the need arises, without resistance. It power-houses its way over any urge to resist, and when it destroys a man's natural tendency to resist when pushed, it has a soldier. There is very little flag waving in basic—it is all so contrary to what the boys of America have been brought up to believe about their country that it would only cause a reaction if there was any pretending about "God being on our side." The sign out in the lawn at B.C.T. [Basic Combat Training] says that the men are trained to the highest degree of personal integrity and professional skill —and the very drill sergeants whom this is supposed to speak for start every lecture with some filthy joke and illustrate their points in references to illicit sexual activities. These same drill sergeants make no effort to hide the fact that cheating is the rule on the rifle range tests. . . . Some of the boys that I have been in confinement with were so situated because they had expected to find honor and integrity in the Army, and in seeing the truth, lost respect for the armed forces and would have lost their self-respect had they continued to be a part of it all.

May 17: I am the proud protector and provider for 1,040 blond females—white leghorn hens. I feed them, clean the house, collect eggs, and all the things one does for a harum of that nature. So far I enjoy it. I get a real kick out of gathering eggs—and I get to gather 700 plus, daily.

July 11: I've got a couple of little rabbits for pets now.

November 22: . . . it's apparent that I'm sort of sad tonight. . . . The voices I hear about me are so loud and so empty—so cruel and so lost . . .

I'm tired of being in jail. There is no fellowship here—and I am lonely.

[*No date, December:*] . . . I live on the farm in my own private egg house—have a radio, a cat, and seldom even see an overseer except when I go up to eat or for afternoon count. . . . I have a job that doesn't take over four hours a day . . . I go to bed when I please and get up when I please, as long as it's by 9 A.M. The place is cheerful. There is no harassment. I can read pretty near anything, write as much to as many as I want; if I really want. . . . I can study more than time even permitted in college and . . . I have seven translations of at least portions of the Scriptures. I have a 300-pound set of Olympic weights at my disposal day and night. Two TV's, two pool tables, two movies per weekend inside the castle,—regular movies. Also, tell anyone who thinks I will definitely be home soon that there is no assurance that this is so.

Everyone that writes me is constantly telling me not to lose hope, to have courage. I think I am more in need of prayers for patience than anything else. I have at no time even felt my hope challenged in this ordeal, nor have I felt any lack of courage. I made my mind up to do what is right a long time ago, and this whole thing has just been a part of that. The times that I got shook was when I heard so many respected voices saying that my stand was wrong. . . . I cared greatly to be certain that I *was* doing what was right—but no one has shown me any reason to believe that there is any other way to stand on this issue scripturally. When I was assured that there was no opposing view that I had not considered in light of the scriptures, there was no problem going on. The times I have been depressed—sad—have been when the barrenness of those about me has been big in my heart, when one hears only filth and blasphemy he feels a greater awareness of a need to be within a fellowship—at these times I have felt lonely. Lately I have had times when I have been very lonely for Barbara. Prayers that my judgment will improve, I would appreciate—that I grow to be more sensitive to the needs of others.

[*No date:*] Im comin home, Im comin home, Im comin home, Im coming hom—home I'm comin home—comin home from across the Sea"

Juan M. Rivera-Negrón

MOBILIZE THE PEOPLE

WE WON'T GO INTO THE ARMY

On this twenty-third of September, the ninety-eighth anniversary of the proclamation of the Republic of Puerto Rico, we Puerto Rican youths declare before our people and the whole world our firm and determined purpose of each and every one of the undersigned to not serve in the United States Armed Forces under any circumstance.

In this way we express our repudiation of the tyrannical law of the Obligatory Military Service (Selective Service System) which is imposed by the North American imperialism on Puerto Rican youth as part of the colonial subjugation of our country.

Moreover, we declare our solidarity and support of the heroic struggle waged by the National Liberation Front of South Vietnam for national independence, neutrality, peace, and territorial integrity.

We are willing to face the consequences in making our decision hold, as we are convinced that we are legally and morally in the right.

¡VIVA PUERTO RICO LIBRE Y SOBERANO!

Lares, Puerto Rico, September 23, 1968

Over a thousand young men in Puerto Rico signed this "We Won't Go" statement which was initially published with 800 signatures in September 1966.

The account by Juan M. Rivera-Negrón was written in response to the questionnaire for this book. The author is a full-time political activist from a Black peasant family in the coastal zone of Puerto Rico. He attended the University of Puerto Rico and has a B.A. in Sociology.

On trial for draft resistance, Rivera and others, with the aid of the American Civil Liberties Union and the Emergency Civil Liberties Committee, are challenging the legality of the draft in Puerto Rico. Puerto Rican representatives have no vote in the United States Congress, hence the question being tested is whether compulsory military service can be required of unrepresented citizens.

Rivera is a member of *Liberación*, a youth project which trains full-time volunteers who live in rural or urban working class communities, to "organize at grassroots level against various aspects of the colonial situation with emphasis on resistance to the draft and the war in Vietnam." One of their organizers explained that they refuse "to enter the U.S. armed forces on the grounds that it is an imperialist army of a foreign country which invaded us in 1898, and since then have ruled our nation by the use of force."

The pledge and account were translated from Spanish by Marimar Benitez.

I HAD MADE UP my mind not to enter the U.S. Army. With this purpose in mind, I sought orientation from people who knew the law and from others who had refused induction. When I was summoned for induction, I presented a sworn statement of my decision not to enter the U.S. Army—although this would mean long years in prison. That day I was isolated from the rest of my companeros, so they did not know of my refusal. When they took me to take the step forward, I was accompanied by four persons, among them a man dressed in civilian clothes and the rest in military uniform. I refused three times in a row to step forward. Then they pretended to leave me in the military quarters. I said I wanted to see my lawyer. About a half hour later they let me go.

I decided to refuse induction because I believe that Puerto Ricans don't have to enter, either voluntarily or compulsorily, into foreign armies. If we Puerto Ricans have to fight we must do so against imperialism which exploits and oppresses us. My contact with youths rebelling against the imperialist power in Puerto Rico helped me make this decision; besides my own personal desire to combat in a militant way the law of the Obligatory Military Service.

The only alternative I contemplated was not going. Now, within this, I had the possibility of doing several things: to submit myself peacefully to the federal jury which would condemn me to jail (in case they thought it convenient). This possibility I considered to be the only one. But then I realized that if I went to jail without raising any fuss, as the Nationalists had done before, this would in no way advance the struggle against imperialism and its odious Selective Service law for Puerto Ricans. It was then that I asked myself the question of whether this was the only alternative or whether there was another which would be more effective and useful to the cause. Then I started to think of other alternatives: to flee and find refuge in foreign countries did not seem to me the more just decision, as this would necessarily entail my forsaking the cause for many years, maybe even for life.

With the help of my revolutionary friends, I took the stand that has been my concern for the last four months. We realized that the most important thing is to mobilize the people: youth, parents, community by community, in committees against the Selective Service. The only way we can combat the law is by organizing the people. Isolated from the people, we will only suffer defeat and frustration.

The pressures to which I was subjected were many: from my family, my neighbors, and even pressures of a moral and economic kind. The harassment was much stronger when we started to refuse induction and started exhorting others to do the same. The FBI and the CIA started to visit my neighborhood, the boarding house where I live and the one where I had lived, the places I often go to, the place where I used to work. The visits of these men have not brought fatal consequences. While they intimidated a few, they enraged most people. And the people start gaining consciousness of the unabashed persecution which befalls their sons who do not want to be sent in chains to war.

I belonged to the Pro-Independence Movement (MPI), which

did not have a clear policy toward the Selective Service. The MPI did exhort its youth to refuse induction, but its only possible tactic was the legal struggle. The MPI envisioned the mobilization of the people only in terms of pickets and meetings in front of the jails. It was necessary that our group make the self-criticism of MPI's position, which resulted in the formulation of the correct position.

For acting according to my principles, I am being judged by a federal jury in San Juan. We hope to have many communities organized before Imperialism announces its verdict.

I feel calm and confident, as we will win.

To me the most important thing is to obtain the support of the people in this as in other struggles.

I want the people to see the Selective Service law as one of the impositions that are binding them. I want the people to see that this is a just and legitimate cause, and because of this, for them to act in our benefit.

My message to all the youth of draft age, especially black and Puerto Rican, is to remind them that you, as well as I, are suffering the oppression of a system that exploits us and discriminates against us. You, as I, have the obligation of fighting this system. We have the strength necessary to defeat them—if we organize. "What is important is the will to fight, the decision to conquer."—Che.

David Nolan

THE QUESTION OF LOYALTY

David Nolan chose to comply with the Selective Service System in order to maintain his own freedom. He describes two encounters which the system permits: refusal to sign the Armed Forces Security Questionnaire and a personal appearance before his draft board regarding his conscientious objector application.

The Armed Forces Security Questionnaire (DD 98) is presented at the preinduction physical examination. (Registrants already classified I-O are exempted. See CCCO memorandum on the Armed Forces Security Questionnaire, address on p. 325.) Army Regulation 601-270, Appendix IV, describes the purpose of the Armed Forces Security Questionnaire as follows:

> . . . *The security questionnaire makes considerably easier the difficult job of detecting, removing, and where appropriate, punishing subversive and disloyal persons. . . . When such persons are identified before entering the service, their acceptance will be held in abeyance until the individuals have been cleared or complete determination made that they are unsuitable for service in the Armed Forces.*
>
> . . . *However, in the interests of national security and in protecting you against those who would undermine and destroy our Nation and individual freedom, the Armed Forces will not accept for enlistment or for immediate induction those persons who refuse to satisfactorily accomplish the security questionnaire; claim protection of the Fifth Amendment, or those who admit membership in organizations listed on the security questionnaire form.*

Some men refuse to sign, not because they have anything to hide but because they think it is not the business of the government to inquire about an individual's associations.

The personal appearance before the local board is the only opportunity provided within the Selective Service System for a conscientious objector to plead his case in person. From that point on, all decisions are based upon the written contents of the applicant's Selective Service file.

Some lawyers believe that there are many procedural inequities and violations of constitutional safeguards in Selective Service administration which could be challenged. No transcript is made during personal appearances before the local board, witnesses are not always permitted, and legal counsel is denied. Advice to registrants is frequently inadequate or misleading, forms and regulations do not reflect court decisions, and yet the burden lies on the registrant to secure information and prove his eligibility for deferment or exemption in a matter which may lead to possible criminal prosecution or the giving of his life.

I WAS A STUDENT at the University of Virginia from 1963 to 1965, engaging more in extra-curricular movement-type activities than studies. In the summer of 1965, a group of us began working the black-belt communities of southside Virginia as the Virginia Students' Civil Rights Committee, a predominantly white SNCC affiliate. At the end of that summer I felt very strongly that we had not fulfilled our commitment or our promises to the people who sponsored us in southside, and decided not to return to school.

My primary gripe with the draft at that time was that it would not permit me to do what I thought was important, but decided for me that I should either go to school or serve in the Army. I was not familiar with the fine points of applying as a conscientious objector, and let the matter slide, albeit with much worry, until mid-November when I received an order to report for a physical in New York City.

I reported for the physical after consulting with some SNCC people and some pacifists I knew. Dave McReynolds [of the War Registers League] showed me a memorandum on the legality of the loyalty oath [Armed Forces Security Questionnaire]. I had no intention of pledging my loyalty to this country in view of its world position.

I took my physical. The atmosphere was somewhat like a concentration camp—where you are not only being sent to your death but expected to be an accomplice in the act. I noticed several guys there who had graduated at the bottom of the high school class I had been at the top of, and I knew that their being there did not grow out of any conscious choice they had made about their future. It depressed me to hear them talk about when they expected to be called, because I had already decided that I could never serve in the Army.

The last item on the agenda was the signing of the security questionnaire, a four-page manuscript with about twenty questions. The sergeant in charge gave us the forms with the order, "The first question will be answered 'yes,' all the rest will be answered 'no.' Hand in your forms." When everyone else had handed in their forms I went up to him and told him that I wouldn't sign it. He jumped back as if I had the plague and said he would have nothing to do with me, that I would have to see the FBI. I went through three different offices, where soldiers and civilians alike told me that I had to sign the form or I would be inducted immediately, imprisoned immediately, or detained indefinitely on the premises—all of which I knew could not happen. So they eventually sent me to the lady who handles problem cases, and after several hours of filling out two forms in quadruplicate (one explained why I wouldn't sign the security questionnaire, the other explained why I wouldn't answer questions as to why I wouldn't sign the loyalty questionnaire—bureaucracy!) they let me go, saying that I would hear from my draft board in three to six months. The clerk who typed out the forms was a Negro and was obviously embarrassed that I listed my occupation as "civil rights worker."

Shortly afterwards I filed a Form 150 for conscientious objectors with my draft board, which was rejected in January, 1966. I applied to the board for a personal hearing, and when I got there they told me that they couldn't do anything because the report from my physical was not in, as my loyalty was still being investigated.

In the next few months I was visited four times in Lawrenceville, Virginia, where I was working, by Army intelligence investigators. I think that by applying nonviolent principles and killing them with kindness, while at the same time refusing to cooperate with them, I made their life as hard as possible. Finally that fall, for some unknown reason they cleared me and I received a notice from my draft board that I was fully acceptable for induction into the armed forces. So I went to the draft board office to see what the status of my CO application was, and nobody seemed to know anything more than that I should apply for another personal hearing. I did that. . . .

On Tuesday, April 18, 1967, I was ordered to report for an interview with Local Board No. 66, with regard to my status as a conscientious objector.

After waiting about an hour I was called into a room where there were four men sitting behind a desk. They did not introduce themselves.

I handed one of the men a letter of reference . . . which he looked at and then placed in my file.

One of the men asked me when I had become a conscientious objector. I told him that I had filed Form 150 about a year and a half ago, when I was nineteen. He said, no, that wasn't what he meant. He wanted to know how long I had been a conscientious objector. So I said that if he meant how long had I held these beliefs, it went back a number of years. He said, no, that wasn't what he meant—he wanted to know how long I had been a conscientious objector.

It seemed to me that there were only two possible answers to that question, and I had already given them, so I was puzzled. Then he asked me why I hadn't signed the little box for conscientious objection when I filled out my original classification form. I told him that at that time I knew nothing about the legal provisions for conscientious objection (indeed, I knew nothing about Selective Service, as is evidenced by a letter in my file sent to the local board shortly before my eighteenth birthday, asking them what I was expected to do). I remember having been warned that many young men made the mistake of signing the CO blank, and was told to be sure that I didn't do it.

The gentleman on the board told me that I had been ill-advised, with which I readily agreed—though obviously he felt that the blame should be placed on me, while I think it is the board's fault that young men are not properly advised of their rights under the Selective Service law.

Another man asked me what my father did. I replied that he was a vice president of the Chase Manhattan Bank. They asked if he was a veteran, and I said that he was not, because he had polio.

They asked me why I was a conscientious objector and I replied that it was because I was opposed to killing and to an organization whose purpose is ultimately to kill—namely the army.

One man asked me if I believed in our form of government. I have studied political science and it seemed to me that the question was so broad as to be meaningless. So I answered with a puzzled look: "I suppose."

He said, "Don't give me any of this 'I suppose' stuff. Do you or do you not believe in our democratic form of government?" Since he added the word "democratic," I happily answered "Yes."

They asked if I believed in obeying the law. I said I did if I felt the law was just. They said that Selective Service was the law of the land. I said that that law also provided legal status for conscientious objectors.

One man said that our glorious country wouldn't be what it is if there had been too many conscientious objectors like me during the revolution. I replied that there was no conscription law during the revolution. I could also have mentioned that great patriots like Thomas Jefferson and Benjamin Franklin did not serve in the armed forces during the revolution.

They said that there was a draft during the civil war and that CO's had bought their way out. I objected, saying that there was a difference between conscientious objection and buying your way out of the army, as Grover Cleveland did. I said I did not consider the latter method to be too honorable. Their only reply was that it had been legal at the time.

One man asked: "If we were invaded, would you defend your

country or would you join the other side, since you don't care anything about your country?"

I objected to his statement that I did not care about my country—I care enough about it to try and make sure it does the right thing. I said I would defend my country, but would not kill or join the Army.

They could not see that the country could be defended except by violence. I pointed out that people usually thought President Johnson was defending the country, but he was not serving in the armed forces. . . . I told them that I rejected the concept that the only way you could defend something was to kill.

One man asked me if I had ever considered working for the Peace Corps or VISTA. I said that I had considered it. He asked me if I had ever served. I said no, but that I had been working for the past two years for social service organizations not connected with the government. Another man asked me if I would name those groups.

I replied that during 1965 and 1966 I had worked for the Virginia Students' Civil Rights Committee. He wanted to know if this was a group that was against war, or what.

I replied that it was formed in December 1964 by a group of students from white and Negro colleges in Virginia, who were opposed to segregation. They asked me how I felt about segregation, and I said I was against it.

One of the board members said he was interested in pursuing my ideas on the race problem further, and asked me how I felt about interracial marriage. I said I was not opposed to it—I felt that if two people loved one another they should marry.

They asked what other organizations I was affiliated with. I said I was a member of the Southern Student Organizing Committee.

The man who had asked about interracial marriage then asked if this wasn't the group that was opposed to everything that the democratic university stood for.

I replied that it certainly was not, and briefly described the group's activities in behalf of peace, civil rights, university reform, and anti-poverty work.

They asked me if I would go to jail rather than go in the army, and I said yes.

They asked if this was because I was afraid to go in the army. I told them it was not a question of fear (indeed, I think fearful people are the most likely to carry guns) but rather of opposition to killing. I pointed out that two weeks before a bomb had been placed on my front porch, and that my safety had been endangered several times while I was a civil rights worker in southside Virginia, but this had not deterred me.

They asked me what I would do if I was attacked. I replied that I had been beaten by members of the Ku Klux Klan and had not retaliated. I referred them to a clipping of the incident in my file. One of the board members said that he was not a member of the KKK (he felt it necessary to mention this) but he wanted to know how I knew it was Klansmen who did this. I replied that it had taken place at a Klan rally. Two of the men were Klan security guards in full uniform—a third was a Klan official in red robes.

The same man then said that he was puzzled that I hadn't mentioned religion, and would I please comment on that. But before I could answer, he made another statement. The members of the board said they had heard all they needed to to make a decision, and I was asked to leave the room.

If I had been permitted to answer the question about religion I would have told them that I believed the essential message of Christianity and other major religions was that of peace and brotherhood. And I believe that it is incumbent on those of us who hold to these religious ideals to do a little more practicing and a little less preaching of them—that this was what I had dedicated my life to.

I would have told them that I was disillusioned with the institutional church because I feel it is hypocritical about peace and brotherhood—in good times they preach them, but in hard times they allow themselves to be led astray by evil men and wind up supporting war and racism.

I would have told them that for this reason I didn't think the churches were the repositories of religion, but rather men like Gandhi who have dedicated their lives to this practice.

I felt that the members of the board were overly hostile in their questioning and found many of their questions insulting. I felt that they were treating me as a criminal rather than as a person applying for a legal classification within the Selective Service System. Ample time was not given to answer each of their questions.

I also got the impression that the members of the board were not completely familiar with the legal aspects of conscientious objection, with the Seeger decision, and other relevant cases.

After the interview I was classified I-A. I am now appealing to the state appeal board for the I-O classification.

. . . If I am ever ordered to report for induction I shall not go, but I am not too interested in hurrying the process.

Perhaps three years ago, when there seemed to be such hope of changing America I would have felt differently about prison than I do now. But I think we have clearly reached the point where suffering is unredeemed, where America is tired of having its moral weakness pointed out, and where these actions do not have much effect.

My original point of departure for opposing the draft was that it would not allow me and my compatriots to do what we wanted with our lives. I was at the noncooperators conference in New York and the reason I didn't sign the statement [see pages 8–9] was that I felt too much that some people were trying to break into jail. This did not solve my dilemma of how a man could live freely in this country, because a man is no more free in jail than under the thumb of schools, or whatever else is necessary to obtain deferments. There are times when a man, to be honest to himself, may wind up in jail, and I don't think that one should shy away from actions that are right because of the fear of jail. I suppose this could be just an apologia for why I am not a non-cooperator, but I think I honestly feel that the issue is whether or not you go into the army. I use my draft card to prove that I am of drinking age, and I am determined that if my draft board thinks they can lay a hand on me they are going to have a damned hard time doing it. I advise everyone I can on how to fight or dodge the draft or screw up the system. I do not feel a Gandhian need to be honest and open with the system—if a person does not feel he is strong enough to go to jail, I would much rather see him obtain a IV-F by any means, than go into the army. And I think that IV-F is preferable to I-O because I don't feel that two years alternative service is necessarily the best way to stop America.

So—I think the draft should be abolished. I refuse to pay taxes. I would like to see this country with no armed forces— morally because I am a pacifist and politically because I don't think that America is capable of doing anything but evil with them at this time. . . .

Malcolm Dundas

IN PEACE & LOVE

> *If I am to be a pacifist, then my life will reflect that attitude
> and no directive of any government agency can make me one
> or not make me one. The government agencies do not have
> the moral right to decide whether a man is a pacifist or not
> —only he within himself can and will know that.*

Malcolm Dundas wrote most of his account in January 1967,
between arraignment and conviction for refusing alternative
service. His mimeographed statements and an interview on radio
station KPFA received public attention in the spring of 1967, but
are largely omitted here. Dundas drew upon the tradition of
Jefferson and Thoreau to support his views about civil disobedience and involuntary servitude, and on international law to
condemn the war in Vietnam.

> *I can not abide by the position of conscientious objector
> because to do so would be to subscribe to a system that sends
> others to death in my place—it would give the system a
> legitimacy that no slave system should have.*

He defended himself in court and pleaded not guilty.

> *I think that the whole war and the people that perpetuate
> the war and accept it, are as guilty as I am. . . . I am not
> guilty of a war crime. I am guilty of an infraction of Selective
> Service law.*

There is some question as to how a "war crimes" defense can
ever be tested in civilian courts, due to the following pattern
of rulings: Selective Service is empowered to raise armies but
has no control over how the armed forces will be used, hence
the Selective Service System is not responsible; the legality of
the war is not relevant to whether a man violates the Selective
Service law because any particular serviceman might not be
sent to Vietnam. Before induction a man does not know whether

he will be ordered to commit war crimes, and after induction he cannot raise the question in the civilian courts.

Dundas was aware that the issues he was concerned about would probably not be considered by the court. He expressed his desire to communicate with the judge as a person. On May 17, 1967, he began to serve an eighteen-month sentence. His letters close with the words, "In PEACE & LOVE."

THE DECISION to refuse is not something, for me, that is so concrete, so solid, that it never changes. . . . It evolves, revolves, grows, changes form and stature.

The draft seems so overpowering—places one in such a help-less position that it is very hard to tell another person what to do. The hardest thing about resisting is that you just do not win (in the legal/political sense). Morally, perhaps, but, still, the draft goes on. Jail or exile does not stop wars directly. It gives a strong voice to dissent and to personal courage. It is not a question one can answer once and for all time—yet, in the terms of the law, one our age must!

My resistance to the draft is mostly a personal stand. It has ramifications outside myself—but the choice to resist, and the avenues, are personal. That is the nitty-gritty of the whole ques-tion. When the banners are gone, it is you, personally, who must face exile or prison.

I think the greatest stumbling block to one's becoming free to act is fear. Fear of an unknown and seemingly harsh path. I grew up with no knowledge of the CO position. People with such ideas did not exist in the Central Valley of California. In these forma-tive years, I had only my brother, books, and animals as com-panions. I guess the mystique of the farm and rural life was a great factor in my subsequent attitude towards people and later wars. I played some war games, but, when school began, I was never involved in the usual wrangles of kids my age. Their quarrels and battles seemed so useless and silly. It is hard to say from here what experiences (like these) were the shapers and pushers. I was always an "outsider." . . .

After my collegiate senior summer, I was again outside; ivory towers were behind me. Then came the Peace Corps. I had, until then, never considered myself as being much of a variant (politically) from the totality of persons my age. But, while in training for the Peace Corps, I began to realize that my ways were not accepted, dogmatic ones. I became a spokesman for the "radicals" in the group.

Once overseas, I became more and more aware, and alarmed, by the discrepancy between the United States' avowed positions and the actual facts of deceit and lies that were the stock in trade of diplomacy.

Perhaps the most irrevocable change in my life came with Johnson's ordering the bombing of the northern sector of Vietnam [February 7, 1965]. I heard the news late—I was away on a trip at the time. The lie—the stink of the whole thing—deeply upset me. I tried, in my mind, to reconcile my serving as a token helper along side the massive lies and military destruction in Vietnam. I questioned, read, and fought to find answers which could satisfy my ideals, and my repugnance to the acts of genocide. Finally, in early April, I sent off two letters—one addressed to the Peace Corps Director in Tanzania, and one to a friend in Peace Corps Washington. I told them of my feelings: I did not think that I could continue as a Peace Corps volunteer, but that I was hoping I could remain on my own as a teacher under the local authority.

The letters created a furor in Washington and Tanzania. . . . The Ministry of Education . . . would hire me if I could terminate my ties with the Peace Corps. Peace Corps Washington sent a long cablegram requesting my presence in Washington, immediately, for what were purported to be talks. I left Tanzania . . . There was no question in the minds of the Directors as to the final outcome. . . . It was then clear to me, also, that these talks were just window-dressing, and the decision had been made beforehand. There were repeated attempts to try and return on my own, but the failure to get a passport ended those faint hopes.

The full impact of this action pushed me more and more into the realm of thought and action one would consider radical. It was not out of bitterness so much as out of disillusionment with the liberal panaceas.

I turned then to the Movement for an outlet, for my desire to help. But, since I was white and since the movement was moving in the direction of black, I was out again. Finally, I heard of a job—organizing farm labor in Visalia, California.

During that summer I began again to re-think the draft question. I attempted to explore again and again prison, cooperating, their effects and hazards. I explored job possibilities, and began to realize how narrow the range was for alternative service.

In the fall, I worked at Turn Towards Peace, in Berkeley. Then, on a whim, I suppose, I headed East for NECNVA [New England Committee for Nonviolent Action]—to the day, one year after I had embarked on the Peace Corps training trip.

At NECNVA, for the first time I met people who were politically, at least, close to me. I met people who had been to jail; who were actually living what were just ideas for me. The people who influenced me the most (draft wise) during this period, I guess, were Paul Salstrom and Roger LaPorte.* Paul, because I could talk to him and because he knew from recent experience what prison was like. Roger, because I never knew him, and because he gave his life, while others, like myself, worried about one-to-five-years in prison. A young man who had so much to give, Roger gave all he could in complete honesty and without banners or marches. I do not think I can ever forget the day he immolated himself—the complete and total lack of words—the silence that screamed in our ears—his message of total faith and love.

These two events—the Peace Corps termination (the way), and the death of Roger LaPorte (the experience of others who had given) set me on the road to self-realization and that of absolutism.

The actual act of resistance took several steps. I was classified as a conscientious objector. Then I faced a choice of limited alternative service or noncooperation. I requested a hearing. At that hearing, I presented a two-page statement of noncooperation (March 5, 1966). While there, I attempted to return my draft

* Roger LaPorte immolated himself in November 1965, in an attempt to turn the United States away from violence in Vietnam.

cards to the board—they refused to accept them. I then signed a document stating that I would not do any form of alternative service. On April 15, 1966, I received an order to report for alternative service—dated for April 20, 1966. I returned that order and explained that I felt myself no longer under their jurisdiction—that I could not possibly accept their orders. In August of 1966, I was visited by two FBI agents. They informed me of their mission and my rights. I agreed to answer their questions. . . . They asked me if I would cooperate and I reiterated that I didn't feel I could cooperate with an illegal and immoral law. On December 9, 1966, I received a letter requesting that I appear for arraignment on December 12, 1966, in Sacramento Federal Court. I appeared, acting as my own defense counsel. The case was transferred to San Francisco, on my request. [*Trial date was April 29, 1967, and on May 17, 1967, an eighteen-month sentence was pronounced.*]

When I first took out the CO papers, I was, I felt at the time, doing the most radical, sincere act I could. When I received the I-O status with no appeals, I relaxed again. No thunder bolts or such had torn my life apart—I was no different, outwardly at least. I still had a respect for *laws*. I felt that the law itself *was* the law of the land and therefore someone should obey it. But I began to see what it was doing to people in the South, and in Africa, and throughout this country, and I began to know that it had to be abolished, that you can't make a slave system more equitable. You have to abolish it and start with something where all people are free. I was romantically and intellectually ready for prison, if my beliefs were not received with concern and justice.

I have fluctuated many times and still do. My position has changed somewhat—I am more anarchist than radical—more love-orientated than political. . . . After years of a scoffing agnosticism, I have broadened my personal witness to the forces of Love/God everywhere. . . .

Legally, I am attacking the Selective Service Act on constitutional grounds. Namely, the Thirteenth Amendment, which prohibits involuntary servitude. To back it up I am using the

United Nations Charter and the Declaration of Human Rights;
the Army Field Manual; the Nurnberg Tribunal decisions; the
London Treaty; the Geneva Convention of 1954; and the Kellogg-
Briand Pact. [See Appendix C, pages 318–324.] The latter treaties
support the struggle against this war in particular. They are
useful in providing evidence that the war is illegal, genocidal, etc.
After that I will attempt to prove that by complying with Selective
Service, one becomes a party to the crimes of genocide and
illegality of the war. Unfortunately, it is pretty clear that I will
not be able to bring this evidence in testimony. . . . You are
faced with the court saying, well, you broke a law and that is
the only thing that is relevant; . . . the Vietnamese war itself is
a political question and therefore not arguable in court.

So the only arguments left are those of moral persuasion. I
want people to question their too ready acceptance of atrocity
and government edicts as their law. I want people to think about
the record of lies and evidence of deception that is this war in
particular and all wars in general. Then I want them to question
themselves as to their role in the making of war or living off the
death and destruction of others for a profit. I want to reach people—as a person, not as a case number. If my case gave one other
person the courage to *be*, then a revolution would have been
accomplished. . . .

Externally, the trial has just begun. Internally, there is a tur-
moil of doubt and anxiety—I feel never really sure that what I
feel or say about anything is really mine, and not the result of
unknown forces. It is a doubt and fear that never subsides, and
perhaps never will be resolved. The hardest thing to live with, I
feel, is the not knowing when it will end—when you will know
what the result of your case will be. The delays—the long periods
between acts of civil disobedience and the response of the draft
board or government. You see friends going and coming and you
feel that you cannot move. Always dangling—that is the worst
feeling for me.

I have found, though, more friends than I counted on beforehand. People who come up to you on the street, or write words
of encouragement to you. The silent people who come to the

trial as a testimony. People come through in their own ways.

I am a poet and I have found especially now, that I cannot write. The spiritual drain has been very great. A sense of hope-lessness—a sudden realization that legally one has not a chance to change anything; that prison is now a cold reality. . . . I resent having my life too ordered, but, with the choice of non-cooperation came a whole slew of channeled actions that I was only dimly aware of beforehand. I have come to accept many of them now, but, for a time it was a rough go. . . . The sense of being alone is very difficult to adjust to. It is a very lonely stand.

The greatest pressure I feel is doubt. The dull, pounding, nag-ging feeling of doubt. The helpless feeling one has when faced with the magnitude of wars and a government's power. The feel-ing of not being able to gauge one's actions to the scale of the war and all its ramifications. It is horrible to realize that your voice, your protest, doesn't stop people from killing and being killed. People want so much to see the effect of their actions, and for the noncooperator that is not possible. The war, the grossness of the way of life based on war, keeps me in my position of oppo-sition to any such acts by the government. I guess I feel as Debs did, or St. Francis, that one's place is always with those who are not free or are not filled. It is the mark of a human being: the need for *love;* the ability to be not one of the poor or enslaved, but to feel responsible, to evoke concern on the part of others, to be a witness to one's faith in love or humanity or God—that is the pressure that keeps one going on.

Sometimes I say, "I wish I had ——," but I know that that is not true. I feel depressed, but not as a result of belief or action (on that I am clear) but at the seeming intransigent nature of the forces I am trying to wield, alter, or abolish. I am not sorry I did this act, I don't think I will ever regret it. I try to live in the present—not becoming tied to the past or planning too hard for the future.

The choices I had to make? Well, economically, I guess, one must give up most career plans which may depend on govern-ment grants and/or large corporations. But, then, one who is about to become a noncooperator is generally not interested in such offers anyway, since they constitute a support of the war system. In addition, most public school teaching jobs are not open. . . . For myself, these were important considerations at first. I had plans, then, of being involved in law, or some such work, or professorial position. Though these are still not totally excluded . . . I relish internal freedom too much to sweat out a lifetime of chasing money.

. . . What can I say to one going the same route, or contemplating such a route. Politically it's a good move—for the movement—but when all the speeches are over it is you who must do the time or fight to avoid doing time.

Read all you can about what others have done—question others about their stands—but, sift it all through your perception of what is right and wrong for *you*. You will never fully be sure, but you should be as aware of all the ramifications of your actions as you can be. When you have done this, then make the choice. If you find then that you can't stick to it, then drop out of the action—don't place an unwanted burden on your life out of a sense of duty or such—your life is your life and not a movement's.

I guess that my case is just that, my case. A record of what I have done in one aspect of my life. A record of an act of faith and, I trust, *love*. I am not hateful of the government—"pity" is more the word. They are trapped too—impotent to do anything beyond the execution of laws and rules. In short, they are not free to be alive. The years of power and "liberalism" are telling on them. Rhetoric is failing them and now brute force replaces dialogue. Somehow we must reach them—behind the fist is still a man and he can be reached and his ideas changed. He need not agree with you, but, he should be aware that you have as much a right to believe, free of repression, as he does—it is a mutual liberation. I hope, then, that my words may reach some people—help them, give them a chance to *be*.

June 13, 1967: County jail life is very dull and monotonous. One rises very early, 5:30 A.M., and then one eats at 6 A.M., then nothing till lunch at 11:30. Sometimes one has an interview, or commissary, but generally—nothing. Lunch passes, then one exercises for the afternoon till 3:30. Dinner is at 4, and lights out at 9 P.M. The block I am in is composed of fifteen cells—$3' \times 9' =$ 2 man. Food is not much to speak of—mostly starches, soups, and mass-feeding things. You can predict generally the week's menu. All lighting is artificial, as is the heating and cooling. I haven't seen any daylight in two weeks. There is a library, mostly discards and grammar school level. If one tries hard one can scrounge up fairly adequate reading. No books can be sent in from the outside. Many prisoners are here awaiting various stages of trial. Most are poor and so can't afford bail. Most rely on public defenders—most are found guilty. Lawyers are hard to afford, so one settles for what one can get. Now there are many young people—drug cases. The deputies are mostly ex-military but, surprisingly fair (at least to me). It is hard to ignore what they represent though, and bitterness is most common. Letters in and out are looked over—unlimited correspondence—but only two pages per letter out.

From all reports the Prisons (Fed) are much better. I am looking for that. I am fairly well, health-wise. Though the fact I am a vegetarian makes it very hard to get adequate nutrition.

One has lots of time for memories, especially here in the intern period before the "pen." I am faring better than I expected. I have much time for writing and I am making use of it. . . .

I still feel I made the right choice. I don't know if there is time now to effect the necessary changes, or if indeed anyone can do so. Jails are very clear mirrors of this society; and if one has ever spent any time in them, one realizes our danger.

August 31, 1967: Is it worth the price? Given the choices, yes; but one can't really do a comparative. My life is my communication—the prison is the unaware, unloving world of systems and hatred.

It's a martyrdom because most people are afraid—either of the time spent or social ambitiousness lost through stigma.

Given the reality of no real freedoms I encase my body/soul because I feel I am freer than the unaware blind fearful man in the outside plastic world. I choose this "slavery" because others attempt to coerce my life.

Robert Luftig

SUING THE ARMY

Robert Luftig tells at length of his experiences after bringing suit for an injunction to prevent the Army from sending him to Vietnam. The legal basis of the case was similar to that of the Fort Hood Three. In both cases Stanley Faulkner, the lawyer, challenged the constitutional authority of the government to send soldiers to fight in an undeclared war. He cited the Supreme Court decision in *Youngstown Sheet and Tube Co. v. Sawyer*. In a concurring opinion in the Youngstown case, Justice Jackson held that the President as Commander in Chief had "no military prerogative, without support of law, to seize persons or property because they are important or even essential for the military and naval establishment." Faulkner argued that since the war in Vietnam is undeclared and illegal, it is unlawful to "seize persons" to fight in it. The significant difference between the Fort Hood Three and Luftig cases was that Luftig filed his suit before he was assigned to go to Vietnam, on the assumption that any soldier might be sent during a period of escalating warfare.

This case went as far as the Supreme Court, but Luftig completed his tour of duty as a cook and was discharged in September 1967. The issue was never decided; again it was not possible to introduce evidence to establish the illegality of the Vietnam war.

Bob Luftig was born in the Bronx and grew up in New York City. His parents were both labor union members. His father had fought in the Spanish Civil War and also in World War II. Bob read a great deal, especially history, and slowly formed his own opinions, with the help of his mother and father.

When he entered the Army he made a high score on the test for Officers Candidate School, but declined to be an officer.

The entire account is taken from an interview on December 26, 1966.

WHEN I GOT my draft notice, I thought of refusing the whole idea of the draft. However, after thinking about it, I decided that had I been drafted in 1942, during the Second World War, I would gladly have went and fought. And I would fight in certain wars—which would not sound good to some people, but to me it is. So I decided not to oppose the draft.

At that moment I did not know, exactly, if I would go to Vietnam if I was ordered. I hadn't made up my mind yet and I still was indecisive. But as I got in the Army I saw what the Army was like, and how the Army treated everybody, and what we were expected to do—just to kill anybody that was the enemy. They said at that time: if you go to Vietnam you're going to be expected to kill women and children; and you know, it may not sound good to you now but the women are armed and nobody's a child in Vietnam if they carry a gun. They are trying to make it sound like it's OK to kill because they're going to kill you anyway so kill them first.

However, as I was going back to the barracks, I think I discussed it with other guys. . . . You know, we couldn't see ourselves shooting women and children, whether they had a rifle or not because, you shoot a woman—and maybe she does and maybe she doesn't have a rifle. And if she doesn't that would be a terrible feeling, at least for me, at least for most people that have any feelings whatsoever. . . .

That's how I believe it, it's just that the war itself is between the Vietnamese, the North Vietnamese and the South Vietnamese. And it's just as if . . . take our Civil War, of the North against the South; we would have tremendously resented any government coming in and helping. . . . We fought our Civil War among ourselves, and I think they should be allowed to fight their civil war among themselves. And if the North happens to win the civil war and takes over, well that's what the people must want. And it appears to me that we are losing, or are not winning, because the people want Ho Chi Minh to be their leader. . . . After consideration, I thought that to go there and to shoot and kill people who are just trying to get independence for themselves, for trying to change the government, however they feel, would be morally wrong.

So after I finished my training, I made up my mind not to go to Vietnam. I had heard about Mr. Stanley Faulkner, a lawyer. So I went down there and talked with Mr. Faulkner for a few hours, and he just told me why the war in Vietnam was illegal from a legal standpoint. . . .

By then, I had been transferred to California and the court case had to start out in California. That was January '66. . . . Actually, Mr. Faulkner had a lawyer in California start the suit, and that's when all the fun . . . began.

. . . I was in Fort Ord and I had no orders whatsoever when I started the court case. I thought that I was going to Vietnam anyway because I was in Fort Ord, and that's usually where you go—from Oakland Army Terminal. And I wasn't going to take any chances. If I would have waited until I got the orders to go to Vietnam, Mr. Faulkner explained, the court case would be silly because it would turn into a court-martial. And it would just be mere refusing orders and . . . it's just 99 per cent that you're going to be found guilty. It's a very simple case the Army has: They give you an order and you refused it. So the whole idea was to refuse it before I got the order—so I did it that way.

. . . I went to the office of this other lawyer in Berkeley, California, named Peter Franck. And I signed an order seeking a temporary injunction and a restraining order for Secretary of Defense McNamara, Secretary of the Army Resor, and the Commanding General of Fort Ord (that was just to make sure we didn't leave anybody out), I think that was a General Ferguson. And so I had to go to court and just file it there, to show my opposition. . . . And that's when all the repercussions began in California.

. . . When I made the choice [to bring a court case] Mr. Faulkner had said to me, you're going to get a lot of trouble. And you're going to get harassed by the Army, which I believed. They are going to put a lot of pressure on you, and maybe they never intended you [to] go to Vietnam and you'll do this case and they'll just order you to Vietnam so they can avoid the case,

he said. That might happen. And then again they might not
do it. You can't tell what they're going to do, the Army. They
might not put you in Vietnam. They might put a lot of pressure
on you. However, he said, can you withstand the pressure? . . .
I said that I could.

And when I did the case, the day I did it I was called in front
of the company commander, a Captain Baker. And I knew what
it was. . . . So when I got up in front of Captain Baker, he said
to me, "What do you think you are doing?"

I said, "What do you mean?"

He went on and said, "What are you trying to do? Act like
you don't know what's going on?"

I said, "What do you mean?"

So he said, "Are you crazy?"

I said, "No, I'm not crazy. I'm in the Army, aren't I?"

He said, "You must be crazy to sue the Secretary of Defense
and the Commanding General of this post to stop yourself from
going to Vietnam."

At that point I said, "No, I don't think I'm crazy to do it. I
wanted to do it. I feel the war in Vietnam is unjust."

Then he interrupted me very quickly, and he was very angry.
And he called me a traitor to the country, first, and in a pretty
loud voice, a communist. . . . "We fight a war for people like
you. What's the use of fighting for people like you?" He went on,
for a few minutes I'd say, like that. It sort of scared me because
he had a lot of voice. And he called me all these names.

And when he finished I said, "Well, I still did it."

And he mentioned my parents, "Your parents are probably
disgraced by you."

I said, "No, . . . my parents know what I did and they're
proud of what I did. And I think the majority of people in the
United States secretly are proud of what I did, and I think the
majority of soldiers like what I did. They just don't happen to
have the fortitude or just don't want to do it, but they believe
in what I did." And we went on discussing it and he sort of
calmed down then.

And I said more about the war. And he mentioned a little

bit about how the Viet Cong cut off the heads of the village
chiefs who'd opposed them. So I said, "I never been there but
I wouldn't agree with that. But we use napalm on civilians, and
we bomb and we shoot civilians, and we are just interrupting
their revolution. Let them have their revolution like we had
ours." And so we went on a little bit like that.

And then he had a phone call, told me to wait outside. I found
out later it was from the Adjutant General which is the lawyers
of the Army. All of a sudden when I came back in, he was like
a changed person, said to me, "Sit down." Then he said, "That's
enough discussing. You got a right to your own opinion and you
can do as you please." And he got very friendly and he said,
"Now listen, there might be certain people around here that are
really going to resent your doing something like that. Do you
want some MP's to protect you?"

So I said, "No. I don't need any MP's. I feel as though my
fellow soldiers understand what I did and I don't think I need
any protection."

He said, "Are you sure?"

I said, "Right."

He said, "Don't worry, everything will be all right. The Army
will take care of you."

So I said, "Thank you," and then I left.

And the reaction of the soldiers was just as I expected. Not
one soldier, not one, ever came up to me and said anything bad.
I'm talking about the regular soldiers I was with. I'm not talking
about the sergeants—career soldiers. I'm talking about guys in
for two or three years, who joined, or, mostly guys who were
drafted. They sort of laughed it off as being a crazy stunt, but
they said to me that it was a good idea and they wished they
would have done it. They wished they didn't have to go to Vietnam too. They said to me that they don't know what they're
fighting for. They can't understand themselves what we're fighting for in Vietnam. That would be a majority of the guys I was
with. And nobody ever said anything to me like, "You're a traitor
to the country;" or nobody ever threatened to hit me, or

anything like that. I had reports; my friends would come back to me—about this sergeant wants to see me and punch me in the nose. And I said to tell them, "They know where I sleep and if they want to come to see me they can!" But that was only a report. . . . Nobody ever came and saw me, or nobody ever tried to hit me or punch me in the nose or tell me I was a traitor to the country.

Life went on for me pretty well around Fort Ord when I wore my fatigues with my name on it, which struck me as sort of strange. I went to the snack bar one time and I was sitting there with a couple of my friends and . . . two colored soldiers came over to me.

One said, "You're Luftig, right?"

And I said, "Right."

So he put out his hand and said, "I want to shake your hand for what you did."

I said, "Thank you."

"I would have done the same thing. I just can't see myself doing it," he said. "I'm from"—I forget where, I think some place in the South. He said, "And if I fight, if I do go to Vietnam and fight, my heart's not going to be in it." And he said, "I should really do what you did, but I just can't do it."

The other soldier said he was from the North, and he agreed with me too. [He] said, "Negroes are going to go over there and fight and they come back here and they still can't live where they want or vote in certain areas or have the rights of a usual citizen, so why should they go over there and get the Vietnamese freedom? We're supposed to get the Vietnamese freedom when we ourselves don't have the freedom."

So . . . I spoke to him warmly—not to say, "You stick by me and I'll get you out of Vietnam," . . . or, "You're right, let's all get together." [The lawyer] had told me not to say anything [like that] and just say, "Well, that's all right" or "That's good." So that's all I usually would say if somebody came up to me and complimented me on it. I said it was a good idea. And I said to these two soldiers that, "You can do as you please, you know.

If you don't want to go to Vietnam then don't go. But there's not
much I can do for you." I said, "I did what I wanted and you
have to make up your own minds." So they left.

And I came out pretty well in California after that. There was
one sergeant, a platoon sergeant. He sort of kept it going, the
tension, as far as I was concerned. . . . See, he thought I was a
pacifist. I never argued with him. I'm not a pacifist, but he probably thought I wanted the famous line. He's talking to all the
soldiers about, "I think you may want to act violent towards this
person," and so on and so forth, "but don't." The thing was, they
weren't going to do anything. They kept laughing when he was
talking to them about this. . . . But he kept sort of egging them
on. . . . Maybe he thought they were going to do something if
he kept talking to them. . . . He went into his own discussion
of pacifists. He said, "You know those type of guys who if their
mother is getting raped by somebody wouldn't do anything about
it." And I sat there. And I got disgusted at that statement. I
wasn't going to give him the satisfaction of telling him I wasn't.
So I stood up and I threw my hands up and just walked out
while he was talking to the group. Maybe I could have got in
trouble. I didn't. I just happened to walk out. I just said to myself
I couldn't take it any more. So I just walked out instead of getting
in an argument with him. And the other guys came back and said,
"Don't listen to him, he's a fool anyway, that sergeant."

. . . There's one more thing that happened just before I left for
Fort Benning. We were taking physical training which is exercises. If you make a mistake you're supposed to do ten push-ups.
I don't mind doing it. If I make a mistake I do them too. . . . I
made a mistake. It looked like they were watching for me to
make one. And I was doing the ten push-ups. I didn't mind that
because [the sergeant] did catch me making a mistake but then
he made a remark like, "I'm glad I caught you, Luftig. It's about
time you did something for the country, and it's about time we
caught you." And then I stood up and said two words that weren't
Happy Birthday to him. Then they thought they had me. All
these sergeants that were gathered around said, "We got you
now."

So I said, "Right. I said it. And I'll say it again to him." (I really was mad that day.) "He's got no right to add his two cents. If he's going to throw in something, I'm going to throw in something."

And I went in front of the first sergeant, and he said, "Did you say it?"

I said, "Right, I said it. I admit when I say something." And I said, "He deserved it."

And he said, "Well, OK, you weren't supposed to curse."

And I said, "Well, he wasn't supposed to add his two cents in was he?"

So he went back and I thought to myself this might be a lot of trouble. However, the Army always needs four witnesses. It happens to be that some of my friends were gathered around near that spot. So they called the four of them in. They said, "Did you hear him say it?" And none of them would say that I said it. To me later on they all admitted that I said it. They said, "Why should we get you in trouble? They're just looking to get you in trouble." . . . So when they did call me back in they said, "Your friends don't admit your saying it." So then I said, "Well maybe I didn't say it then." He said, "Well, we'll let you go, since your friends say you didn't say it."

. . . Just one more incident that happened out in California. I was only out in California for eight weeks and all this was crammed into about three weeks, all these incidents. They kept asking me if I wanted to see a chaplain. Finally I said, "OK, I'll go see one." I wanted to see what they had in store.

They said, "What religion are you?"

And I said, "Jewish."

They didn't have a rabbi or anybody on the post.

"No, you don't?" I said. "That's not right."

They said, "Well, he's away in Vietnam. What religion would you like to choose next?" Just like that!

So I said, "What choices do I have?"

"You could see a Catholic priest or a Protestant minister."

So I said, "I'll take the Protestant minister."

That was just the way they put it, too. It was just like you got a choice: if you can't get this kind of food, do you want this or that? You can see either the Catholic priest or the Protestant minister. So I said, "I'll take the Protestant minister."

They said, "OK."

I had to deal with a lieutenant colonel. . . . And he started, "Why did you make a decision like that?" And he had been to Vietnam and he was listing the towns—like he had an extreme knowledge of Vietnam: . . . The Viet Cong killed four civilians I saw in this town; three civilians here; beheaded this one person.

And I let him go on for a while. I said, "Right. You been there and I haven't. But just because you were there doesn't absolutely make you an expert. I believe I know something about it. You might know more about the little technicalities in each village. But there's bigger things than that." I said, "That's a revolution. In our revolution we *must* have killed innocent people." I said, "Nobody is going to say we didn't. We killed people who supported Britain, loyalists on their side. And every revolution there is, is always innocent people killed." I said, "It's unfortunate. I don't say it's right for the Viet Cong to do it. But they can't be choosy. Those people are government men. Maybe they don't deserve to be killed. But maybe that's the point the Viet Cong have been driven to." So I went on about this napalm. I said, "So, we use napalm indiscriminately on villages. You've been to Vietnam. You must have seen the effects of that napalm."

And he said, "Very much. I've seen them." And he smiled.

And I got sort of surprised. "To me," I said, "it wouldn't be too funny to get burnt alive like that." I thought, as a minister, he wouldn't laugh like that.

And he went on like, "We're fighting for freedom," and so forth.

So I said, "We're only fighting for freedom in our sense of the word. Everybody has their own definitions of democracy and freedom. . . . So much in being able to vote. To them they want to have food and land at the moment, and they don't have that. And that will come later on, the other parts. They're interested in the basic necessities of life." And I said, "Everybody else has their definition of democracy. And maybe what we have won't work for them."

And he went on about how we got to fight communism: "Now it's eight thousand miles away, but next week it will be in Hawaii" (just like Johnson would say) "and the week after that it will be San Francisco. We got to stop them now."

I just said, "Well, I think every man should have a right to choose about certain things. That's his conscience. A man has a right to choose, I think, about whether he wants to kill or doesn't want to kill. That's the ultimate point in life. They may not have to choose little things. But that's such a major decision that a man should be able to make up his mind whether he wants to kill someone or he doesn't."

And then he went on a little bit more.

And finally I saw that it was getting sort of ridiculous, because I kept saying certain things and he'd go back.

So I said, . . . "I probably would go to Vietnam, and go will-ingly, if I saw a perfect democracy in this country. . . ." And I said to him, "How many soldiers do we have in Vietnam?"

And he said something like, "Three or four hundred thousand."

I said, "All right. That's a lot of soldiers." I said, "How about if the American Army sends two thousand soldiers, that's all, just two thousand, to Mississippi and Alabama and make sure that the Negroes vote in the next election, just make sure that they vote."

So then he got very mad and said, "The Army has nothing to do with that."

I said, "I know the Army officially has nothing to do with that, but the Man who runs the war in Vietnam could do that if he wanted to, but of course Mr. Johnson wants to get elected again so he wouldn't do anything like that. Like the rest of the politi-cians we have, all they are interested in is getting elected. They are not interested in the people." And I went on a little bit like that.

And he said, "There's no use talking to you, Luftig. You might as well leave."

So I said, "Well, maybe there isn't."

And I got up and left. Sort of an angry interview, it was. It ended on that point.

. . . When I was sent to Fort Benning, nothing much hap-

pened. When the case came up again—and it got in the papers
in Columbus—I was a cook in an outfit for guys who were in
paratrooper training. . . . The Army got all excited again. So we
went through the same thing again. And I went to see this battalion commander, this colonel. He wanted to talk to me. . . .
And he had a young lady to take notes on what I said; a Catholic
priest, a psychologist, and the company commander there besides
myself and him.

And he started in a real fatherly approach, "This is ridiculous
what you're doing," and this and that. "Be a good young son.
Be a good man." And, "Stop all this foolishness. You're not going
to Vietnam anyway. You're going to stay here."

So I said, "Well, I may not be going to Vietnam at this point.
Maybe I'm not. But I'm not only doing it for myself. I'm doing it
for other people. Maybe if I do it and I get out of the Army and
they realize I am, then soldiers say, 'Well, why don't I do it? He
didn't go to Vietnam. He knew how to do the court case.' Maybe
I'll convince fifty soldiers."

He said, "You really want to do something like that?"

I said, "Yes. I would like to convince [them] just on this principle, just on my court case. . . . I would like to see more soldiers do it."

So he sort of seemed surprised, and he went on a little bit more
discussion of Vietnam. He had the same old lines about freedom,
and how vicious the Viet Cong is, and said the same things about
the napalm. We discussed it for a while and then it just sort of
ended.

And then I got transferred from the paratroopers group because
they said it wasn't safe for my health. The paratroopers were too
gung-ho. They were going to Vietnam and he said that most of
them would feel, "If I go to Vietnam and he's not going to Vietnam, that isn't fair." So they wanted to transfer me. So I said,
"All right." I was transferred to this other place where guys who
have been in Fort Benning will stay . . . for the rest of their tour
—until they are out of the Army.

So since I've been here I've gotten along real well. Everything

has gone smooth. I'm just about positive I won't go to Vietnam.
. . . So the Army will never know whether I would have went to
jail instead of to Vietnam. . . . I made up my mind that I
wouldn't go to Vietnam, but I never really told anybody that.
. . . I was going to refuse the order to go to Vietnam. I was, in
the beginning at least, going to try and face up to see if I could
go to jail. But if I could have lasted as long as Mora and the rest
of them [see "The Fort Hood Three," pp. 181–202], I don't know
but I at least was going to take the first step. In my mind I was
fixed that I wasn't going to go to Vietnam no matter what. . . .

. . . The main issue [in the Luftig case] is that some time
during the Korean War the government, when Mr. Truman was
President, seized a steel mill in Youngstown, Ohio, and they said
they were going to nationalize the steel mills or at least this steel
mill. . . . The steel mill started the case. They lost at the beginning. When it got to the Supreme Court, the Supreme Court said
that the government had no right to take this steel mill since the
government was not officially at war. During Korea the United
States government never declared war. It was just a UN action.
So they had to give the steel mill back to them. Faulkner said to
me, if they couldn't take a steel mill the government shouldn't
have a right to seize people who take precedence over private
property, take a person and send them to fight a war which is
not declared. . . . It seems like you should win. You're right and
you shouldn't lose. However [the judge and the government at-
torney] keep saying it is not [their] jurisdiction. It's up to the
Army. They don't even want to discuss that point. . . . The Army
takes care of their own.

. . . Once I get out of the Army that's the end of the case
because the case only applies to soldiers. . . . As long as you're
in the Army, [Mr. Faulkner] said, he has a case because everybody in the Army is very likely to go to Vietnam. So the case
will end as soon as I get out of the Army. . . . I don't think you
can win because if I won nobody would have to go to Vietnam if
they didn't want to. That would change the whole foreign policy
of the United States. And that's not going to happen.

[*Bob Luftig was asked what it was about himself that made him think he could take the pressure and harassment while others could not imagine themselves doing it.*] Well, I thought I was a strong enough person. Since I believed in something so strong, since I believed in not going to Vietnam, and I knew I was doing the right thing, that's why I thought I could take it. A lot of people said, "You'll never do it." . . . But I thought that I could just keep believing that I was doing the right thing, that I was doing something for the benefit of all people. So I keep those high thoughts in mind, that I could make it.

Why other guys couldn't make it is maybe because their parents would say, "You're crazy . . . What are you trying to do? Ruin the family and ruin your lives when you get out of the Army?" That's what the Army also said to me, some of the officers . . . like Captain Baker—"You're going to ruin your life. When you get out of the Army, you'll never get a job," and this and that. . . . The only reason the parents might back them up is because it's their son. They don't want to leave their son, but that would be the only reason. Politically they wouldn't back them up. I knew I had that on my side.

. . . I feel it was about the best thing I've ever done in my life. Really, the most important thing I've ever done in my life is this court case. And I'm glad I did it. . . . The only thing I regret is that more soldiers didn't do it, or so far haven't done it. . . . That's the only unfortunate thing that happened to me.

. . . Everything else was great. I enjoyed doing it. And I really enjoyed the soldiers' reaction, how I was right. I had told my parents, I know young people up to a point and I can tell you, I don't think anything is going to happen to me. And it never did. I never had any violence or anything. . . . I'd like to see a lot of soldiers refusing to go, but it takes a lot of courage. . . .

Dennis Mora, James Johnson, and David Samas

THE FORT HOOD THREE

Pfc. James Johnson, Pvt. Dennis Mora, and Pvt. David Samas became known as the Fort Hood Three when on June 30, 1966, they made public their intention to refuse orders to go to Vietnam. They announced that they had filed a suit which challenged the orders on grounds that the war in Vietnam is illegal and requested an injunction to bar the Army from sending them to Vietnam. (See headnote to Robert Luftig's account, page 168.)

High-level conferences at the Pentagon were held to decide what to do with the three soldiers. On July 3, the *New York Times* reported that the senior legal counsel for the Defense Department had indicated that members of the armed forces who refused to fight in Vietnam might, in extreme cases, be sentenced to death.

As the men were on their way to a public meeting on July 7, they were intercepted separately and given amended orders to "proceed immediately to Fort Dix, New Jersey, . . . for the convenience of the government." Mora and Johnson were put in handcuffs and all three were driven in military police cars to Fort Dix. There they were held for "investigative detention." No charges were filed against them. They had stated their intention but had not yet refused any direct order.

On July 11, attorney Stanley Faulkner attempted to present arguments for the injunction before the Federal District Court in Washington, D.C. The judge did not allow Faulkner to finish his presentation, denied the suit, and dismissed the hearing, saying that the war and foreign policy were the province of the President and not of that court.

The suit is in reality a suit against the United States and the United States has not consented to be sued. In addition,

*it is not the function of the judiciary to entertain such litiga-
tion which challenges the validity, the wisdom or the propri-
ety of the Commander in Chief of the Armed Forces abroad.
The issue presented involves a challenge to the conduct of
not only diplomatic, but foreign affairs, over which the President is exclusively responsible.*

On the evening of July 13, the three were separated from each
other and on July 14 each one was ordered individually to board
transportation for Vietnam. When they refused they were put in
solitary confinement in the maximum security area of the Fort
Dix stockade.

A defense committee was organized to publicize the case and
to enlist support among servicemen, men facing military service,
and the public at large. The Fort Hood Three Defense Committee maintains that men and women in the armed forces are
citizens of this country and "must not be deprived of their rights
as citizens to freedom of thought, of conscience, of expression in
all matters, including those relating to the war in Vietnam."

The same legal grounds were used to defend the soldiers in
the military courts and in the civil suit, namely, violations of
international treaty obligations and assurances, the U.S. Constitution, and provisions in the Army Field Manual which hold
that the individual soldier is responsible if he commits war
crimes. (See Appendix C, pages 318–324.) The petition for hearing by the Supreme Court of *Mora et al. v. McNamara et al.* asks,
in effect, whether the courts as well as Congress will abdicate
their responsibility to the President by claiming that the issues
are political and not justiciable. The Supreme Court refused certiorari on November 6, 1967, but this time two justices stated
that the Court should hear the merits of the case. The significant
dissent of Justice Potter Stewart follows:

*Mr. Justice Stewart, with whom Mr. Justice Douglas joins,
dissenting.*

*The petitioners were drafted into the United States Army
in late 1965, and six months later were ordered to a West*

Coast replacement station for shipment to Vietnam. They brought this suit to prevent the Secretary of Defense and the Secretary of the Army from carrying out those orders, and requested a declaratory judgment that the present United States military activity in Vietnam is "illegal." The District Court dismissed the suit, and the Court of Appeals affirmed.

There exist in this case questions of great magnitude. Some are akin to those referred to by Mr. Justice Douglas in Mitchell v. United States, 386 U.S. 972 [*See pages 103–105.*] *But there are others:*

I. *Is the present United States military activity in Vietnam a "war" within the meaning of Article I, Section 8, Clause 11 of the Constitution?*

II. *If so, may the Executive constitutionally order the petitioners to participate in that military activity, when no war has been declared by the Congress?*

III. *Of what relevance to Question II are the present treaty obligations of the United States?*

IV. *Of what relevance to Question II is the joint Congressional ("Tonkin Bay") Resolution of August 10, 1964?*

   (a) *Do present United States military operations fall within the terms of the Joint Resolutions?*

   (b) *If the Joint Resolution purports to give the Chief Executive authority to commit United States forces to armed conflict limited in scope only by his own absolute discretion, is the Resolution a constitutionally impermissible delegation of all or part of Congress' power to declare war?*

These are large and deeply troubling questions. Whether the Court would ultimately reach them depends, of course, upon the resolution of serious preliminary issues of justiciability. We cannot make these problems go away simply by refusing to hear the case of three obscure Army privates.

I intimate not even tentative views upon any of these mat-
ters, but I think the Court should squarely face them by
granting certiorari and setting this case for oral argument.

**Sources for this account were made available by Stanley Faulk-
ner, attorney, the Fort Hood Three Defense Committee, and
Grace Mora Newman, sister of Dennis Mora. Several of the
letters to Mrs. Newman were published in *The National
Guardian*.**

Joint Statement: We are Pfc. James Johnson, Pvt. David Samas,
and Pvt. Dennis Mora, three soldiers formerly stationed at Fort
Hood, Texas, in the same company of the 142 Signal Battalion,
2nd Armored Division. We have received orders to report on the
thirteenth of July at Oakland Army Terminal in California, for
final processing and shipment to Vietnam.

We have decided to take a stand against this war, which we
consider immoral, illegal, and unjust. We are initiating today,
through our attorneys, Stanley Faulkner of New York and Mrs.
Selma Samols of Washington, D.C., an action in the courts to
enjoin the Secretary of Defense and the Secretary of the Army
from sending us to Vietnam. We intend to report as ordered to
the Oakland Army Terminal, but under no circumstances will
we board ship for Vietnam. We are prepared to face court-martial
if necessary.

We represent in our backgrounds a cross section of the Army
and of America. James Johnson is a Negro, David Samas is of
Lithuanian and Italian parents, Dennis Mora is a Puerto Rican.
We speak as American soldiers.

We have been in the Army long enough to know that we are
not the only GI's who feel as we do. Large numbers of men in
the service either do not understand this war or are against it.

When we entered the Army, Vietnam was for us only a newspaper box score of GI's and Viet Cong killed or wounded. We
were all against it in one way or another, but we were willing
to "go along with the program," believing that we would not be
sent to Vietnam.

We were told from the very first day of our induction that we were headed for Vietnam. During basic training it was repeated often by sergeants and officers, and soon it became another meaningless threat that was used to make us take our training seriously.

But later on, Vietnam became a fact of life when someone you knew wondered how he could break the news to his girl, wife, or family that he was being sent there. After he solved that problem, he had to find a reason that would satisfy him. The reasons were many—"Somebody's got to do it," "When your number's up, your number's up," "The pay is good," and "You've got to stop them someplace" were phrases heard in the barracks and mess hall, and used by soldiers to encourage each other to accept the war as their own. Besides, what could be done about it anyway? Orders are orders.

As we saw more and more of this, the war became the one thing we talked about most and the one point we all agreed upon. No one wanted to go, and more than that, there was no reason for anyone to go. . . .

No one used the word "winning" anymore because in Vietnam it has no meaning. Our officers just talk about five and ten more years of war with at least half a million of our boys thrown into the grinder. . . .

We know that Negroes and Puerto Ricans are being drafted and end up in the worst of the fighting all out of proportion to their numbers in the population; and we have firsthand knowledge that these are the ones who have been deprived of decent education and jobs at home.

The three of us, while stationed together, talked a lot and found we thought alike on one overriding issue—the war in Vietnam must be stopped. It was all talk and we had no intentions of getting into trouble by making waves at that stage.

Once back in Texas, we were told that we were on levy to Vietnam. All we had discussed and thought about now was real. It was time for us to quit talking and decide. Go to Vietnam and ignore the truth, or stand and fight for what we know is right.

We have made our decision. We will not be a part of this

unjust, immoral, and illegal war. We want no part of a war of extermination. We oppose the criminal waste of American lives and resources. We refuse to go to Vietnam! ! ! ! ! !

Mora: I was active in the peace movement before I was drafted. The Army knew this and took me anyway.

In May of '64, I refused to answer certain questions on a personnel questionnaire at my induction physical. I was opposed to the "loyalty oath" nature of the questions because they violated my constitutional rights of freedom of association, speech, and political convictions. I was sent home and told I would be investigated.

On November 1, 1965, I was apparently found acceptable and I reported for induction a second time. I wore an anti-war button to the center and got into a scuffle with a lieutenant and some sergeants. I was arrested by the city police and charged with disorderly conduct, assault, and resisting arrest. However, I was sent home from the precinct that same day. Approximately a month went by before I contacted my draft board to find out my status. They, in turn, referred me to the FBI. At the FBI headquarters in New York I was given the treatment and told that they had just gotten my case—failure to report for induction (not reporting the day following my arrest was tantamount to not reporting at all) and they further informed me that I would have the local police charges dropped pending my induction.

At this time I still saw a way out of jail, so I found myself on a troop train on December 6, 1965, going to South Carolina. I figured that Vietnam was a remote possibility and nothing else. . . . Whenever I have been faced with any situation, it is easy to tell the man, no. When I was a kid I lived in a ghetto. I was told all I could do was to work with my hands because I was a Puerto Rican. I had to tell them, no, this was not so. I could not believe that . . . we were living in a tenement because we belonged there—I had to tell the man, no. Whenever the cop on the corner would tell us we had to keep our place, keep within our boundaries at that time, I told them, no. If a man is without a moral code, he is like the sea without water. That is the only way I know how to act.

I will not fight for the blood money of war industries, nor will I give my life so that U.S. corporations can claim as their property the people and resources of Vietnam.

Johnson: On December 6, 1965, I entered the Army reluctantly. Although I did not voice my opposition, I was opposed to the war in Vietnam. . . . I once told a colonel about my opposition to the war. I was told that I was being paid to be a soldier not a politician. . . .

Now, there is a direct relationship between the peace movement and the civil rights movement. The South Vietnamese are fighting for representation, like we ourselves. The South Vietnamese just want a voice in the government, nothing else. Therefore the Negro in Vietnam is just helping to defeat what his black brother is fighting for in the United States. When the Negro soldier returns, he still will not be able to ride in Mississippi or walk down a certain street in Alabama. There will still be, proportionately, twice as many Negroes as whites in Vietnam. Those Negroes that die for their country still cannot be assured of a burial place which their family feels is suitable for them. His children will still receive an inferior education, and he will still live in a ghetto. Although he bears the brunt of the war, he will reap no benefits.

It is time that the Negro realizes that his strength can be put to much better use right here at home. This is where his strength lies. We can gain absolutely nothing in Vietnam. All this is lending to the decision I have made. I know it is my right to make this decision.

Samas: At one time (in Fort Gordon, Georgia) there were six of us who felt that America had no right being in Vietnam. The six of us often discussed this, and we tried to find a way to follow up on our beliefs. We all decided to refuse orders (we were all quite certain of getting them) for Vietnam, no matter what the circumstances.

We had to make a choice of means of action. We knew we could speak out before we got orders, or do some private scheming after we got orders. There are countless ways of avoiding duty in Vietnam; but we felt our beliefs and our purpose to be just, so our means had to be also.

. . . We had thirty days before we had to report, approximately thirty days. I went to Chicago, and I was married in Chicago on June 17. Then from Chicago, on the twenty-second of June, we proceeded to New York.

. . . I've been opposed to American participation in Vietnam from the very beginning, but have never until a few days ago made my feelings public. . . . On June thirtieth . . . I participated in a press conference and read a personal statement. [I] stated my views and [said that] I would refuse to go to Vietnam. . . .

Since that time we have been plagued by federal agents and what can only be called hired thugs. I kept my whereabouts secret from the press and the police, and only my parents and a very few people knew where I was living. The Modesto city police visited my parents in California, saying they had been sent by some "higher authorities" but were not able to reveal those authorities. An officer who my father happened to know approached him in a friendly manner, saying he came to help the family. . . . It didn't prove hard for the police to persuade my parents into believing I was being used as a tool of the Communists. They were told that I was in serious trouble and that the only way for them to help was to reveal my address to the police so that the authorities in New York might get in contact with me and try to help and protect me. My father became terribly upset, fearing for my safety, and gave the police my address in New York. . . .

Although they have absolutely no authority, the Modesto city police . . . had told my father that if I would retract my statement and withdraw completely from the civil action now in progress, that I would receive a discharge from the Army and no serious repercussions would result. . . .

The next morning when we left our apartment we were followed by three men in their early twenties, who made no attempt to be discreet about tailing us. They remained within twenty feet of us all day long, and when approached, would deny any connection with us.

Mora: We never got an opportunity to report. On July 7th I was supposed to attend a meeting at the Community Church in New York. It was a peace rally, and at about 6 o'clock, an hour before the meeting, myself and James Johnson, were arrested, handcuffed, and brought to Fort Dix. We had no opportunity to speak to our lawyer. We were told our orders were changed and we were to be stationed at Fort Dix. We were kept there for a week in administrative restriction.

Samas: On July 7th, approximately 7 o'clock, my wife and I left our apartment. Previously we had been followed for four days by unidentified men, many of them, and there were people behind my house, on top of the house, all around the house. Anyway, on July 7th we left the house and had gotten into the street. This was in the Bronx, New York. We had just started walking down the street. I was a little behind my wife. A man crossed the street, dressed in an ordinary suit. He showed me his badge and asked me who I was. He said he was a city detective. At the same time I saw another badge on my left. I didn't see the man approach, but I saw the badge flash past my face. He told me he was from the CID and grabbed my arm and handed me a copy of my orders. He said my leave was canceled, my orders had been canceled, and said I would report immediately to Fort Dix; transportation would be provided. He started to lead me down the street. I was dressed in civilian clothing. I wasn't prepared to come back to the Army. I said, what about my clothing—if I had a chance to get it. He said, no, that would be taken care of at a later time. I asked if I could give my wife some money because she didn't expect me to be arrested. He let me. . . . When we were at the corner of Aldus and Southern Boulevard an Armed Forces Police car drove up and stopped maybe 100 feet away in the flow of traffic. There was a captain in the car and an Armed Forces Police driver. He led me to the car, and the captain had gotten out of the car to open the door for me. The captain never said a word to me the whole trip down, he never said one word. The CID man said very little.

Q. Did he say you were under arrest for violating any article of the Uniform Code?

A. No, he did not. I asked him why I was arrested and he said he had not done it as an arrest per se. I asked him why he grabbed me, why he used physical means. He said in the car, "That was the most expedient means possible to make sure you complied with your orders." I asked him again why he felt it was necessary to pick me up in the street. He could have knocked on my door and handed me the orders. I said, why grab me in the street like that. He said, "I don't recall the situation," which left no more room for any more questions by me. . . .

We were brought to Fort Dix. . . . I was led into the office and everything was taken out of my pockets. I was frisked and taken into protective custody. I did not know my rights and I asked him what the charges were against me so I could call my lawyer. He said, ask Major Jones. I asked Major Jones and he said he does not have to answer my questions and told me to shut up. Then they put me in a cage in back of the office. While I was there I saw James and Dennis.

Mora:

Q. When is the first time you were informed of formal charges against you?

A. Later that evening Colonel Wesley read a statement to us, which applied to our administrative restriction and told us we were being investigated under Article 134 of the Uniform Code of Military Justice, which amounted to making statements detrimental to the morale of the armed forces. . . . We were now to be stationed . . . in a certain building . . . not to be let out, not to have a chance to talk to anyone concerning the motives for what we had done.

Q. Were you under guard?

A. Yes. There were eight guards, three shifts a day, four men inside. There was just room for four beds. There were four guards inside and at least four guards outside.

Q. Were you permitted to go outside the building?

A. We did go out to take a shower in the building next door where shower facilities were provided for us. We were allowed to go from the building to the shower with two guards. When we took a shower the two guards watched us take the shower. . . .

I would say it was much closer than maximum security in the stockade now, because there were guards over us at all times. We could not go to the latrine without having two guards. We did not have any exercise. We were restricted to the immediate area of our bunks.

[*Excerpt from message to U.S. Army Chief of Staff from Commanding General at Fort Dix:*]

Subject: Plan for Suppression of Anti-Vietnam Activities by U.S. Army Personnel (Mora, Johnson, Samas . . .) . . . 12 July 1966.

PART I

Investigation has been completed this date. I have determined that:

1. With respect to Johnson, Mora and Samas there is sufficient evidence to warrant the preferring of charges alleging a violation of Article 134, uttering disloyal statements with intent to cause disaffection and disloyalty among the civilian population and members of the military forces. My decision is that in the best interest of the service the preferring of charges be deferred to afford EM opportunity to comply with orders to proceed for duty in RVN.

. . .

PART II

In accordance with my decision the following action is contemplated:

1. Movement orders will be prepared by Personnel Center, Fort Dix.

2. At 1830 hours, 13 July, EM will be assigned separate quarters.

3. At 1915 hours, 13 July, unit commander will advise each EM separately that he will depart Fort Dix 14 July, for forward movement to Vietnam. EM will not be advised of particulars of travel at this time. If EM request, permission will be granted to contact families and consult with legal counsel.

4. At 0700, 14 July, movement orders will be presented to EM.

5. At 0720 hours, 14 July, EM will be escorted separately to MAFB to arrive at 0740 hours, 14 July. Aircraft Flt No R743Y will be boarded at 0750, 14 July. Aircraft departs 0800, destination TAN SON NHUT, SAIGON, via ANCHORAGE, ALASKA, and KADENA, OKINAWA. Each stop will be approximately 2 hours.

6. If EM refuse to board aircraft, direct order to do so will be given by unit CO. Should orders be disobeyed, appropriate action will be taken.

PART III

. . .

2. Demonstrations aimed at Fort Dix may be anticipated. Necessary steps will be taken by CG Fort Dix to preclude interference by any demonstrators.

Samas:

Q. What happened on the morning of the 14th of July?

A. That morning I believe Major Moorman was the first officer I saw. I was awakened about 5 o'clock and someone had brought me a suit of khakis along with a tray of breakfast, and I was told to change and to get ready to move, which I did. And then Major Moorman came up to see me and said, "We have grounds to prosecute you under Article 134. We have sufficient evidence. We can proceed with the prosecution, but we will not." I asked him if I could contact my wife and he said, no, it was out of his hands now. He left. Then Captain St. Martin came in shortly thereafter . . . and handed me a set of orders, saying I should board the plane July 14, approximately 7:15. . . . It was enroute to Vietnam and Saigon, but he did not read the orders to me and did not say whether I was in disobedience of orders. He said, "Be prepared to move out at 7 o'clock, maybe 6:30." When he came back again I asked him to read my orders because I wanted to be sure what it said. He did not read it. Everything was in Army abbreviations. I asked him to explain them to me and he did. Then he left again. A short time later I was taken downstairs. My duffel bag and suitcase were packed. I loaded them in the car. . . .

Q. Did you have a chance to call your wife?

A. No. I wasn't allowed.

Q. Where was your wife?

A. My wife was on the post. . . . She was staying down at the guesthouse here on post.

Q. And you asked to talk to her?

A. Yes, I did, and I was denied. I asked if I could do it. Then I asked if he could do it . . . for me as a favor. He said it was out of his hands. He said, "She will find out in due time," which she did when I wasn't there for visiting hours on the next day.

Mora: . . . It was 6 o'clock or so, right after chow Captain DeVera came . . . and read to me the order saying I was to report to McGuire Air Force Base for onward shipment to Vietnam. At that point I asked him to interpret the order and he read the abbreviations and what they meant. I asked would there be any stops before Vietnam. He told me I was to get on the plane at McGuire enroute to Vietnam. He then asked me if I was disobeying the order.

He read the order. I said, "I refuse to go to Vietnam." He waited another five minutes. He read to me the written order, and he read it again, and again I refused. He told me to think it over. He told me to take my duffel bag outside. There was a car waiting outside, an MP car. I carried the duffel bag outside and put it down, and for the third time he asked me if I understood the order. He proceeded to read it. I told him, "For the third time I refuse the order to go to Vietnam." At that point he started writing out a confinement order. I was taken directly to the stockade and put in maximum security confinement. I was processed in the stockade. . . .

[*August 15: The prisoners were formally charged with disobeying an officer's orders in violation of Article 90 of the Uniform Code of Military Justice.*]

[*August 19: The Army refused a motion to postpone courts-martial until after the case was heard in civil court.*]

[*September 6–9: Courts-martial were held at Fort Dix.*]

Mora:

Q. Did you have a reason for refusing the order?

A. My refusal of the order was a culmination of all my beliefs I had about the war in Vietnam. The fact that the war by its very nature is one which began as a civil war; the fact that the Premier of South Vietnam was born in the North; the fact that thousands of Vietnamese from the same towns and provinces are fighting each other—this is in the nature of a civil war. I believe it is the sacred right of any people to determine their own social or political systems without any kind of interference.

I could never be clear as to what our objectives were in Vietnam. We have been told in CI class the objective was to kill as many Asians as we could. That was the substance of what I understood we were told by the CO. We were

told when we reported to Fort Hood, after being assigned
to a regular unit, the reason for going over there was to
help those little brown people straighten out their problems.
I cannot accept that as any kind of a reason for something
that would involve me so directly. . . . This is ten thousand
miles from home, and I just cannot bring myself to believe
we have a commitment.

Samas: I compared the war in Vietnam very much to our War
for Independence from the British Empire. I feel we are putting
the people in Vietnam in the same position. We aren't giving
them a free choice in what kind of government, what kind of
life they should live, or what kind of system they should live
under. We are telling them, we are instructing them by force
. . . to live the way we want them to live. I don't believe we are
giving them the chance, as we had the chance. I believe the war
to be immoral, unjust, and illegal.

Johnson: . . . I felt that if I participated in this war I would
be participating in an illegal war and committing an illegal act.
. . . I felt it was not in the best interests of my country or Vietnam to violate my conscience and convictions, because if I did so
I would lose my humanity and all respect if I would comply with
orders to go to Vietnam. I was especially interested in the Nuremberg agreements which said each man, each soldier, was responsible for his individual acts; and a soldier had not only a right but
a duty not to commit, not to follow any unlawful command given
him. In other words, he should disobey anything he thought was
immoral or illegal. And this is how I felt at the time. I also stated
that I was opposed to the number of Negroes in Vietnam who
were forced to fight in Vietnam against people who were fighting
for the same thing that so many members of their own race were
fighting for right here in this country. . . .

[*Sentences: Mora, three years; Johnson and Samas, five years.
Reduction to lowest rank, total forfeiture of pay, and dishonorable
discharges.*]

Mora, September 13, 1966: They moved us today to Fort Meade, Maryland. A jail's a jail. . . . The food is better here. . . . The clientele's a little different, too, and the ceiling higher. Nevertheless, the Leavenworth special sounds so sweet now. Amazing how you can get used to things. There's more sleep too. Tell Mama not to worry because if she does it bugs me. . . . She must consider Dave and Jimmy her sons now since they are my brothers.

September 20: I have no need for it [a watch that was being repaired]. My clock has only two times on it—nighttime and daytime. This simplifies matters. . . .

I was just reading about a classic martyr. We just don't fit into that category. We will not render unto Caesar what is his because in this case L. B. Caesar wants our lives. We can't turn the other cheek because we've learned enough not to let anybody get that close. As for forgiving our enemies, we are aware that they know exactly what they're doing and we can't let them get away with it. We've also been unable to make a slice of bread anything more than it is, let alone the butter. We just hope we won't be denied three times by Peter appeals. This could be the only thing we have in common with the carpenter.

[*Composite letter, October 7, 1966:*] Two of us are in one cell and the third is in a separate, single cell. The cell is 8' by 10' approximately. . . . My cell is 6' by 8', contains a bunk, a sink, and toilet. . . . We are awakened each day at 0500 hours either by someone blowing a whistle over the P.A. system or someone yelling, "God damn your soul, get-up." . . . From that moment until six in the evening I'm not permitted to sit or lie down. . . . Leaning against the wall, stumbling too close to the bars, talking, singing, whistling are all punishable by push-ups. . . . The confinement officer is quick to make the prisoners do push-ups or confine them to the "box" if he finds anyone violating these rules. The box is a single, unventilated, unlit cell which is reserved for any breach of stockade regulations. Whoever is placed in this cell is also on a restricted bread, potatoes, and water diet.

We are not allowed to talk to any of the prisoners, and today prisoners were forbidden to even look in our direction. . . . I'm not permitted to talk to anyone. I've been given a direct order not to even talk to Dennis Mora, who is my cellmate. . . . The guards also have been instructed not to speak with me.

The heat is irregular and the cement floors are cold and damp. We eat on the floor, and there are flies constantly in our cells. . . . I am allowed to eat breakfast (usually cold) either on the floor or the toilet.

We are not permitted to have shoestrings or razor blades, although we are not considered escape-risks. This means that many days we are not able to shave because it is difficult to obtain a locked razor or razor blades.

We have no reading material except for a Bible, but only either the Old or New Testament. We are not allowed both Testaments. . . . Our mail is unduly delayed, and communications from our attorney, we sometimes never receive. . . . Our exercise is supposed to consist of one hour of walking outside the compound in a fenced yard. This is not given to us on a regular basis and even when we do go out we are further restricted to a corner of the yard. . . . Given these restrictions and rules the only way to pass the time is to shine boots or pace the floor.

That's it until six o'clock when we can take down our displays. Lights out is at 9 o'clock, but at times lights go out about 11.

Samas: Although I am being held in solitary confinement, the prisoners and guards find occasion to speak with me. I was ordered to remove the name tags from my uniforms and from above my cage door. I now exist as the man without a country or a name; this plus instructions for no one to speak with me entices the prisoners and guards to find out my story.

Naturally and eagerly, I am always explaining who I am and why I am opposed to the war in Vietnam. My beliefs as to the illegality and immorality of the war are accepted and (no surprise to me) almost always agreed with. It is simple, indeed, to show the wrongness of American intervention in Vietnam. . . . The facts are easy to deal with and easily understood.

I find that after explaining why I feel the war is wrong, people still don't understand why I refused to go. They ask some very simple questions that are much more difficult to answer: Which is easier, one year in Vietnam or five years in prison? Why didn't you just go AWOL and get thrown out of the Army? Why didn't you refuse the draft? Why did you make it a public issue? And, finally, their most basic question—What is in it for you?

In black and white, judged according to present-day standards, my actions were foolish. One year is easier! AWOL is simpler! Refusing the draft would have been easier! Relative silence would have been easier, and materially I did not gain a thing! In fact, long lists can be drawn showing what I have lost, and I cannot balance this with a numbered list of my gains, no more than I can trace the outline of my soul or tell you where my conscience lies.

After much consideration, I chose to take the hardest possible path because it was, to my belief, the most honorable one. Nothing is hidden and there is nothing that I have meant to hide. The world can listen to and watch Jimmy, Dennis, and me or ignore us; truthfully, it matters little to me what anyone else might think. Conscience is a costly thing, and I am paying dearly for the rights to my mind. Five years—a cement wall and cold iron bars, five years in a very horrible, empty limbo is the price I am paying for real freedom.

I laugh at my masters, but I pity them. I have no contempt for them, but hatred for a system which they are caught up in.

Judge Learned Hand had a much quoted saying—"Liberty lies in the hearts of men; when it dies there, no law, no jury, no judge can save it!" I have taken this and changed it somewhat to help me to endure my prison life. Liberty lies in the hearts of men; when it exists there, no law, no jury, no judge can destroy it!

[*On November 7, the First Army Commanding General reviewed the courts-martial and affirmed the convictions and sentences.*]

Mora, Fort Leavenworth, November 8: Suddenly I am in Kansas! It was done quickly and quietly. In the interests of national security, we are sure. This place has it all over the stockade. We're in individual cells. They are provided with the usual features, plus a spring bed and listen to this, a headset with three outlets for radio stations. Yes, we have sounds! You can keep three hardcover books for three weeks and two soft-covereds, plus a magazine. Paradise itself. . . . Please tell everyone, and emphasize the point that I am in fine spirits. The future looks good. The purgatory is over and I can do this standing on my head.

Mora, November 22: You gain a self-assurance here that, although expensive, is useful. It's simplicity itself to look at a wall and know that it is crumbling even if the process is slower than you would want.

Mora, December 21: Thirty days here without a domicile entry (black mark) and I'll be in a wing that has TV, pool and card tables, and where the doors to the cells are kept open all day. Custody is like a soft sand dune: the higher up you go, the harder it is to move and the quicker it is to slide down. At the top is the parole unit. This is outside the walls, has no bars, and is just like regular duty. The object all along is to give you the illusion of freedom by giving you many of its accessories. . . . Here we pass some time by trying to make a knot in a string weighted with a washer. You can use only one hand. You let it dangle and then flick your wrist.

[*The Army Review Board affirmed conviction on all counts but, on July 3, 1967, reduced the sentences of Johnson and Samas from five to three years, so that the sentences would be equal with Mora's.*]

Mora, August 17, 1967: . . . I should be honest and say that at first my dread of jail was inordinate compared to the "Hey baby, when did you get out?" or "How much time you got, brother?" attitudes that I remember as a kid in Spanish Harlem. It is this reaction of a generally exploited and oppressed people to the violence, brutality, and suppression of the establishment that gives that people its strength [to] endure what is necessary and explode when the limit is reached. In other words, the thing I'm proudest of is that I have behaved according to my working-class roots and have become more class-conscious than before. It has been in many ways a year of learning (Uncle Ho says a revolutionary's best school is jail) more about the sons of the people who will lead this country out of its moral, racist, and violent quagmire.

The comical point in all this and the one that puts everything in place is, of course, the larger-than-life heroism of the Vietnamese. . . . The knowledge that they'll not live as slaves and will secure their freedom at any cost assures them of victory. This is the greatest contribution that has been made in my generation to peace and real social ideals. I am only sharing an infinitesimal bit of it, and it makes me happy to contribute a little. Those who vacillate or doubt, as indeed I often did, the justice of the cause and the part one must play in it as a consequence of that knowledge, should only let their understanding lead them to its own logical conclusion and that is to resist in every way all the time those who think people can be bought or whipped or fooled into becoming obliging slaves.

. . . Anyway, I'm still in a process of unlearning and relearning the ways of the dissenter and insurgent against this degenerate sixth decade, twentieth-century mess called American capitalist society.

For those who are still not sure about what to do regarding the draft and their personal commitment, I submit that the Detroits, Newarks, Spanish Harlems should already have removed much of their doubt. . . . I feel I am contemporaneous with the future, and the winds from those tomorrows are blowing from Vietnam across the Pacific.

Johnson: The basic issue which my case raises is the individual's right to refuse to obey orders which he considers morally or legally wrong.

I believe that the only solution right now is for young men to be as uncooperative as possible with their draft boards. Mass civil disobedience will probably be necessary. If I had to do it over again I would probably begin by refusing induction or burning my draft card.

It has been a trying but very educational experience. I hope others like myself can benefit from it.

Mora: I don't want my action to get people to think, but to do. Simply, opt for jail over and against the Army or the draft. I tried to avoid jail by not taking a stand against induction because my freedom was too sweet to me. Admittedly a compromise, but decisions like this seem to have an irresistible power when they are presented by life and experience and only then.

Besides, facing up to it as a member of the Army enabled me to meet it head-on, and was more valuable than had I been a civilian. Whatever value my action has is enhanced by the fact that it was a rebellion of sorts within the military establishment. Any challenge to an entrenched political system is always most effective if it is done by the citizen acting as a member of the class to which he belongs or to which he feels ideologically bound.

Come on in. Choices and ways out are vanishing so if you are conscience-stricken come to jail.

My only regret is that we didn't have more company.

Samas: I'm in jail now and I guess it's easy for me to tell others, "Come on in, it's fine." But if a man is to follow his conscience and live a principled life in our times then he must be aware of the penalties for doing so!

I regret nothing. Of course I would not like to go through it again but I would if it were necessary. My beliefs have been strengthened. . . . In a great way I too am responsible for the boys who already are in Vietnam. But even as an unaffiliated civilian, I was closer to the peace movement than most soldiers are now. To me the peace movement always looked like concerned students and citizens trying to protect their country from war and nuclear devastation. To a soldier the movement appears very differently. The soldier is very far indeed from the outside world and the normal news media do not usually reach him.

News of the free world reaches him through letters from home, or through his buddies. It often seems that the peace groups are united against the soldier, and that forces the soldiers to cling together and ignore the real issues made public by the peace movement. The stories that reach the soldiers usually show that the peace movement is backing their enemies, and is against the Army, and against the individual soldiers. Upon too many occasions groups have offered aid to the Viet Cong, and too few times have they approached the GI's with help.

The GI should be reached somehow. He doesn't want to fight. He has no reasons to risk his life. Yet he doesn't realize that the peace movement is dedicated to his safety. Give the GI something to believe in and he will fight for that belief. Let them know in Vietnam that you want them home, let them know that you are concerned about their lives also. Tell them you want them to live, not die. Bring home our men in Vietnam!

Student "We Won't Go" Statements

This was probably the earliest "We Won't Go" statement, circulated in the spring of 1964 by members of the May Second Movement, an anti-imperialist student organization. It was signed by several dozen men, mostly from Haverford, Yale, and New York City.

WE THE UNDERSIGNED,
ARE YOUNG AMERICANS OF DRAFT AGE. We understand our obligations to defend our country and to serve in the armed forces but we object to being asked to support the war in South Vietnam.

Believing that United States participation in that war is for the suppression of the Vietnamese struggle for national independence, we see no justification for our involvement. We agree with Senator Wayne Morse, who said on the floor of the Senate on March 4, 1964, regarding South Vietnam, that "We should never have gone in. We should never have stayed in. We should get out."

BELIEVING THAT WE SHOULD NOT BE ASKED TO FIGHT AGAINST THE PEOPLE OF VIETNAM, WE HEREWITH STATE OUR REFUSAL TO DO SO.

The two paragraphs preceding the pledge are from a flier which was distributed with the pledge card, prepared by the Yale Draft Refusal Committee, fall 1967:

Last winter 24 draft-eligible men at Yale signed a "We-Won't-Go" letter which was published in the [Yale] Daily News and in the [New Haven] Register. They were one of the first groups in the country to take such action. The following spring, as large numbers of students began signing pledges across the country, a group of Yale students, most of them not signers of the original letter, began to make plans for a large fall campaign to gather signatures. They sent a letter to the Daily News stating their intention, and, when the response seemed favorable, decided to begin to gather signatures despite the pressures of final exams. In a very brief effort, over 100 Yale students signed their pledge. . . .

Nationally, the draft refusal movement spread extremely rapidly last spring. About 400 students signed a pledge at Cornell, over 300 at Stanford (including one-fourth of its medical students), 350 in the Boston area, and comparable numbers elsewhere. . . . James Reston suggested that the movement had caused U.S. officials to fear mass refusals if they attempted to draft college students. . . .

We are men of draft age who believe that the United States is waging an unjust war in Vietnam. We cannot, in conscience, participate in this war. We therefore declare our determination to refuse induction as long as the United States is fighting in Vietnam.

The following letter was signed by sixteen students and printed in the *Wooster Voice*, April 21, 1967. Wooster is a conservative, church-related college.

We Won't Go

To the Editor:

As American citizens we must accept the responsibility for our nation's actions in Vietnam. We firmly believe that it is our duty to insist that the United States act morally and with justice throughout the world. We are convinced that our present course of action in Vietnam is neither moral nor just nor in the best interests of the United States' relations with the peoples of the world. We make this public statement of conscience concerning our country's involvement in Vietnam as have students at Yale, Wisconsin, Union Seminary, Harvard, Earlham, Chicago, Berkeley and Antioch. If called to participate in the Armed Services during the current war, we will refuse induction. We do not take this step lightly, and we realize the possible consequences, but to aid our government in the execution of this war would be for us an act of disloyalty to our country and to our beliefs.

We urge anyone interested in discussing this statement to contact us.

The following pledge was signed by over 260 medical students, 80 of whom were from Stanford University, in the spring of 1967.

A PLEDGE OF NON-PARTICIPATION

In the name of freedom, the United States is waging an unjustifiable war in Vietnam and is causing incalculable suffering. It is the goal of the medical profession to prevent and relieve human suffering. My effort to pursue this goal is meaningless in the context of the war. Therefore, I refuse to serve in the Armed Forces in Vietnam. So that I may exercise my profession with conscience and dignity, I intend to seek means to serve my country and humanity which are compatible with preservation and enrichment of life.

The following "paid advertisement" was sponsored by the Queens College chapter of Students for a Democratic Society, and was signed by twenty-six students in February 1967.

WE, THE UNDERSIGNED,
DRAFT-AGE MALE STUDENTS AT QUEENS COLLEGE,
WILL NOT SERVE IN THE ARMED FORCES
OF THE UNITED STATES—
FOR VARYING REASONS
AND REGARDLESS OF PERSONAL CONSEQUENCES.

> (Refusal of induction is a
> violation of the Universal
> Military Training and Service
> Act, and may subject offenders
> to penalty of five years
> imprisonment.)

Tom Bell

ORGANIZING DRAFT RESISTANCE

Tom Bell, writing prior to the Spring Mobilization, discusses the formation of the "We Won't Go" group in Ithaca, New York, the group which issued the call for the draft card burning on April 15, 1967, in New York City.

In discussion before the event Tom suggested that effectiveness lies in actions such as draft card burning which push an individual over a certain threshold. From that point on the stakes for him are high; he becomes an organizer. And as an organizer, as one committed, he becomes effective.

> . . . *There is a real agony for me in the dilemma presented by seeing this great opportunity for political organizing and action versus the likelihood that a lot of people are going to be hurt (including myself) by the action being taken. . . . I don't like national actions, but I do want to change America. I like a personal, deep communication type of politics, but perhaps this is not really political. I don't want to manipulate anyone but I feel that it [is] essential for my own struggle and for the development of all of us as human beings that people change.*

This article appeared in similar form in *New Left Notes*.

I WILL DISCUSS one method of organizing resistance to the draft, using the case study of the "We Won't Go" group in Ithaca, New York. . . . Organizers and resistance unions can apply [this information] to their own situations, but it would be dangerous to attempt simply to duplicate this pattern. The organizer should not have preconceptions about specific decisions to be made or steps to be taken past the initial steps. . . .

I. The Decision to Organize

At a national meeting [in] August [1966], two models of draft resistance organizing were put forth and debated. The first called for a massive demonstration of noncooperation (100 to 500 people burning draft cards) to be held late in the fall. Organizing would involve finding the most "committed" people in the movement who agreed with this kind of tactic. These people would come together, probably in Washington, at a specified date and make their demonstration.

The second model called for unions or communities of draft resisters organized locally around the idea "we won't go into the U.S. military, and we will encourage others to do the same." These unions would be autonomous and locally based. Since no one at the meeting had organized such unions, their exact functioning was unclear. . . .

The consensus at this meeting was clear—"we won't go" unions. The choice was made strongly for several reasons. The unions would be a conscious organizing effort to build a movement against the draft, perhaps even reaching proportions to affect military manpower. The unions or communities could reach beyond those who would normally respond to a massive demonstration; they would not be bounded by the existing movement or by the campus. While a demonstration would rely primarily upon the mass media for its effect, the resistance communities would establish their own means of communication in the locality and would bring events directly to draft age people. Growth of the resistance unions would depend on their internal dynamic, resting only minimally on reaction to the decisions of others within the movement or in national or international politics. Starting at a very low level, the unions would provide a constantly growing visible resistance to the draft. In short, the resistance unions, if successful, offered the possibility of a solidly organized political confrontation with the system. The demonstration, even if successful, was seen at that time as a protest with doubtful possibility for continued confrontation.

II. *The Beginning*

My experience as an organizer had been very limited—working mostly with SDS [Students for a Democratic Society] chapters and with demonstrations. For me, the natural thing to do in organizing draft resistance would have been to go to an SDS meeting and propose that the chapter adopt a "we won't go" position; or to make a general announcement that all those interested in draft resistance should come to room X at 8 o'clock to discuss formation of a new group. I rejected these approaches for several reasons.

It would have been impossible to reach a consensus on draft resistance within SDS at Cornell. After weeks of heated discussion we likely would have had less understanding of what we wanted to do than before. In the end, a group of us from SDS would have started a resistance union, but with much delay and considerable bad feeling. The group formed in this way would have been ten or more to start, which I consider to be too large to get the initial solid understanding which has been so important to the development of our group. We would have had to fall back on the "normal" reliance on a single leader to formulate most of our decisions.

The announcement to form a new organization would have brought an unwieldy number of people together (at Cornell, probably about forty). The sheer numbers would make impossible the necessary personal discussion and individual understanding. Within that number, compounding the problem, would be people of a whole variety of positions about draft resistance. Some would proclaim that resistance was martyrdom, therefore apolitical. The same or others would say that we must go into the army and organize from within (a position I do not reject in principle, but which never seems to go anywhere because its proponents never volunteer, and because they are usually unacceptable to the army anyway). One or two hecklers might be present. Certainly, someone would have the position that we should forget all the talk about "union" and organize a massive draft card burning for some time in the next week. Once such a meeting was called, no subsequent meeting would be free of the endless differences. To attempt to reconcile these differences, making action possible, would be a complete waste of time.

The method of organizing actually used in Ithaca is very simple and direct. I had never done it before and had only discussed it briefly with people who have done community organizing. I feel that it could be used by anyone with a fair degree of patience.

Committed to the idea of draft resistance, I began to talk independently to three people who I felt would share my opinions. We discussed the meeting I had attended and the ideas current at that point. There was considerable difference of opinion among the four of us—especially about how to go about organizing draft resistance. We got outside help at this early point, in the form of an experienced community organizer. He talked with us a great deal, raising crucial questions. We were able at this period to begin to agree on a method of organizing and to clarify some of our other points of difference. Our experience was that this outside help was very important.

We continued to meet in sessions of three or four until we came to a pretty solid understanding. We had talked about our personal draft positions, our willingness and reservations about following a course of resistance, the possibilities we saw for resistance organizing, and the next step we would take. There was argument for each of the methods of organizing mentioned above, but we finally agreed that each of us would talk to one or two other people, discuss the idea with them and then all meet together in a week. In this way, all four of us were now organizers, and with considerable success. We managed to reach people, even at this early point, who had not been politically active in Ithaca before, but who were involved personally in the draft question. These people were interested in the type of resistance community which we were trying to build.

With the expanded group—now seven—we had roughly the same discussions as before. This time it did not take so long to reach a solid understanding. The new people, by chance I believe, were *more* turned on to the particular method of organizing. We decided to make the same move as before; each person would talk to someone new, give him an understanding of what we were about, get him to talk with some of the other people already involved, and bring him to a meeting in two weeks. We also decided to discuss the draft among ourselves, outside of a specific meeting, thus getting to know each other better and developing personal communication.

Understanding the risk of prosecution under subversive control acts, seven of us had agreed that under no circumstances would we go into the U.S. military; that we would encourage others to stay out of the military; and that we were all willing to take our stand publicly upon a collective decision on the right time and means. . . . Everybody in the group had essentially taken on the job of being an organizer of the group. Our organizing had relied on long hours of soul-searching discussion and a healthy rejection of the press or already organized groups. The building of the draft resistance community had in no way challenged existing groups nor did it pretend to make decisions for anyone but those people participating in the resistance community.

III. Growth of the Community and Its Composition

In general, a group at this point should have enough internal strength to be making its own decisions. Everyone in the group should have become an organizer, in a limited sense, and the original organizer should either have become an equal participant in the group or have left the group entirely to begin organization of another. If the organizer attempts to become leader (or does not resist the pressure to become leader), he will most likely finish with a group which depends very heavily on him for its existence and which can be pressured by him into making unreal decisions. By "unreal" I mean decisions which do not have the full support of the individuals in the group. Without this support the individuals must be harassed constantly into implementing the decisions. If, however, the group has been organized with real communication between the participants, and if the organizer becomes an equal participant or withdraws entirely, the resistance union will be able to set its own direction and implement its own decisions from this point.

The Ithaca group carried through its decision to talk to more people and then bring them into the group. We were then rather large (fifteen) and it became difficult to have the type of searching discussions we had been having for the previous two months. We decided to try some different things, attempting to build the community of understanding we felt was necessary. We started to get together for meals, or at other times, at each other's apartments. We also decided to take a room in the student "union" once a week for three weeks, from 3 P.M to 11 P.M. Several of us were to be in the room at any given time. In this way we were able to talk among ourselves in small groups. We spread the word that the room was open to people who wanted to discuss problems about the draft in a personal way. The group added some new participants and managed to give some help to several other people, as well as further building a solid group base.

In the process of the day-long sessions, we began to feel the need to learn more about the draft law, and the methods, legal and illegal, of evading it. This information became essential so that we could be useful to people who came seeking help, and so that we would be better informed in our own fights against the draft. It also began to be obvious that we should be talking to the people who most immediately faced induction, rather than almost exclusively talking to each other and to students. To train ourselves as draft counselors, we set up three sessions with experienced men. . . .

IV. Development of Thinking

We all have different criteria of what would be a good personal position on the draft. These criteria for each of us involve a different mix of personal, political, and moral considerations. We found these considerations to be part of a unity. For example, no act could be moral if it had the wrong political content. Nor could an act be political in the right direction if it put us in unacceptable personal situations. From this discussion one thing clearly emerged: in our terms, there is no "right" way to handle one's position with the Selective Service System. Each person sees himself confronted with a set of alternatives *none* of which are satisfactory.

One phase of thinking that the group went through collectively was the question of going to Canada. Fear, and the inability to find a good position, had pushed virtually all of us to the decision to flee to Canada. As we talked, we became more convinced that prison would be immoral—that is, personally damaging and apolitical. As we spent long hours arguing the merits of the position, a complete change occurred. In the first place, we saw flight from the draft as potentially placing restrictions on our whole lives. We could never return to this country; a problem, since some of us see our lives intimately involved in work to change America. We would have some distasteful restrictions in Canada for five years until citizenship, i.e., having to work, no subversive activity, etc. And, our travel might be restricted for the rest of our lives by the possibility of extradition by the U.S. In the second place, we began to talk more seriously about prison. We talked at length with Ralph DiGia and briefly with Arlo Tatum about their experiences in prison. Both men testified that prison does not necessarily "break" a man, and both claimed it to have been a unique and in many ways valuable experience for them, e.g., a totally non-middle-class experience.

After these discussions everyone seemed to decide that they would stick it out in the U.S., and prison became a real alternative. Since that time our thinking has again come to challenge going to prison, this time because it represents a plea to the society for change; a plea, that is, which is within the system and shows a belief in prison as a democratic institution. Some of us no longer believe that America will respond to any such protest appeal. For part of the group at least, our thinking has pushed towards an understanding of where the beginnings of real resistance in America will come: rejection of the draft, and organizing without allowing ourselves to go to prison.

At a fairly early point, Dave Sternes announced that he was I-A, was not applying for CO, and would refuse induction, arguing his court case on the grounds of involuntary servitude.

This was it, as it seemed. We had organized realizing that non-cooperation was in the offing for many of us, and that we were together partially so that we could support each other in time of crisis. Dave, it appeared, would be the first of our group to face prison. We began to discuss with him what we might do to support him. We decided that since his position was shared by us and since it was simply a bureaucratic accident that he was to be called before the rest of us, we would not let him go alone—we would go with him. From the point he refused induction until his arrest, one of us would be handcuffed to him at all times, and we would employ an elaborate system to inform the others of the arrest so that they could get themselves handcuffed into the chain. Fortunately, the plan never got beyond this stage. Some of us had been talking with him about his position and the reality of his decision. We found that he had not considered very seriously the possibility of going to prison (this situation arose rather early in the life of the group). He felt he would win his court case. Some checking discovered that he had very little chance of winning such a case. With this new information, that the refusal of induction meant prison, Dave still felt it was the only course open to him. A number of us felt uncomfortable at this point, and began trying to bring some of Dave's feelings about this action to the surface. As we talked together Dave began to realize that going to prison would be an immoral act for him, and that he honestly could apply for CO. Being *together* in this experience was important to the development of our community.

In another case a month later, Bruce Dancis announced that he was planning to destroy his draft card publicly. Bruce was eighteen, and already a long-standing pacifist. He had registered only because of the provision for CO, but since that time had decided that any cooperation with Selective Service was objectionable to him. He decided to become a noncooperator. For some of us who had known Bruce's position over a period of time, his decision seemed solidly based, and we were not worried that he might be ignoring his true feelings. To others, his case appeared to be very similar to Dave's, though Bruce readily acknowledged that he would have to spend some time in prison. Some tried to dissuade Bruce from his action while others simply accepted his decision. We met to decide how we might support Bruce. We found it all too obvious that the only meaningful support from us would be to destroy our draft cards with him. Not being willing to take that action at the time, we were discouraged, and could only give publicity-type support. Bruce went ahead with his decision. The effect on the group at first was disturbing. While it did raise the level of seriousness, as only an action can, we found no way to be *together* in the action. The group published an ad on the same day as Bruce's action saying, "WE WON'T GO. The undersigned men of draft age will not serve in the U.S. military and encourage others to do the same." This ad was effective in its own right. We were together in it. But it was an action taken independently of Bruce's action.

It seems that Bruce's action, while initially divisive, may have been crucial in the development of the group. It raised . . . the question of draft card burning, which now has become a serious possibility for most of us.

V. Moving into Town

From the beginning, the "we won't go" group had a sense that we should organize in the locality. The people who face the draft immediately with their lives are not on campus, but in town. The first moves into town came independently of any group decision. Two of the people began on their own to leaflet the buses taking people from Ithaca to Syracuse for their pre-induction physicals. They wrote a leaflet which they brought to the group for criticism. The names and phone numbers of all the participants were included in the leaflet, along with a suggestion that potential inductees call if they need some help. Two other guys went to talk with a woman whose son had been sent to Vietnam, and who had written to the Ithaca paper criticizing the government's position. She gave them some names of friends of her son who faced induction but did not want to go. We began to discuss how to approach, in a more systematic manner, the guys in town who faced induction. . . .

A store front would have been ideal for the center, but we did not have the financial resources. The Unitarian Parish House was an excellent possibility because of its location next door to the local draft board. We entered a long negotiation with the Unitarians, which finally resulted in their leasing us a space at a nominal rent. The discussion within the Church was itself a valuable start toward the goal of building a base of adult support. We opened the center in mid-January, for fourteen hours per week. We got a full stock of literature and a telephone and began to advertise in the local papers. . . .

There are two major dangers resulting from the move we are trying to make in the town. The first danger results from having been partially "institutionalized." The Unitarians required that we give them a name for the group, and the names of a president and an advisor, and that we sign an agreement with them. Up until that point we had none of these things, and were not pleased to have to select "leaders." We decided to separate the counseling center from our other activity and to formalize ourselves only for that one function. To the public we became the Selective Service Counseling Committee operating the Selective Service Counseling Center. The tendency, now that we are institutionalized in this partial sense, is to rest on the Center and expect people to come to us. Our slowness in reaching out from the Center to do organizing is at least partially the result of the ease of thinking that we are already organizing in town simply by manning a counseling service.

The second major danger is related to the first: a counseling center in itself is not a radical idea. If we use the Center for contacts to begin organizing, we can do radical work. If we allow the Center to be self-contained, we are on the same path that the civil rights "tutorial programs" eventually took. That is, we will be in the liberal bag of simply trying to "help" people in a specific and limited way. The Center eventually will repel radicals and come to be manned by people who have no desire to organize, but only to "make needed information available" and show what a democratic system the draft is because a select few can get CO.

With the reservations discussed, I think that the move into town is essential to the draft resistance movement and a very significant comment on the method of organizing. Militant resisters, if the movement grows, will and should come from among those people who normally would provide the cannon fodder. Certainly the draft comes into the lives of all young men in very real ways, but militant resistance among students is lessened by the fact that it often seems like martyrdom. . . . There is a dead end for discussion. The move into town and into work with potentially more militant resisters is one very meaningful way to go beyond that dead end.

VI. *Where Do We Go from Here?*

The experience of the Ithaca group suggests one other way to go beyond intimate personal discussion among students. This way again is rooted in these very important personal discussions and on the real communication which leads to real decisions. At the time when Bruce destroyed his draft card there was very little interest among the group for others to follow. . . .

It seems, though, that several individuals in the group have come to an increasingly militant stand. Five individuals, with the support of most of the others, have sent out a call, nationally, for five hundred people to burn their draft cards on April 15, principally in New York City.

Ithaca, New York
2 March 1967

The armies of the United States have, through conscription, already oppressed or destroyed the lives and consciences of millions of Americans and Vietnamese. We have argued and demonstrated to stop this destruction. We have not succeeded. Murderers do not respond to reason. Powerful resistance is now demanded: radical, illegal, unpleasant, sustained.

In Vietnam the war machine is directed against young and old, soldiers and civilians, without distinction. In our own country, the war machine is directed specifically against the young, against blacks more than against whites, but ultimately against all.

Body and soul, we are oppressed in common. Body and soul, we must resist in common. The undersigned believe that we should *begin* this mass resistance by publicly destroying our draft cards at the Spring Mobilization.

WE URGE ALL PEOPLE WHO HAVE CONTEMPLATED THE ACT OF DESTROYING THEIR DRAFT CARDS TO CARRY OUT THIS ACT ON APRIL 15, WITH THE UNDERSTANDING THAT THIS PLEDGE BECOMES BINDING WHEN 500 PEOPLE HAVE MADE IT.

The climate of anti-war opinion is changing. In the last few months student governments, church groups, and other organizations have publicly expressed understanding and sympathy with the position of individuals who refuse to fight in Vietnam, who resist the draft. We are ready to put ourselves on the line for this position, and we expect that these people will come through with their support.

We are fully aware that our action makes us liable to penalties of up to five years in prison and $10,000 in fines. We believe, however, that the more people who take part in this action the more difficult it will be for the government to prosecute.

Such action, in terms of the dynamic of our group, clearly goes beyond the potentially terminal point of personal discussion and the public statement, "WE WON'T GO." This decision on the part of most of our group seems to open the way for real draft resistance. Our discussion has centered on the question of whether such an action would be simply a protest or whether it could be useful as one of the steps in initiating a resistance movement. As a protest, the action would be one of the most militant we can think of. It would gain publicity, and it would demonstrate the seriousness of at least a small group of people. The protest might stimulate a wave of similar action and help to communicate broadly the idea of draft refusal, especially among the non-urban poor and middle class youths who now have no notion of it.

The question in debate among us has been whether the protest should be continued by acceptance of prison, or whether we should also try to resist going to prison. The argument for going to prison stems from the long-standing belief that "public opinion" will then work to change existing conditions—will end the war. . . . People supporting imprisonment are saying that when all else has failed (rational argument, letters to Congress, appeals to conscience, and all of the milder forms of protest) our bodies on the line in prison will finally put the democratic process to work. Other opponents say that America has rendered us powerless at our present level of organization, and that even by going to prison we are powerless to make change. These people say we should burn our draft cards if it will help to build a resistance movement, but that we should do everything possible to join that resistance movement ourselves—inside the country and outside of prison. We have not been able to see clearly how such an "underground" could function, but we sense that we are at the beginning of such a movement. Just as the first freedom riders were breaking the ground for protest without a clear idea of where or how it would lead them and America, so are the first "prison refusers" setting off on a course for which they have little or no experience. . . .

VII. Evaluation

This technique of organizing requires two to three months of continuous effort on the part of the organizer. He must hold the group back from making unreal decisions, and he must make every effort to establish real communication among the participants. He must understand that if he is successful the group will gain its own dynamic, and that he will be unable to direct it to decisions of his own choosing. This time and effort might be seen as a weakness as compared to campus organizing techniques which form a forty-member action group in two weeks. I believe, however, that there are in this method very important strengths which justify this time and effort.

The draft as an organizing issue lends itself well to the formation of groups where each person has equal participation and influence. Each person has his own experience with Selective Service, and each person's opposition can be respected and discussed by the whole group—no one has the special "authority" or the greatest "experience." To organize in the way done in

Ithaca realizes this possibility. It builds a solid group (call it union or community) where each person relies on himself for leadership. . . . It is very rare, in my experience, where this self-reliance has occurred in a grassroots type group. As Americans we have been systematically miseducated to rely on leaders, things, others—anything but ourselves—for our decisions.

An equally important strength is that a group organized in this way seems to generate its own dynamic, independent of any one or two participants. This dynamic propels group thinking to a level that one leader and a number of followers can rarely achieve. The dynamic also propels implementation of decisions which come out of the real communication established, and seems to inspire individuals to implement their own ideas on their own.

The radically democratic nature of the group and the self-reliance which results has very important "internal education" type results. Each person in the group grows in his ability as an organizer, and each person goes through a radicalizing process. So often, radicalization comes from travel—to the third world, to Europe, or to the American South—where a view of the true nature of American society is more obvious. The draft is an issue where people are radicalized by organizing to fight their own fight. Their foe is an authoritarian American institution which they can see in a very real way, without ever leaving their own home area. . . .

In political terms, . . . a group organized in this way might well move in directions which avoid direct political confrontation and which emphasize individual morality, experience, etc. The organizer has no more power than anyone else to steer this direction. There is, I believe, a natural tendency within such a group to move out to the people most directly threatened by the draft. Such a tendency, if followed, probably leads itself to initiating a dynamic for political confrontation out of solidarity with those facing induction. . . . Our group is definitely trying to take the path of political confrontation.

Martin Jezer

SHEEP MEADOW GRADUATION

The event which Martin Jezer describes took place on April 15, 1967, at the Spring Mobilization to End the War in Vietnam in New York City. This was the largest anti-war demonstration to date, estimated to be on the magnitude of 200,000 participants.

Martin Jezer is an editor of *WIN Peace & Freedom Through Nonviolent Action,* a magazine originally published by the New York Workshop in Nonviolence and the Committee for Nonviolent Action, and later, by the War Resisters League.

This account was taken partly from articles which appeared in *WIN,* as well as material written for this book.

UP UNTIL the night before April 15th, no one was sure how many people would burn their draft cards at the Mobilization; indeed, we were not at all sure whether the action would even take place. About 120 people had signed the pledge to burn their cards if 500 others did it at the same time, so the pledge was not binding. Moreover, the Spring Mobilization Committee had disowned the draft card burners and were pressuring them to postpone or cancel their plans. Many Mobilization leaders support civil disobedience, but they were afraid that a radical act like draft card burning would scare away many people new to the Movement.

At a meeting the night of April 14th, we decided to burn our cards in the Sheep Meadow at 11 A.M. despite the Mobilization's opposition. We also decided that 50 would be the minimum number of burners to make it an important political act. There was a tense moment when Bruce Dancis asked, "How many will burn their cards if 50 do it at the same time?" Hands shot up around the room. The count was 57. We were in business.

That night I hardly slept. I recalled how it was the night before my graduation from college. . . . That was a celebration of my ability to get good grades and to conform, intellectually, to the current catechism of uncritical Americanism. Although I was something of the campus radical, by contemporary standards I was just a good, harmless white liberal, impressed with and convinced of my own powerlessness, prepared to allow politicians, generals, and corporate managers to make decisions over my life. . . . Burning a draft card, I thought, would be a more meaningful graduation. I had finally begun to be educated, to see through the myths of the American propaganda machine.

The next morning we gathered on the rocks in the Sheep Meadow. Friends of ours, veterans, women, and pacifists, linked arms and attempted to clear space for us. There were no uniformed police in sight. Soon the press, FBI men, and all kinds of ill-mannered people began pushing, shoving, pressing through the protective circle. Confusion reigned; an orderly demonstration seemed impossible. So we began burning our cards. Someone held up an empty tin can of Maxwell House Coffee with flaming paraffin inside. We lit our cards with matches, cigarette lighters, and from the flames of each other's cards. It was a pretty sight, draft cards—burning. Gary Rader, from Illinois, materialized from out of the crowd and set his card aflame. It was a wonderfully courageous act. He's an Army Reservist and was wearing his "green beret" uniform. Photographers trampled us to get his picture. He seemed very happy; smiling, shaking hands with those near him. Then, to bring some order to the demonstration, we all sat down.

The photographers fell back, our protective circle was restored. We began singing freedom songs and chanting, "Resist! Resist!" and "Burn Draft Cards, Not People." People in the audience were applauding us, shouting encouragement. Then some guys began to come out of the audience with draft cards in hand. They burned them. Alone, in pairs, by threes they came. Each flaming draft card brought renewed cheering and more people out of the crowd. Someone passed us daffodils. "Flower Power," we cried happily. . . . Some of the draft card burners were girls, wives or girlfriends of male card burners. . . . It lasted this way for about half an hour. About 175 people burned their cards. This was more than had signed the pledge. . . .

The Cornell contingent, numbering in the thousands, was led by its "We Won't Go" organization and draft card burners under a large banner, "WE WON'T GO" emblazoned in the school colors. Locked arm and arm, they were literally dancing down the street, joyful, defiant, irresistible. "Hell, No, We Won't Go," their words vibrated between the sterile buildings on Madison Avenue and echoed up and down the canyon-like side streets. . . .

Burning my draft card was a recognition that I had finally learned something. But that I decided to commit what the U.S. government considers a heinous crime is due to a large degree to those responsible for my education. They instilled in me a sense of values, principle, and morality. They taught me that we were a peace-loving democracy, and I believed them. The education of Martin Jezer is the realization that if this *is* to be a peace-loving democracy, functioning on principled, moral values, it is for us, for me, to make it so.

My education from one graduation to another, from college grad to draft resister, began slowly but accelerated after 1964. I spent a year and a half in graduate school studying journalism because I wanted to write, and didn't want to go into the army. I abandoned my thesis to go to Hazard, Kentucky, with a friend who was doing a book on the wildcat coal mine strikes. The trip had a decisive impact on my life. For the first time, and at firsthand, I identified with the struggles of the oppressed. But though shaken, I was still in the liberal bag. The only hope, I thought, was for massive federal aid. The miners, I felt, couldn't do it for themselves.

I returned to New York, got married, and worked as a copywriter and then as an encyclopedia editor. I also joined CORE, but my chapter was inactive and I had neither the will nor the experience to make it otherwise. Nonetheless, I came to identify more and more with the Movement.

Quitting graduate school led to my being classified I-A and then I-Y for medical reasons. I knew nothing about principled draft refusal or noncooperation. I would not have known how to go about filing a CO application. . . . I thought you had to be a Quaker or a Mennonite to become a noncombatant. I also knew nothing about pacifism. I thought the kids boarding Polaris submarines were kooks. So if drafted I'd have gone, believing that in fighting communism I was fighting a noble cause. I'd not have liked it though. A brief experience in ROTC and my own anarchical tendencies make militarism anathema to me.

I campaigned for Lyndon Johnson in 1964. The complete acquiescence of Congress, the press, and all informed public opinion to his obvious violation of all his campaign promises shocked me. From the Gulf of Tonkin to the Sheep Meadow, my radicalization was fast and furious. The American government completely alienated itself from my concept of common human decency.

In progressive order I wrote my Congressmen, the Vice President and the President. The *New York Post* published my irate letters to the editor. I marched in my first peace parade, walked picket lines, leafletted and vigilled. When the U.S. resumed its bombing of North Vietnam in February 1966, I sat down in Times Square and got busted for the first of three times. I finally came to the conclusion that only mass civil disobedience could stop the war. My own position became clear. To do nothing, or to fiddle around with petitions, peace candidates, and other respectable means of protest while Vietnam burns and we plunge madly on in our insanity, is intolerable. I have to resist in the most direct way possible, for myself, and to set an example for others. When the call for a mass draft card burning on April 15th arrived from the organizers at Cornell, I signed it at once. I had no doubt that this is what I had to do, even if the proposed 500 draft card burners did not show up. Not to have burned a draft card April 15th would have been tantamount to living in Boston in 1773 and not to have dumped tea in Boston harbor. I'd not have missed it.

Despite my enthusiasm for the action and my personal commitment to go through with it no matter what, I was filled with fear. I agree with Thoreau that there are times when the only place for an honest man is a jail, and I accept the dictum that walls do not a prison make. But out of fear, and also for personal and selfish reasons, I did not want to go to jail. . . . My life was changing for the better. This was no time to interrupt it with a long jail sentence. But *any time* is the wrong time to go to jail, and I knew full well that to give in to my selfishness would be a far greater sacrifice than two or three years of my life. Moreover, all my friends supported my intention to burn my draft card. By April 15th I was positive I was doing right and events that followed have reinforced this view. But, of course, there are times, as I wait to be indicted, that I am scared—and selfish. . . .

When I burned my draft card, I thought that this was enough of a witness. I would publicize my act to encourage others and face up to the consequences. Now I believe that it is politically necessary for some of us to carry resistance into the courts and into jail, if necessary. The one weapon the government holds over us is prison. To be effective we must overcome our fear of jail. The civil rights movement helped shake this fear; it is for us to destroy it. For once imprisonment becomes an honorable alternative to the military, something to be sought rather than avoided, resistance to the draft can become massive. In order to strike at this fear, some of us will have to face imprisonment with joyous defiance.

. . . The most important effect of the draft card burning was that it changed the lives of those who took part. I've been told many times that the Movement can't succeed, that you can't change people's hearts, that social change is gradual, and that we New Leftists are doomed to become frustrated, old, radicals. This is not true, for to the degree that the Movement has led its participants to change their lives, it has been successful. It has given people the insight to drop out of a brutal and dehumanized society, and it has given people the strength to devote their lives toward the creation of a community where love of one's fellow replaces the profit motive as the highest value.

Love is a word new radicals use often. I've had to overcome a lot of cynicism before I could use the word honestly, and not in the kind of rhetoric that American politicians use when they speak of democracy. Love, in all its wondrous manifestations, is the New Left's most positive contribution to political thought, and commitment to love, more than any other innovation, distinguishes it from the Old Left. The New Left is concerned with moving individuals as individuals into a better world, not in creating blind mass movements that seek only power, without an accompanying change of consciousness. For me, the burning of my draft card was, symbolically, my graduation or entrance into this world.

To destroy one's draft card, to place one's conscience before the dictates of one's government is in the highest tradition of human conduct. This country was not created by men subservient to law and government. It was created and made great by civil disobedients like Quakers who refused to compromise their religion to suit the Puritan theocracy; by Puritans who openly defied British authority; by provo-type Sons of Liberty who burned stamps to protest the Stamp Act and who dumped tea in Boston harbor; by abolitionists who ignored the Fugitive Slave law, by slaves who refused to act like slaves; by workingmen who insisted, despite the law, on their right to organize; by black Americans who refused to ride in the back of the bus; and by the more than one hundred young Americans already in prison for refusing to acquiesce in the misguided actions of their government.

So when people tell me that I have no respect for law and order and that I do not love my country, I reply: "Jefferson, Tom Paine, Garrison, Thoreau, A. J. Muste, the Freedom Riders, these are my countrymen whom I love; with them I take my stand."

Muhammad Ali

THE CHAMP

The World Heavyweight Boxing Champion, Muhammad Ali, was convicted in June 1967, and sentenced to five years in prison and a $10,000 fine for refusing to be inducted into the armed forces. Appeals are pending.

Ali, whose "slave name" was Cassius M. Clay, Jr., registered for the draft in 1960. He was classified I-A in March 1962 but was reclassified I-Y [qualified for military service only in an emergency] after a physical. Again in March 1964 he was examined and classified I-Y. At about this time he became a member of the Muslim faith. As the result of another physical in January 1966, Ali was classified I-A. Immediately he filed a Form 150, claim for conscientious objector status. He was retained in class I-A after his personal appearance before his local board, and he appealed to the State level.

This account was taken from a transcript of the administrative hearing on August 23, 1966, before Judge Lawrence Grauman, who was appointed by the Justice Department to be the Hearing Officer for Ali's appeal. (Justice Department hearings have been eliminated for CO appeals filed after June 30, 1967.) Excerpts from this hearing were published in *The National Guardian.*

. . . I WAS RAISED as a Baptist and while being raised as a Baptist I never understood the teachings of the Christian preacher, and I never understood why Heaven was in the sky and I never understood why Hell was under the ground and I never understood why the so-called Negroes had to turn their cheeks and have to take all the punishment while everyone else defends themselves and fights back. . . .

I never understood why when I went to the Olympics in Rome, Italy, and won the Gold Medal for great America and came back to Kentucky, I couldn't go in a downtown restaurant, and I always wondered why everything in it was white.

I always wondered these things and I am saying this to tell you why I accepted the religion of Islam the minute I heard it when in 1961, while I was walking down the streets of Miami, Florida, a Muslim walked up to me and asked me would I like to come to Muhammad's Mosque and listen to the teachings of Islam and listen to why we are the lost people . . . and this sounded interesting and, by me being a person of common sense, I went to the Mosque to listen and immediately, on entering the Mosque—I would say the first half hour after being there—I immediately wanted to know what I could do to become a member. . . .

The minister of the Mosque was preaching on the subject of why are we called Negroes. . . . I asked questions and he gave me good answers and he also said that we do not have our own names . . . and all intelligent people on earth are named after their people of their land and their ancestors. . . . We call ourselves Culpepper, Mr. Tree, Mr. Bird, Mr. Clay, Mr. Washington, and he said these were names of our slave masters, and by me being an intelligent man and the Lord blessing me with five senses, I have to accept it because there have been write-ups in the Louisville papers where my father and [I] were named after a great white slave father named Cassius Marcellus Clay.

So, I had to accept this, and he also told us that the proper name of God is Allah and that the Honorable Elijah Muhammad was taught by Allah for three and one half years to teach the so-called Negroes the true knowledge of his God, the true knowledge of his religion, true knowledge of his names and his future and not to force himself on whites and not to beg whites to come to clean up the rats, but to clean up our own neighborhoods, respect our women, do something for ourselves, quit smoking, quit drinking, and obey the laws of the land and respect those in authority.

Immediately, I had to check and see who is Elijah Muhammad. . . . So after finding out who he was, I had to convince myself that he was a divine man from God because I knew that I would have to give up a lot . . .

. . . At least six hours of the day I'm somewhere walking and talking, or going to schools or colleges all over the country, Muslim temples, and there are some fifty odd mosques all over the United States that I am invited to minister at right now, and constantly—in Chicago, I have this thirty-passenger bus that, daily, we go out bringing in busloads of people to the Mosque. And now I'm talking to the Blackstone Rangers, which is the worst Negro group in the wilderness of North America who have killed at least one hundred boys since they've been in Chicago, and the police—nobody could handle them and I was blessed with, all praise due to Allah, I was lucky enough to round up the twenty-one of the ringleaders and . . . they say they are ashamed for the way they been shooting and killing and . . . I've convinced them to come together. So, this is what I do as far as ministering and talking is concerned. . . . But when I'm really in training and in camp for fights, a week or two before the fight I don't have time, not too much time, because I really burn a lot of energy debating and answering questions, so during training we don't do too much ministering. . . . When they say that, "You would not bring in five hundred people," inasmuch as I do sometimes, "You would not bring these five hundred people if you were not the champ," well, if it was not for Allah and the teachings of the Islam, I would not be champ and I could not hold my title so strongly after being the champion. . . . On the average it's about thirty people a night.

. . . It's the teachings of Islam that has given me the proudness and boldness to say, "I'm the Greatest," and lift my chin and which has enabled me to be one of the most popular athletes on earth . . . and this is the only thing now keeping me out of night clubs and places that serve alcoholics like liquor and demonstrations where I could become popular in leading people.

. . . I have, I would say, and excuse the expression, caught more hell for being a Muslim, even before the Army talk came up, with my wife and boxing, and the movie rights that I turned down, the advertisements, the TV commercials, the royalties and endorsements that I have had to turn down and I have done all this before the Army came up and it's not just saying that I would not participate in war, but we actually believe it and feel it. . . . We are awfully serious in anything we say about fighting a war, adultery, or fornication, or drinking alcohol, cursing, using profanity, or anything that is against the teachings of the Holy Qur'an and the Honorable Elijah Muhammad, and Allah is who we really fear. . . . I was registered as a Muslim about three weeks prior to the first Sonny Liston fight and then if I had gone to any type of a war or done anything morally or spiritually that wasn't in accord with the teachings of the Honorable Elijah Muhammad I would be cast out or severely punished by himself, but I would say I . . . was a conscientious objector the hour that I first heard the teachings of the Honorable Elijah Muhammad. . . . But I would be lying to you if I said to you that at that moment I was determined that I would be a conscientious objector because war was not pending at that time. I had nothing to worry about and I had nothing about war on my mind . . .

. . . The only time that I really thought about it—the only time that I was conscious that I would have to make a decision was the first time that they mentioned going to take a physical. . . . The first time I failed I had no need to say anything. They said I wasn't fit. The second time . . . I took the test in Kentucky and they advised me and said I wasn't fit. Then, when they reclassified me [I-A] I came out with that outburst and my lawyer went in with the conscientious objector bit and it was known then. . . . I had no need the first two times that I was called up, because they never accepted me, but I'm sure that if they had called me when I was in Miami and I had passed the test then I would have had to just say I'm a conscientious objector. But I know nothing about the law and if I knew the right procedures at the time I would have moved accordingly. But I'm new—I'm learning each day about how this appeal and things go, but I didn't know at the time. I had no idea how they worked.

. . . When I go in a ring, my intention is not to be violent in the way of fighting to kill, or going to war, or hurting [anyone] physically; it's not my faith. We have a referee in the ring, and I'm known as a scientific fighter and as a fast, classy boxer, and we have three judges and we have an ambulance and we have doctors and we are not one nation against another or one race against another or one religion against another. It's just the art of boxing, and more people get killed in at least ten other sports than they do boxing. But I don't consider myself a violent man because next month I will be in the ring with Carl Mildenberger of Germany, prancing and dancing and moving and jabbing and if he hit me low, points will be taken away. In a war you shoot, you kill, you fight, and you kill babies and you kill old ladies and men and there's no such thing as laws and rules and regulations.

Mentally, some fighters are violent; mentally, some fighters go in the ring angry and they have a grudge and they are violent in their approach towards a fellow and many of them lose their head and get beaten, but I never get violent. I never lose my head and I'm known for being a calm, cool boxer and I never feel as though I'm violent and I never fight and act like I'm violent. . . . I don't consider them blows of violence, not me. . . . Now, football players, they elbow each other and they run over each other and they cleat each other and break each other's backs and they are paralyzed, and I don't think that's referred to as intentionally going out to do violence. As far as hitting a man is concerned, my intention is not to really hurt [anyone]. In war it's your intention to kill and to hurt and put the other man out. . . . It would be no trouble for me to accept conscientious objector [status] on the basis that I'll go into the armed services boxing exhibitions in Vietnam, or traveling the country at the expense of the government or living in the easy life and not having to get out in the mud and fight and shoot. . . . If it wasn't against my conscience to do it, I would easily do it. I wouldn't raise all this court stuff and I wouldn't go through all of this and lose and give up the millions that I gave up and my image with the American public, that I would say is completely dead and ruined because of us in here now, and so I wouldn't turn down so many millions and jeopardize my life walking the streets of the South

and all of America with no bodyguard if I wasn't sincere in every
bit of what the Holy Qur'an and the teachings of the Honorable
Elijah Muhammad tell us and it is that we are not to participate
in wars . . . on the side of nonbelievers, and this is a Christian
country and this is not a Muslim country. . . . The Holy Qur'an
teaches us that we do not take part . . . in any part of war unless declared by Allah himself, or unless it's an Islamic World
War, or a Holy War, and it goes as far (the Holy Qur'an is
talking still) as saying we are not to even as much as aid the
infidels or the nonbelievers in Islam, even to as much as handing
them a cup of water during battle.

. . . Many people confuse the teachings of the Honorable
Elijah Muhammad with the teachings of hate, and the only
hate I know, as far as the teachings of the Honorable Elijah
Muhammad is concerned, is that we hate the way that we've
been treated for four hundred years. We hate the way that our
pregnant women are being kicked around the streets; we hate
the way the innocent Negroes have been shot and lynched and
killed outright, but the killers are not—never been caught. We
hate that we're the first fired and the last hired and we hate
the way we have served so faithfully for the country in all wars
and have spent three hundred and ten long years [in] enabling
America to have fifty of the richest states on the planet. . . . We
do not hate white people. We hate the way certain people have
treated us and we also, now, have a better knowledge of ourselves. We have a better knowledge of nature. We have a better
knowledge of where we should go, where we shouldn't go, what
we should do, what we shouldn't do.

So, we are taught by the Honorable Elijah Muhammad that
if a wild lion broke in, say this courtroom now, I would break
out—not because I hate lions. I don't have a chance to hate the
lion. I just know his nature is not like mine and we can't get
along. . . .

So, we do not hate white people. We want to go for ourselves
and do for ourselves and get some of this earth that we can call
our own like other intelligent civilized humans do on the planet
Earth. . . . We are not haters. [The Honorable Elijah Mu-

hammad] teaches us to love. We don't break laws. We are in no
riots, no demonstrations. We pray five times a day. We fast three
days a week and we constantly worship at the Mosque three
nights a week. We are peaceful people and we are not haters,
but we are the victims of hate.

. . . The Holy Bible . . . teaches that though I dwell in the
valley of the shadow of death I fear no evil, and we are taught
by the Honorable Elijah Muhammad that [no] one dwells more
in the shadow of death [than] the so-called Negro is here in the
wilderness of North America. . . . So, by our teaching and by
we believing in God, whose law is self-preservation, we are taught
not to be the aggressor, but defend ourselves if attacked, and
a man cannot defend himself if he knows not how, and we are
taught that not only America, but all countries, all civilized
governments have armies and have guns around their shores, not
necessarily to attack or to be the aggressor, but to defend America or our country or whatever it may be if we are attacked. So,
we, the Muslims, to keep in physical condition, we do learn how
to defend ourselves if we are attacked since we are attacked
daily through the streets of America and have been attacked
without justification for the past four hundred years.

. . . We are only preparing for the war of Armageddon
divinely. We are taught that the battle will be between good and
right, truth and falsehood, and we are taught that the battle will
be between God and the Devil. . . . If it will be a physical war
we will look foolish with what we call military training, which is
judo and learning how to wrestle and box and run. The war of
Armageddon will be a real nuclear war, and nothing that judo
can do and nothing that karate can do or take part in. So therefore, this is for our health and self-defense while we are here if
we are attacked. But when Armageddon itself comes . . . we
won't participate in putting out physical energy ourselves.

. . . It is impossible for us to prepare for Armageddon since
we don't make bullets, we don't make guns, we don't control
food. It's foolish for us, or for an intelligent government to think
that we, the ten per cent of America, are hiding in some secret
little meeting places in this country preparing to fight these atomic

bombs, these jets, these helicopters and all types of guns you have that haven't been revealed to the public yet. . . . But as far as us putting it out in a war, it would be like a beanshooter running up against a big German tank, so we are only preparing for Allah in a spiritual way.

. . . We just hope that we are spiritually and physically and internally and mentally and morally able to get on the side of Allah and the Honorable Elijah Muhammad when Armageddon starts. . . .

According to a letter from T. Oscar Smith, Chief of the Conscientious Objector Section of the Justice Department:

The Hearing Officer concluded that the registrant is sincere in his objection on religious grounds to participation in war in any form and he recommended that the conscientious-objector claim of the registrant be sustained.

[However, the letter concludes:]

With due regard for the recommendation of the Hearing Officer, the Department of Justice finds that the registrant's conscientious-objector claim is not sustained and recommends to your Board that he be not classified in Class I-O or in Class I-A-O.

[Reasons given include:]

It seems clear that the teachings of the Nation of Islam preclude fighting for the United States not because of objections to participation in war in any form but rather because of political and racial objections to policies of the United States as interpreted by Elijah Muhammad. . . .

It is therefore our conclusion that registrant's claimed objections to participation in war insofar as they are based upon the teachings of the Nation of Islam, rest on grounds which primarily are political and racial. These constitute only objections to certain types of war in certain circumstances, rather than a general scruple against participation in war in any form. However, only a general scruple against participation in war in any form can support an exemption as a conscientious objector under the Act. . . .

It would seem from . . . remarks made by the registrant immediately after his having been classified I-A in February 1966, that his claimed objections to military service are based in part upon an objection to fighting the Viet Cong, with whom he has no "personal quarrel," and to his objection to the Muslims getting involved in the Vietnam war. . . .

The main thrust of registrant's letters to his local board following his reclassification from I-Y to I-A appears to be more of an argument for one of several classifications other than I-A, rather than valid support of his conscientious-objector claim. . . .

The burden of clearly establishing his conscientious-objector claim is upon the registrant. . . . The Department of Justice concludes that this registrant failed to sustain that burden.

Two days after the CO appeal was denied, the local board refused to consider evidence that Ali was a full-time minister and might be entitled to a IV-D exemption. Ali had submitted 92 petitions signed by 3,810 Muslims testifying that he was a full-time minister who taught the faith wherever he went. When called for induction in April 1967, Ali based his refusal on grounds that he should be exempt as a Muslim minister.

Although stripped of his title by the World Boxing Association, Ali was undefeated as Champion.

Gene Fast

AWOL

Although there are provisions for discharging servicemen who develop conscientious objection to participation in war after they enter the armed forces, it appears that virtually no discharges have been granted on these grounds since May 1966. Frustrated when their applications for conscientious objector status have been denied, a number of men have gone AWOL (absent without leave) or refused to wear a uniform. Many soldiers are in stockades for petty offenses which they committed in order to avoid duty in Vietnam.

The consequences for many have been more severe than for Gene Fast, who tells his story here. In some cases, legal advice at an earlier point could have prevented needless complications. Stanley Faulkner was Fast's attorney for the first court-martial.

[I WAS DISCHARGED] from the Army on January 12 [1967] as undesirable. This was several months before my sentence expired.

It was the latter part of August 1965, when I was ordered to report for induction. My first thought was to refuse to report and take the consequences. However, after some thinking, an attempt to have my local draft board reclassify me as a conscientious objector, and pressures from the family, I decided to accept induction and try to use my administrative remedies in the service to gain discharge as a conscientious objector.

After my induction and initial processing I was finally assigned and shipped to a basic training company. It was at this time that I decided to make my beliefs known to the commanders involved. Their first reaction was to try and intimidate me with threats of imprisonment and fines. When I persisted in my claims, they then looked for the appropriate regulation under which to process my case. This was Army Regulation 635–20; my application for discharge as a Conscientious Objector was sent forward, on its way to the Department of the Army headquarters.

The processing took about five months, during which time I was assigned to the battalion headquarters as a clerk and runner and general handyman, doing painting and cleaning, etc. The papers were finally returned with a disapproval. The commanding officer of the battalion was an unusually fine person for the Army and he called me in, talked to me, and decided to re-initiate the application with his letter asking them to reconsider and grant the discharge. This, of course, was turned down after about four more months, and the choice was left to me as to what to do. After the time I had spent at the headquarters, I knew most of the ways to attain discharge. This was the reason that I decided to use AWOL, instead of a refusal of a direct order, to gain my discharge.

The first AWOL was for twenty-two days; when I returned to the base I remained at the company area until tried by a Special Court-Martial, at which I was sentenced to three months confinement at hard labor and a fine of sixty dollars a month for three months. After one month in the stockade, half of it spent in solitary confinement, I was released by my commanding officer, upon the promise I would go to training.

The following day I was released from the stockade and returned to the company. I hung around long enough to get a couple of dollars for bus fare and then went AWOL again—this time for forty-eight days.

On my way back I was picked up in the Port Authority Bus Terminal in New York City by the Armed Forces Police, and spent a night in the 54th Street Precinct Jail, awaiting shipment back to Fort Dix.

When I got back to the post I was taken to the stockade and placed in there on a vacation of suspension of sentence pending additional charges. They finally charged me with AWOL and desertion to shirk important service (Basic Combat Training), and put me up for a General Court-Martial. However, I had a good military lawyer at the investigation, to see if the charges were of sufficient strength to be placed before the General Court.

The outcome of this was that the desertion charge was dropped and I was tried on only the AWOL before a Special Court-Martial.

Shortly after the court-martial I had an interview with the head shrinker who stated that he could see no reason for my further retention in the service and that he would press for my discharge. This, plus my record, finally forced the commanding officer to initiate discharge proceedings. . . . Even though I refused to accept my pay until discharged, it had little or no effect upon the outcome of my case.

This statement is from the first Court-Martial on June 17, 1966:

I believe that war and preparation for war is immoral. Military training and service has but one purpose and that is learning to kill and injure other human beings. Regardless of the branch of military service one is in, he is directly or indirectly supporting a system designed to snuff out human lives. My duty to humanity overrides all other duties for to me humanity is the supreme being. Perhaps this is somewhat different to the conventional way of defining a supreme be- but it is to me my religion. . . .

The [next statement] is from the second Court-Martial of November 23, 1966:

. . . For me, my moral beliefs constitute my faith and therefore are just as valid as any organized religion.

The Regulations of the Department of the Army and Selective Service have violated the constitutional rights of myself and others like me by limiting what may or may not constitute a religious belief.

This leaves me with no choice but to break various laws of the established order, to attain a redress of grievances through discharge.

The Resistance

Initiated in the San Francisco Bay Area, the statement "We Refuse to Serve" was distributed on April 15, 1967, at the Spring Mobilization in San Francisco. The following three selections were written during the summer prior to the first Resistance action on October 16, 1967. According to Martin Jezer in *WIN*,

> *On October 16th, 1,158 draft-age men returned their draft cards to federal authorities in 18 cities. This act of civil disobedience, punishable by up to five years in prison and up to [$10,000] in fines, signified their refusal to cooperate in any way with the Selective Service System. At the same time, hundreds of women and men over draft age turned in anti-draft cards, making public their advocacy of draft resistance and stating their intent to stand with those draft resisters brought to trial.*

On December 4, 1967, cards were returned in approximately thirty cities.

The philosophy of The Resistance has elements in common with the pact which Gene Keyes described in his account (see pages 15–32): noncompliance, open confrontation, mutual solidarity. However, the scale of participation and repression of adult support created a qualitatively different situation.

I. *We Refuse to Serve*

IN THE PAST few months, in many parts of the country, a resistance has been forming . . . A resistance of young men— joined together in their commitment against the war. . . .

We will renounce all deferments and refuse to cooperate with the draft in any manner, at any level. We have taken this stand for varied reasons:

opposition to conscription

opposition only to the Vietnam war

opposition to all wars and to all American military adventures.

We all agree on one point: the war in Vietnam is criminal and we must act together, at great individual risk, to stop it. Those involved must lead the American people, by their example, to understand the enormity of what their government is doing . . . that the government cannot be allowed to continue with its daily crimes. . . .

There are many ways to avoid the draft, to stay clear of this war. Most of us now have deferments . . . but all these individual outs can have no effect on the draft, the war, or the consciousness of this country. To cooperate with conscription is to perpetuate its existence, without which, the government could not wage war. We have chosen to openly defy the draft and confront the government and its war directly.

This is no small decision in a person's life. Each one realizes that refusing to cooperate with Selective Service may mean prison. Again we agree that to do anything but this is to effectively abet the war. The government will not be permitted to use us on its way to greater crimes and destruction. We prefer to resist.

The organization is an action committee, composed of those who make this commitment. We stand all-for-one, one-for-all. We are prepared to act together to support anyone singled out for arrest by every means possible, including civil disobedience and unified, public violations of the Selective Service Act. As the resistance grows, the government will either have to allow the draft noncooperators to go free and thereby swell our ranks, or fill the jails. . . .

II. *The Politics of Resistance*

. . . The government's success in countering the challenge of the anti-war movement is directly related to its ability to co-opt the ideals and strategy of the movement. . . . The challenge presented by the peace movement has become assimilated into the dominant structure of power, and hence transformed into an integral part of that structure. . . . To accept the bounds of the established structure of authority and to define the political action of the movement in terms of that structure, means to accept political emasculation and the inevitable co-optation of the movement's spirit and energies.

The stance of resistance is active, rather than passive, offensive, rather than defensive. The aim of resistance is to provoke continual confrontations with the governmental institutions linked to the war. The resistance confronts the government with an unresolvable dilemma; to prosecute and imprison us, which will generate new waves of protest and dissent, of unsurpassed intensity; or to set us free, which will provide greater impetus for the expansion of the movement. . . .

III. *Going Beyond Prayers to an Unjust King*

. . . It is becoming increasingly clear that peace cannot be attained unless some fundamental change is first effected within American society, that there is something about the functioning of the American "system" that does not permit it to respond other than violently to the yearnings of the people it oppresses. . . . One cannot appeal to a repository of justice that does not exist. The incantation of protest must become resistance if we are to avoid the co-optation, invisibility, and sheer impotence that have, up to now, been our experience with regard to the war and the whole issue of the garrison society in America. There is, however, one potential repository of justice, and that is "the people."

. . . If the normal day to day pattern of American life were sufficiently disrupted, people in large numbers would have to begin thinking about the nature of their lives and the society around them. . . . People and societies have a hard time existing out of equilibrium. If we can succeed in breaking the emptiness of the current equilibrium of American society (and it is already being severely threatened by a monstrously confusing war, and by bewildering revolt in our own cities) a new equilibrium will have to be found. . . .

. . . Noncooperation must be seen in its larger context: a seizing of control of our own lives and a conscious effort to redirect the movement of American society.

. . . If all the issues can be clarified and tied together by competent community organizers, if viable courses of action can then be charted by an organized people, we will again see America moving in the direction of justice and democracy. . . .

IV. *The Resistance*

Since the United States is engaged in criminal activity in Vietnam,

Since the major instrument of that criminal activity is the American military establishment,

Since the machinery of the military cannot effectively function without the acquiescence of the people it is supposed to represent,

Since we are young Americans who still believe in the ideals our country once stood for,

The RESISTANCE has been formed to organize and encourage resistance to, disruption of, and noncooperation with all the warmaking machinery of the United States.

The RESISTANCE is a nationwide movement with organizations in New York, Illinois, Massachusetts, Iowa, Ohio, Wisconsin, Michigan, Oregon, and California.

ON OCTOBER 16, 1967, WE WILL PUBLICLY AND COLLECTIVELY RETURN OUR DRAFT CARDS TO THE SELECTIVE SERVICE SYSTEM IN MAJOR CITIES THROUGHOUT THE COUNTRY. We will clearly challenge the government's right to use any young lives for its own nefarious purposes. Our challenge will continue, and we will openly confront the Selective Service System, until the government is forced to deal with our collective action. After October 16, we will organize campuses and communities for similar waves of resistance in December, March, etc. We have gone beyond the "We Won't Go" statements in that we are renouncing all deferments, joining the forces of those who can and those who cannot afford deferments, and forcing an immediate confrontation by practicing total noncooperation with the military establishment. By turning in rather than burning our draft cards, we will be proudly giving our names to the public at large, and to the powers that be. Our hope is that upon our example every young man in America will realize that *he* must decide whether to resist or acquiesce to the draft and the war. We are confident that many will resist. . . .

[*Report by Marjorie Swann in* Direct Action, *the newsletter of the New England Committee for Nonviolent Action.*]

It was a beautiful, sunny day on October 16th on the Boston Common, thousands of miles away from the jungles and paddies of Vietnam, where men and women and children were dying at that very moment. I walked around with a sign, "They Are Our Brothers Whom We Kill," watching between 4,000 and 5,000 people assemble for the ceremonies known as The Resistance. . . . An attractive, blonde woman . . . carried a sign, "LBJ Killed My Son." . . .

Amid some heckling, the speeches got underway, and professors, clergymen, and young resisters gave their reasons for resistance and supporting the resistance. . . . We lined up then, the young men and clergy first, and walked the long way around the Common to Arlington Street Church, which has a history of harboring war resisters. There were so many of us that at least a thousand stayed outside, lined along the sidewalks and filling the corner of the Garden, listening through loudspeakers placed on the spire of the church.

Inside there took place what must have been a most moving service. Perhaps what was the most exciting for some of us was the sense that the church was finally coming into its own—doing what a church and its representatives should be doing in a society wracked by violence and injustice. . . . The Reverend William Sloane Coffin, Chaplain of Yale University, offered on behalf of a number of clergy to provide sanctuary in churches and synagogues to draft resisters. A "breaking bread together" took the place of communion. Then draft age men were invited to come to the altar and turn their draft cards in to representatives of various faiths (including humanist and atheist) or to burn them in the flame of the altar candle. A moment of silence called in memory of all the victims of war even brought silence for at least half a minute, from the right-wing hecklers and the multitudes of police standing out on the street corners with us. Approximately 180 young men turned in their cards, and 80 more burned theirs. A final hymn and carrillon chimes ended the service, and the young war resisters filed out of the church to the applause of the outside listeners.

The October 16 Resistance was billed as "a beginning." . . . Maybe this is a beginning of fulfillment of the old adage, "Wars will cease when men refuse to fight."

V. *A Footnote on Community*

Many Resistance members are deeply concerned with the formation of community, and in some instances our common commitment is leading to the development of strong communal bonds. For at least two reasons this must continue to be a central concern. First, it would be impossible for most of us to face up to the tasks ahead, particularly the prospect of prison, were it not for the strength which derived from the experience of community. The Palo Alto Resistance, which has revolved around the life of a remarkable intentional community for more than a year now, is the clearest and most formal achievement of the community we seek. But, in less formal ways, the same patterns of interdependence are emerging elsewhere.

Secondly, the formation of community may bear an essential relationship to the shape of the future. . . . If radicals are to remain faithful to their own values, then they must create mechanisms in which those values can not only be expressed but also *experienced* in the present. . . .

In the context of . . . 1968, it is possible to assert that the most political option before us is the act wherein thousands of young people reclaim possession of their lives from a System which seeks to manipulate those lives for the purposes of death and repression. Many of us are beginning to recognize that peace is more than a function of government; it is a way of life that must begin with ourselves, our relationships, and our communities. The formation of community grows out of that recognition, and it does not serve as a substitute for engagement. Rather the experience of community sustains us in the political struggle which must be waged relentlessly if we are to make America safe for the world. We urge you to join us, brothers. It's your struggle too!

Michael Senecal

I-A-O IN VIETNAM

Conscientious objectors who go into the armed forces with a I-A-O classification take basic training, the same as other draftees, except that they are not required to train with weapons. (They may have to do long hours of KP while the other men take weapons training.) After basic training, I-A-O's are usually assigned to the medical corps.

The medical corps "contributes to the success of the military effort, through . . . Conserving Manpower [and] . . . Preventing Adverse Effects of Unevacuated Casualties on Combat Efficiency. . . ." "The primary task of medical troops as of all other troops is to contribute their utmost to the success of the command of which the medical service is a part." (Army Field Manual, FM 8-10.)

This account was taken from a letter which Michael Senecal wrote in February 1968, several months after his discharge from the Army.

I WAS A MEMBER of the Army Medical Corps in Vietnam.

During my four years of High School I was a member of the ROTC. Out of a freshman class of over three hundred who enlisted in the program, I was one of twenty-two who were selected in the senior year to become cadet officers, and obtained the rank of First Lieutenant. By this time, although I still felt quite a feeling of pride in the organization, an indefinable seed of doubt and discomfort began to disturb me as I tended to encourage my peers to challenge uniformity. I began to read and listen and think.

About the end of 1964 I felt that I couldn't purposefully train to, and, in actuality, destroy fellow men. About that time I obtained literature from a close friend about conscientious objection and pacifism. In a ten-page essay to my draft board I described as best I could my feelings toward actively taking arms against other human beings. The draft board didn't even call me up for an interview, and sent me my I-A-O rating about two weeks after my application.

During my entire Army term I experienced no real "tough" harassment; and except for a few threats in Vietnam, where firearms were about in abundance, did I ever get concerned.

Some of my daily tasks consisted of scrubbing blood, intestines, brains, and human matter in general from the canvas litters outside of the emergency room. The actual tasks themselves, like scrubbing the vomit, excrement, etc., from a young lad who had finally lost his mind, didn't disturb me; but the entire "feeling" that a war zone emits (its human components) disturbed me so entirely that, even today, I at times feel psychologically disorientated.

After talking to about 400 GI's in private, while preparing their wounds for the surgeons, about 90 per cent of these men (mostly draftees or nonprofessional soldiers) said that from their experience in the field, they had observed no real victories or accomplishments of significance. The entire aura of mechanical obedience and arrogant blasphemy of the basic rights and respect of other human beings, combined with the gore, and horror connected with the chaos of war, drove me out of the emergency section of the hospital to a malaria ward, and finally away from medical work entirely. I spent the last few months of my tour working as a stake-holder for an army surveyor collecting data for a topographic map of the area.

Perhaps one might pose the question now of why didn't I just refuse to join the Army if I felt that killing was wrong. At eighteen years of age I just hadn't seriously thought of all the details of my ideas—like I would still be killing people if I joined the Army; or how much or "how strong" did I believe. Also, the pressures of years of training in schools, at home, church, and in most of society still had me partially convinced that during certain periods of time, a man must abandon personal beliefs for the best interests of society, no matter what those beliefs might be.

I was not a member of any draft resistance group. Had I been, before I went to the draft or at least known then what I understand now, I would not have gone into the Army or any other military force. The way I see the world, there are millions upon millions who would have better benefited if I had gone on a constructive rather than a destructive errand. And right in this country *now* we have conditions which most certainly should be corrected before we spend 55 million a day on an irrational and unreasoned war halfway around the globe.

Every time I get in a conversation about present politics or philosophies, I find people undecided on "what is right." Well, some way, somehow, I want to help them to learn what they believe to be right—it's as if people were existing in a limbo and just sort of abandoning some part of themselves—which is very important to a whole life. . . .

David Nesmith

ALTERNATIVE SERVICE IN VIETNAM

David Nesmith, son of a Methodist minister, was recognized as a conscientious objector. He went to Vietnam to do alternative service under the auspices of the International Voluntary Services. His major assignment was working for a Government of Vietnam Animal Husbandry Station in a northern province of South Vietnam. Subsequently Nesmith was moved to Saigon where he became a technical specialist in charge of orientation and training of new IVS volunteers coming to Vietnam.

A letter dated January 23, 1967, to friends at the Episcopal Peace Fellowship records some of the initial agony which Nesmith perceived:

> *Do you understand what it means to be a sustenance farmer, just growing enough rice for the family to live on for a year? And do you understand how it feels to watch a plane fly overhead spraying chemicals on your field just before harvest, and then watch that field become brown, and then black? Would you like to watch your family starve to death because of some nebulous fight that does not matter? Do you know why it does not matter? Because the very thing that the U.S. seeks to preserve (freedom and abundant life) is that which it destroys every day. . . .*
>
> *What does it matter that I work from dawn far into the night trying to increase production so that we can distribute more chicks to the countryside when there is no way to assure the farmer of adequate feed supply, and a simple quirk of war could wipe him or his family off the face of the earth?*

Discontent among volunteers working for IVS and other social service agencies in Vietnam became widespread. They circulated eye-witness accounts of American attacks and expressed their anti-war views publicly. A letter of protest to President

Johnson was signed by forty-nine IVS volunteers: "to stay in Vietnam and remain silent is to fail to respond to the first need of the Vietnamese people—peace." In October 1967, the director and three staff members of IVS in Vietnam resigned because they refused to yield to pressure to silence the protestors. With the U.S. military effort driving Vietnamese civilians from the countryside at the rate of 100,000 a month, the obvious need, they stated, was to stop making refugees. Those who have not offered to resign continue as witnesses to what is happening in Vietnam.

> *I like to think that the letters that I write home and the things that I talk about . . . when I send tapes . . . begin to make people think about what's happening here so that my presence is in a very small way justified, even though I know damn well it is not justified as far as the Vietnamese people are concerned.*

This account was recorded on tape in November 1967, and deals specifically with David Nesmith's evaluation of alternative service in Vietnam.

THE FIRST THING I want to talk about is why I came to Vietnam. . . . My draft board was after me to do alternative service after I'd finished four years in college. I hadn't gotten my degree yet, but they wanted me to do my alternative service. So I was looking around and checking into alternatives. The ones that I was actively looking into were a Delta Ministry Project with the National Council of Churches, working in civil rights down in Mississippi; a job in urban church work in San Francisco; working with the Goodwill Industries, or working in [a] state hospital in California. The other alternative was International Voluntary Services.

I chose IVS for a great many reasons. One of the major ones was, the war disturbed me tremendously and I wanted to try to provide in Vietnam some kind of antithesis to the American foreign policy effort that was being made there in terms of the war. I wanted to see if I couldn't to some extent turn the consequences around so that, instead of suffering, at least a few Americans might bring balm. I wanted to be able to try to help a few of the eternally downtrodden peasants of any country, but especially the ones who have suffered in Vietnam. I expected to be able to do it keeping completely away from the military effort and the U.S. foreign policy effort being made in Vietnam. This was my hope when I came.

I've worked in Vietnam now for almost a year and a half and my contract is over in September [1968]. I work in Hue, Thua Thien province, the second to the northernmost province in South Vietnam, in agriculture, primarily with the Government of Vietnam Animal Husbandry Station here in the province. These are all reports that I know of personally or have received firsthand from some other IVSer.

As far as my feelings as a CO is concerned, I've tried to forget about my conscientious objector-ness because I can't be a CO in Vietnam. It's a hellish load. You can't be ideologically consistent and be in Vietnam. Because an American in Vietnam is an *American* in Vietnam. In the eyes of the Vietnamese, except for maybe a half a dozen of your closest friends, you are part of this whole American effort here. And if they agree with the American effort here, they'll like you. And if they disagree with it, they'll dislike you; and for most of the Vietnamese, they'll dislike you, of course. When I drive down the streets of Saigon, I'm not a different American, even though I have a beard and long hair. I'm just another God-damned round-eyed American driving a vehicle that adds to the unutterable chaos that is Saigon traffic. When I ride my bicycle down the streets of Hue I'm not, for ninety-nine per cent of the people, anything except another American who threatens the beauty and tranquillity and the very way of life of the Vietnamese. It would be impossible for them to distinguish, well, this one's an IVSer, he's a nice guy. So that I can almost hear Vietnamese grit their teeth as I pass them. I'm hated because I'm an American. And it's a feeling I can only understand and mourn for its effect on me, but not for any feeling of injustice. It seems to me the only way a CO could remain in Vietnam and work is by hiding his head. I just do my job and I don't consider the political consequences of my actions. This is the only way that a CO could remain in Vietnam and keep his ideology intact.

I'm over here with International Voluntary Service, which is supposed to be a private nonprofit organization, working in underdeveloped lands on a people-to-people basis. This is practically a quote from their pamphlet. It isn't that. It's just not true. We're not private because a great deal of our independence has been impinged upon. We still maintain more independence than most organizations in Vietnam, but if we were private, nonpolitically involved, we would not be in Vietnam now.

You can't escape the military because you can't drive on the roads and so you have to fly airplanes—and there's only three sets of airplanes to fly in Vietnam: that's Air Vietnam, which is the commercial airlines; the military flights, which is obviously directed by the military; and Air America, which is a USAID [United States Agency for International Development]-sponsored thing, but is under CORDS—which is the Civil Operations and Revolutionary Development Support program, which is, of course, part of the American effort. And since Air Vietnam is not open to us because of the high prices and our low salaries, in transportation we are utterly dependent on the military and the foreign policy effort in Vietnam.

The community development worker in Vietnam works in two areas: youth work or refugee work. A community development refugee worker in many cases becomes involved in working right with the American effort, finds himself involved completely with the task of taking care of the Vietnamese generated by American search and destroy missions and large offensive sweeps, using USAID commodities, USAID transportation, building with USAID tools, and so forth and so on.

In agriculture, the field that I'm in, there is no way for me to help the farmer as an individual. I have to work through government agencies, Vietnamese and American. When I go out to a village, if I am to help the farmer with feed, medicine, training, improved livestock—everything that I do has to be approved.

Largely I work through the Government of Vietnam. Their entire animal husbandry effort in my province this last year has been directed to revolutionary development—a part of this pacification program which, in so many instances and particularly in Thua Thien province, has failed so miserably. The only hamlets that are given food, feed, medicine, improved animals, and farmer training are the revolutionary development hamlets who are receiving so much aid already and who are clustered right around Hue.

The work that needs to be done here on the farm is remodeling, rebuilding, getting new machinery, rewiring the farm, and so forth. All of these things require USAID support. And this means that we've got to be doing things that USAID wants us to do, that is, revolutionary development programs. So that even if GVN [Government of Vietnam] was not forcing the farm to do things, we would have to do them to get support from USAID.

The only works I've been able to do by myself—that I've been able to justify in terms of helping people in a nonpolitically involved, nonmilitarily involved way—was that the first half of this year I spent about half my time working in about six hamlets, way out toward the foothills that climb into the mountain chain that divides Vietnam from Laos. They were hamlets that the animal husbandry cadre would not go to because they were too insecure, and for which the GVN would provide no support because it would fall into Viet Cong hands. I'd spend time just talking with the farmers, helping them rebuild the chickenhouse, learning how they do things—just spending time. I can't say that I helped them any. I know they helped me a lot. They kept me sane. But then, towards the end of spring and early summer and on through summer [1967], one by one the hamlets were taken over by active Viet Cong control, to the point where those with whom I worked would have suffered reprisals if I had continued to come out and work with them. So that all six hamlets by August were closed to me. . . . Another one I tried to get into and work with, the first day I was in, talking with people, American combat jets bombed the next village and destroyed any possible rapport.

So that now I am faced with the prospect of working completely within the military effort—because that's the only effort that is being made in Vietnam at this time. There is no effort to help the Vietnamese peasant. There is an effort to win the war, and all of America's agencies' efforts are bent in that direction. To be sure, people are being helped as a result of this effort sometimes. Refugees are being fed. Improved livestock is being taken out to the hamlets. But refugees needn't be made. And with the lack of training (the training that we don't have time to give or we refuse to give to the farmers who get the improved stock), most of the improved stock get what we call "Tet disease," that is, at the Vietnamese New Year celebration, the animals are killed for food.

Most of my experience has been with refugees. I've seen war-injured people, civilians. I see them almost every week. The effects of phosphorus grenades and napalm bombs and land mines and machine guns is something that cannot be described.

> [Napalm] explodes and spreads a jelly all over everything in the vicinity. This jelly is on fire. It burns through clothing and destroys the skin with burns. It leaves the people not already dead to die a horrible death by burns. It burns trees, houses, everything. . . . A phosphorous bomb . . . gets on the body and burns; and it does not stop burning until it reaches bone. What does it feel like, I wonder, to have phosphorous on your face and feel it eating away right down to the skull.

. . . Almost ninety per cent of the refugees in Vietnam are refugees of U.S. fire power. . . . We call the refugees people who are under Government of Vietnam control. And I tell you they are under the South Vietnamese Government's control not because they want to be, but because they have been forced to be. They are pro-American when the American USAID officials come around because that's the only way they can stay alive. You can bet that if they are ever resettled . . . they are going to be very close listeners to any Viet Cong propagandist that might come around.

. . . The [refugee] camps are usually situated on unwanted ground because this is the only land that is readily available to the GVN. So most of the camps I have seen are infertile, hilly, sandy, land where water is not readily available—just totally undesirable land. Usually the rice allowance and the daily piaster allowance is siphoned off, so the refugee sees little or none of either because of the corruption within the Government of Vietnam. A refugee has no way of supporting himself unless he can get some kind of a job. And the only jobs available, usually, are jobs in nearby American bases. To get a job at an American base you have to have a Government of Vietnam Security Police check run on you. And this check, while supposedly free, costs 2000 piasters for a routine check, and if they find anything questionable in your past it costs more. So if a Viet Cong spy wants a job at an American base it may cost him 10,000 piasters but he can get the job; whereas a refugee who is poor and needs only 2000 piasters [for a routine check] usually can't get it because he's just plain penniless.

Spraying of rice crops, which is an . . . ongoing policy of the United States, seems to me to be one of blatant genocide. . . . When rice crops are sprayed those who suffer are not the Viet Cong troops, nor are they even the neutral young men who might perhaps live in areas affected by spraying of crops. Those who are affected by it are children and women and old people, those who are least likely to be involved in fighting. I've seen children particularly who are just starving to death. Their families were finally forced to leave the area and go into refugee camps, where they are completely dependent on American and Government of Vietnam aid to stay alive. `

A refugee camp that I worked in, in the past had been adopted by a United States battalion who had bought some hogs for them and were sending in several pails of garbage to feed the hogs every day. The hogs were starving to death. And yet the garbage cans came back, in the words of the Captain, "finger-licking clean"—because the people were starving to death and the garbage was their major source of food. These people are not going to love Americans as soon as they get a chance to be off by themselves and independent again.

Five woodcutters were out cutting wood when a helicopter dived at them and they ran. The machinegunner opened up and killed two, wounded the other three. When protest was made about what was being done, the commander of the helicopter flight said, "Well, you've got to give the gunner credit. He got five for five."

The free-strike zones which are now taking up so much of the geography of South Vietnam are another interesting thing. Anyone found in them is considered suspect and liable to being shot at, bombed, strafed, rocketed, or anything else. Anyone found looking suspicious in insecure areas is liable to be shot at. That means that if you're in a Viet Cong-controlled area and you're the pilot of a helicopter, you can dive at a group of people who are walking along a road, and if any of them run or fall into a ditch or do something that seems suspicious, it is OK for you to shoot at them. Seasoned Viet Cong combat soldiers are not going to run when a helicopter comes chopping and clunking and diving down out of the sky. But a simple peasant is very likely to run. So that here again, civilian casualties are going to be high.

In general terms, I would like my actions to influence people in the United States to begin to think differently as a nation. If they could begin to realize the utter horror of war . . . maybe we could begin to change the attitude of a nation which thinks so much now in terms of solving problems by violence. Maybe if we could get people to change their attitude about war, maybe they'd begin to think more seriously about internationalism, so that we'd be more willing to strengthen the United Nations rather than ignoring it when it suits us. I really don't expect this to happen, but I'd like whatever I do to move those who I influence in this direction.

What I mainly want to do is try to bring the horrible agony and suffering of Vietnam into the daily lives of some Americans. . . . When I hear of Hubert Humphrey and Lyndon Johnson and Dean Rusk saying the things that they say, it reduces me to a quivering bundle of seething rage. That men can be this far removed from the realities of what they are doing to Vietnamese just seems to me to be impossible—that they cannot see the effects of what they are doing.

One thing that being in Vietnam has done for me: it has made me a hell of a lot more radical than I was when I left the States. . . . Then, I thought the government had the right to force men (and women) to serve two or four or five or six years in government service. Now I think that a government who misuses this right as blatantly as ours does, loses that right. . . . And I think that the Selective Service law, as it is now, is immoral. And if I wasn't so damned afraid of jail I'd disobey the law. But after spending a day in jail in Mississippi, I don't think I'd like five years in jail.

It's really difficult to talk about the problems of a conscientious objector in Vietnam because the problems are mostly internal. How do you reconcile the ideals with the reality which is so terribly different? And the reconciliation is usually something that requires a great deal of compromise and in some people's definition, it might be a great deal of copping out that is required.

There are many CO's working in Vietnam; I talked to a lot of them, and what they say is that they are over here to help the Vietnamese people. And they view this in a narrow sense. They are helping a half a dozen or twenty or thirty Vietnamese, training them in agriculture or teaching them English, or something like this. The long term effect of their presence—that it helps the American effort here—is something that is not relevant to them. If they do admit that their presence here is inconsistent, they merely say, "I just want to stay here and finish up and then go home and forget about it." As for myself, I cannot really place myself within these two groups or outside of them. I can't really consider myself a CO anymore because of the tremendous compromises that I've had to make simply to be here.

Why do I stay here? I guess because I want to see war. I want to see what it does to people so that when I do get back to the States I can take the face of American-white-middle-classdom who hold the power in the United States and rub it, without pity, in the blood and gore of what they are doing to the people of the world. I want the horror of this thing to be so indelibly impressed in my mind and in my life that those who are around me will never forget what our country has done to Vietnam and what it is beginning to do in Laos and what it is preparing to do in Thailand and Bolivia and Peru and Venezuela. And I guess this is why I am here, and why I stay. So that people in the United States will never forget what horrible things they have allowed their government to do.

Dale E. Noyd

PARTICULAR WAR OBJECTOR

*Petitioner is an Air Force officer who became a conscientious
objector after eleven years of honorable service, and whose
application for recognition as a conscientious objector, and
either discharge or reassignment to duties not conflicting with
his conscience, was denied by his military superiors. . . .
. . . Capt. Noyd stated that he would be available to
accept any duty assignment, anywhere in the world, however remote and however hazardous, except for assignments
which would directly or indirectly involve his participation
in the Vietnam War, in violation of his conscience.* (Noyd
v. McNamara, et al. *Petition for a Writ of Certiorari.*)

Dale E. Noyd was a Distinguished Military Graduate of the Air
Force ROTC program at Washington State University in 1955.
After completing training he served for three years in England
as a fighter pilot with a nuclear delivery capability, and he received an Air Force Commendation Medal for landing a severely
disabled plane. From 1960 to 1963 he was a graduate student at
the University of Michigan under the Air Force educational program, and thereby became obliged to serve in the Air Force for
six additional years. From June 1963 until January 1967 he was
an instructor and then Assistant Professor of Psychology at the
Air Force Academy.

This account presents excerpts from Noyd's Tender of Resignation, December 8, 1966. In January 1967, the Captain was
removed from his teaching position and a promotion to Major
was withheld. His efforts to be recognized as a conscientious
objector were repeatedly denied, even though there was no
question as to his sincerity or depth of religious conviction.

With the assistance of the American Civil Liberties Union,
Captain Noyd brought a suit to test whether he was entitled to
conscientious objector status. Several questions were at issue but

the most significant ones had to do with the "selective" nature of Noyd's objection. Noted religious authorities testified: "universal pacifism and discriminating pacifism . . . are equally religious," ". . . if the law were to exempt universal pacifists while denying exemption to discriminating ones, it would discriminate religiously—by *content* of belief—against some religious views and in favor of others." The language describing the categories I-O and I-A-O was used to illustrate that "the words, 'in any form' more naturally modify 'participation' than 'war' . . . The I-A-O only objects to a certain *form* of participation."

> . . . *It is religiously informed conscience itself*, in the matter of war and killing, *rather than some conscientious scruples of a particular formulation or content, which national policy undertakes to respect.* . . . *An unwarranted discrimination based on the content of different religious beliefs— between those opposing all wars and those opposing only such as are deemed unjust—would violate both the First Amendment . . . and the due process mandate of the Fifth.* . . .

As of this writing, the merits of a "particular war" objection have not been judged by the Supreme Court.

Capt. Noyd was assigned to take instructor training in F-100 jet fighter aircraft, a type currently being used in Vietnam. He moved with his wife and two children to Cannon Air Force Base, Clovis, New Mexico. For several months he was protected by a temporary injunction and assigned to noncombatant duties. But after a "limbo" period of waiting, with alternately hopeful and disappointing legal and administrative moves, the Captain was ordered to begin the training. He wrote the following to his commanding officer on August 28, 1967:

> *I am not conscientiously opposed to recurrency training in the F-100 or to all flying assignments in that aircraft. I am convinced, however often I attempt to deny it or rationalize it away, that the training of RTU pilots for Vietnam is a direct and significant contribution to the war*

*and as such is the same affront to my conscience as killing
Vietnamese. . . . If I were to perform duties as an instructor
pilot, I could be almost certain that any skills I imparted to
a student pilot would soon be employed in the killing of
Vietnamese. Doubly tragic would be the constant awareness that any young man whom I would be training may for-
feit his life in a cause that I believe to be immoral and
worthless. . . .*

*Your orders have now put me in the position wherein it
appears that I shall inevitably be confronted with duties—
those of instructor pilot—which would violate my conscience.
Again these I would be compelled to refuse. . . . I shall,
however, if ordered to begin training, attempt to suppress
the resultant feelings of anger and futility and to satisfactorily
fulfill the assigned duties. This I shall continue to do, as I
have both at the Air Force Academy and Cannon AFB until
I am up against the wall with an order which violates my
conscience and which I shall be compelled to refuse.*

On December 5, 1967, Captain Noyd refused a direct order to
fly as an instructor. He was formally charged with disobeying an
order and court-martial proceedings were begun. The Supreme
Court as well as the lower federal courts said they did not have
jurisdiction to consider Noyd's civil case and refused to consider
the question whether an "in-service applicant for conscientious
objector status, who has exhausted all his administrative remedies, must commit a crime and submit to a military court-martial
before gaining a federal review of his constitutional claims."

On March 9, 1968, Captan Noyd was sentenced to one year at
hard labor, forfeiture of all pay and allowances, and dismissal
from the service.

I, DALE EDWIN NOYD, Captain, . . . hereby voluntarily tender my resignation from all appointments in the USAF. . . .
Because of the unusual nature of my circumstances, and the
complexity of the issues involved, I shall attempt a somewhat

more extensive explication of the reasons underlying my resignation.

I am opposed to the war that this country is waging in Vietnam; and for the past year . . . I have considered various stratagems that would obviate my participation in, and contribution to, that war. Among other alternatives, I have considered grounding myself or seeking an assignment other than in Southeast Asia. But these choices were not an honest confrontation of the issues and they do not do justice to my beliefs. The hypocrisy of my silence and acquiescence must end—I feel strongly that it is time for me to demand more consistency between my convictions and my behavior. Several months ago I came to a decision that would reflect this consistency and sought counsel on what alternatives I might have. This letter is a result of that decision. Although I had intended submitting this resignation at a time better suited to the requirements of the Academy, the welfare of my students, and my own convenience, the issue was forced by my recent notification that my assignment here has been curtailed to June 1967.

Increasingly I find myself in the position of being highly involved and *caring* about many moral, political, and social issues—of which the war in Vietnam is the most important—and yet I cannot protest and work to effect some change. Not only may my convictions remain unexpressed and the concomitant responsibilities unfulfilled, but I am possibly confronted with fighting in a war that I believe to be unjust, immoral, and which makes a mockery of both our Constitution and the charter of the United Nations—and the human values which they represent.

Apart from the moral and ethical issues, and speaking only from the point of view of the super-patriot, it is a stupid war and pernicious to the self-interest of the United States. . . . Because of the gravity of my circumstances and the unusual nature of my resignation, I shall state some of the observations and premises from which I have made my judgments.

First of all, in a nation that pretends to an open and free society, hypocrisy and subterfuge have pervaded our conduct and policy in Southeast Asia at least since 1954. This is not only in relations with the Vietnamese and in our pronouncements to the other nations of the world, but also with the American people. One need look no further than our public statements in order to detect this. I insist on knowing what my government is doing and it is clear that this right has been usurped. Although I am cognizant that an open society may have its disadvantages in an ideological war with a totalitarian system, I do not believe that the best defense of our freedoms is an emulation of that system.

After the Viet Minh assisted in expelling the Japanese from Indochina in World War II, the United States supported the French in their reestablishment of colonial rule. This support of the French continued in the form of weapons and aid in their futile attempt to resist the nationalism, the desire for self-determination, and the social progress of the Vietnamese. The Viet Minh was dominated by Communists but this does not mitigate the following facts: that it represented the aspirations of the people, it was the only popular political force, and it represented *change*—not unlike the status of the NLF today. Although the United States would prefer that it not be brought to their attention, the Vietnamese have not forgotten that in their struggle against the French one million Vietnamese died—died facing weapons supplied by the United States.

This country has made it abundantly clear in the last twenty years, on several continents, that the political freedoms and social aspirations of other peoples are not the principal considerations in the determination of our foreign policy. We have been opposed to any social change that carried the taint of the political left, especially any change that could be labeled "communistic." We have supported fascists, dictators, and military juntas—anyone who professes "anti-communism"—no matter how oppressive and reactionary, no matter how they retard the legitimate aspirations of the people, as long as they served the perceived temporary self-interests of the United States. We have become the caretakers of the status quo.

Anti-communism is an inadequate substitute for a rational and humanitarian foreign policy; we should express a concern for people and not only their ideology. . . . The world of the "good guys and the bad guys" may be less complex, less troublesome, and problems seem to be more easily resolved, but it simply does not exist. And, unfortunately, we sometimes confuse the labels. I am no apologist for Communism or any other totalitarian system, but let us not refuse to recognize that there are instances in which such a political force may represent self-determination or social progress for a people. If we must intervene in the affairs of other nations, and thereby in this age risk the human species, let us do so on the basis of a coherent and consistent set of principles and values—a moral philosophy which is endemic to the American people but which seems to have been temporarily anesthetized.

Since the Geneva Accords of 1954 [see excerpts in Appendix C, pages 321–322], the United States has supplanted France as the supporter of the status quo in South Vietnam. We have maintained a succession of dictators whose only political base is the same coterie of oligarchy and Mandarins who were allied with the French. Their obvious vested interest has been to oppose land reform and all other forms of social progress, paying only intermittent lip service to these principles in order to appease the democratic concern of the United States and thus guarantee their continued power. This self-interest was epitomized by the most flagrant of the early violations of the Geneva Accords, the U.S.-backed Diem refusal to allow national elections in 1956 which would have reunified Vietnam under the leadership of Ho Chi Minh.

One hardly need comment on the hypocrisy of our protestations concerning our belief in the principle of self-determination. Aside from the minority of Ky supporters in South Vietnam today, there appears to exist two other identifiable groups. The first, and perhaps the majority, are those politically indifferent peasants who want only a share of the land, enough to eat, and an end to twenty years of war with its coercion, conscription, and killing. The other group is the latter-day Viet Minh—the NLF and the Viet Cong, who have opposed the French, the Japanese, the French again, a succession of U.S. supported dictators, and now principally the United States. The NLF is the only popular, indigenous, and viable political force in South Vietnam, and it has continued to represent nationalism and social change. It is a *civil* war, and no amount of specious argument nor emphasis on the recent direct support of the Viet Cong by the North Vietnamese can obscure the fact that our principal opponent is a South Vietnamese peasant who has taken up arms in an attempt to better his life and evict non-Vietnamese.

. . . Never in several generations has there been so much uncertainty and divisiveness over the course of this nation. We find anxiety and opposition not only on the steps of Sproul Hall in Berkeley and on the diag in Ann Arbor, not only among our most respected historians, social scientists, and international analysts, not only in the halls of Congress but also among the American public who are understandably slow in condemning our acts while increasing numbers of coffins are unloaded in California. . . .

. . . This country is capable of achieving for its people, and encouraging in other nations, enormous social advancement, but we are now throwing our riches—both of material and of purpose —into the utter waste of the maelstrom of increasing military involvement. If we as a nation really care about people, then we had best make concepts like freedom and equality *real* to all our citizens—and not just political sham—before we play policeman to the world. . . .

Our behavior in Vietnam is immoral for another set of reasons which concern our conduct of that war. As many newsmen have witnessed, time and again we have bombed, shelled, or attacked a "VC village" or "VC structures"; and when we later appraise the results, we label dead adult males as "VC" and add them to the tally—and fail to count the women and children. Our frequent indiscriminate destruction is killing the innocent as well as the "guilty." In addition, our left-handed morality in the treatment of prisoners is odious—we turn them over to the ARVN for possible torture or execution with the excuse that we are not in command but are only supporting the South Vietnam government. Again, this hypocrisy needs no explication. Also frighteningly new in American morality is the pragmatic justification that we must retaliate against the terrorist tactics of the VC.

Perhaps most devastatingly immoral about the war in Vietnam are the risks we are assuming for the rest of the world. Each new step and escalation appears unplanned and is an attempt to rectify previous blunders by more military action. The consequences of our course appear too predictable, and although we as a people may elect "better dead than red," do we have the right to make this choice for the rest of mankind?

I am not a pacifist; I believe that there are times when it is right and necessary that a nation or community of nations employ force to deter or repel totalitarian agression. My three-year assignment in an operational fighter squadron—with the attendant capacity for inflicting terrible killing and destruction—was based on the personal premise that I was serving a useful deterrent purpose and that I would never be used as an instrument of agression.

This, of course, raises the important and pervasive question for me: What is my duty when I am faced with a conflict between my conscience and the commands of my government? What is my responsibility when there is an irreparable division between my beliefs in the ideals of this nation and the conduct of my political and military leaders?

The problem of ultimate loyalty is not one for which there is an easy solution. And, unfortunately, the issues are most often obscured by those who would undermine the very freedoms they are ostensibly defending—by invoking "loyalty" and "patriotism" to enforce conformity, silence dissent, and protect themselves from criticism.

May a government or nation be in error? Who is to judge? As Thoreau asked, "Must the citizen ever for a moment, or in the least degree, resign his conscience, to the legislator? Why has every man a conscience, then? I think that we should be men first, and subjects afterward. It is not desirable to cultivate a respect for the law, so much as for the right. The only obligation which I have a right to assume, is to do at any time what I think right. . . . Law never made men a whit more just; and, by means of their respect for it, even the well-disposed are daily made the agents of injustice."

The individual *must* judge. We as a nation expect and demand this—we have prosecuted and condemned those who forfeited their personal sense of justice to an immoral authoritarian system. We have despised those who have pleaded that they were only doing their job. If we are to survive as individuals in this age of acquiescence, and as nations in this time of international anarchy, we must resist total enculturation so that we may stand aside to question and evaluate—not as an Air Force officer or as an American, but as a member of the human species. . . . We must not confuse dissent with disloyalty and we must recognize that consensus is no substitute for conscience. As Senator Fulbright has stated, "Criticism is more than a right; it is an act of patriotism—a higher form of patriotism, I believe, than the familiar ritual of national adulation. All of us have the responsibility to act upon this higher patriotism which is to love our country less for what it is than for what we would like it to be."

Aside from the issues of loyalty and violation of conscience, one might question the wisdom of my action in that the personal costs overwhelm any possible contribution or support to a cause which I believe to be just. The cynic might argue that only the fool sticks his neck out in today's world; the individual act is futile and absurd. . . . It is only recently in man's history that he has come to realize that the given order is not the necessary order—that at least some of the banes of the human condition are not immutable. . . .

Pessimism is pernicious in that it is not only a mood but an act; the concomitant apathy and withdrawal makes it a self-fulfilling prophecy because it denies the reality of alternatives. This unwillingness to act upon one's best intuitions and to speak out as an individual has two consequences. The first is the insidious attack upon his sense of self and his potentiality for becoming a real person. . . We grow only as we express what we are. The second consequence of pessimism and withdrawal, of course, directly affects the future of our nation. . . . One popular answer to counteract the feelings of impotence, futility, or meaninglessness is an "escape from freedom" to the role and meaning defined for you by a particular political, ethical, and social system. . . I find that I am incapable of acquiescing and living within that system as it exists—that if I attempt to do so, I cannot live with myself. When confronted with the ubiquitous injustices of this world, the only possible individual morality is activism.

I have attempted to sincerely state the values and beliefs that are both most meaningful in my life and relevant to my present dilemma. It would appear that I am no longer a loyal Air Force officer if this loyalty requires unquestioning obedience to the policies of this nation in Vietnam. I cannot honestly wear the uniform of this country and support unjust and puerile military involvement. Although it may be inconsistent, I have been able to justify (or rationalize) my position here at the Academy by my belief that my contribution in the classroom has had more effect in encouraging rationalism, a sense of humanism, and the development of social consciousness than it has had in the inculcation of militarism. My system of ethics is humanistic—simply a respect and love for man and confidence in his capability to improve his condition. This is my ultimate loyalty. And, as a man trying to be free, my first obligation is to my own integrity and conscience, and this is of course not mitigated by my government's permission or command to engage in immoral acts. I am many things before I am a citizen of this country or an Air Force officer; and included among these things is simply that I am a man with a set of human values which I will not abrogate. I must stand on what I am and what I believe. The war in Vietnam is unjust and immoral, and if ordered to do so, I shall refuse to fight in that war. I should prefer, and respectfully request, that this resignation be accepted.

Appendix A

THE SEEGER DECISION

Section 6 (j) of the Military Selective Service Act of 1967 defines a conscientious objector as a person who "by reason of religious training and belief, is conscientiously opposed to participation in war in any form." The 1948 law, as amended, had specified that, "Religious training and belief in this connection means an individual's belief in a relation to a Supreme Being involving duties superior to those arising from any human relation . . ." This "Supreme Being" clause was cut from the 1967 law, presumably in an effort to circumvent the effects of the Seeger decision. However, the Seeger decision remains significant for its broadening of the application of "religious training and belief" to include beliefs which are not traditional and not theistic. "While the applicant's words may differ, the test is simple . . . namely, does the claimed belief occupy the same place in the life of the objector as an orthodox belief in God holds in the life of one clearly qualified for exemption?"

The law further stipulates that "the term 'religious training and belief' does not include essentially political, sociological, or philosophical views, or a merely personal moral code." With regard to a "merely personal moral code," the court distinguished between "a moral code which is not only personal but which is the sole basis for the registrant's belief" and a claimed religious belief which is "parallel to that filled by God of those admittedly qualified for the exemption."

Any individual who earnestly wishes to be classified as a conscientious objector is urged to state on the Form 150 the values by which he lives and show how he acts on those values. Draft boards vary considerably in how they deal with such claims.

UNITED STATES v. SEEGER.

CERTIORARI TO THE UNITED STATES COURT OF APPEALS FOR
THE SECOND CIRCUIT.

No. 50.   Argued November 16–17, 1964.—Decided March 8, 1965.*

These three cases involve the exemption claims under § 6 (j) of the
Universal Military Training and Service Act of conscientious objectors who did not belong to an orthodox religious sect. Section
6 (j) excepts from combatant service in the armed forces those
who are conscientiously opposed to participation in war by reason
of their "religious training and belief," i. e., belief in an individual's
relation to a Supreme Being involving duties beyond a human
relationship but not essentially political, sociological, or philosophical views or a merely personal moral code. In all the cases
convictions were obtained in the District Courts for refusal to submit to induction in the armed forces; in Nos. 50 and 51 the Court
of Appeals reversed and in No. 29 the conviction was affirmed.
Held:

1. The test of religious belief within the meaning of the exemption in § 6 (j) is whether it is a sincere and meaningful belief occu-
pying in the life of its possessor a place parallel to that filled by
the God of those admittedly qualified for the exemption. Pp.
173–180. [279–286]

  (a) The exemption does not cover those who oppose war from
a merely personal moral code nor those who decide that war is
wrong on the basis of essentially political, sociological or economic
considerations rather than religious belief. P. 173. [279]

  (b) There is no issue here of atheistic beliefs and accordingly
the decision does not deal with that question. Pp. 173–174. [279–280]

  (c) This test accords with long-established legislative policy
of equal treatment for those whose objection to military service is
based on religious beliefs. Pp. 177–180. [283–286]

2. Local boards and courts are to decide whether the objector's
beliefs are sincerely held and whether they are, in his own scheme
of things, religious; they are not to require proof of the reli-

---

*Together with No. 51, *United States* v. *Jakobson,* on certiorari to
the same court, and No. 29, *Peter* v. *United States,* on certiorari to
the United States Court of Appeals for the Ninth Circuit.

gious doctrines nor are they to reject beliefs because they are not
comprehensible. Pp. 184–185.[290–291]

   3. Under the broad construction applicable to § 6 (j) the applications involved in these cases, none of which was based on merely
personal moral codes, qualified for exemption. Pp. 185–188.[291–294]

326 F. 2d 846 and 325 F. 2d 409, affirmed; 324 F. 2d 173, reversed.

Solicitor General Cox argued the cause for the United
States in all cases. *Assistant Attorney General Miller*
was with him on the briefs in all cases. *Ralph S. Spritzer*
was with him on the briefs in Nos. 50 and 51, and *Mar-
shall Tamor Golding* was with him on the briefs in No. 50.

Duane B. Beeson argued the cause and filed a brief for
petitioner in No. 29.

Kenneth W. Greenawalt argued the cause and filed a
brief for respondent in No. 50.

Herman Adlerstein argued the cause and filed a brief
for respondent in No. 51.

Briefs of *amici curiae,* urging affirmance in Nos. 50 and
51 and reversal in No. 29, were filed by *Alfred Lawrence
Toombs* and *Melvin L. Wulf* for the American Civil Liberties Union, and by *Leo Pfeffer, Shad Polier, Will Mas-
low* and *Joseph B. Robison* for the American Jewish Congress. Briefs of *amici curiae,* urging affirmance in No. 50,
were filed by *Herbert A. Wolff, Leo Rosen, Nanette
Dembitz* and *Nancy F. Wechsler* for the American Ethical
Union, and by *Tolbert H. McCarroll, Lester Forest* and
Paul Blanshard for the American Humanist Association.

Mr. Justice Clark delivered the opinion of the Court.

These cases involve claims of conscientious objectors
under § 6 (j) of the Universal Military Training and
Service Act, 50 U. S. C. App. § 456 (j) (1958 ed.), which
exempts from combatant training and service in the
armed forces of the United States those persons who by

reason of their religious training and belief are conscientiously opposed to participation in war in any form. The cases were consolidated for argument and we consider them together although each involves different facts and circumstances. The parties raise the basic question of the constitutionality of the section which defines the term "religious training and belief," as used in the Act, as "an individual's belief in a relation to a Supreme Being involving duties superior to those arising from any human relation, but [not including] essentially political, sociological, or philosophical views or a merely personal moral code." The constitutional attack is launched under the First Amendment's Establishment and Free Exercise Clauses and is twofold: (1) The section does not exempt nonreligious conscientious objectors; and (2) it discriminates between different forms of religious expression in violation of the Due Process Clause of the Fifth Amendment. Jakobson (No. 51) and Peter (No. 29) also claim that their beliefs come within the meaning of the section. Jakobson claims that he meets the standards of § 6 (j) because his opposition to war is based on belief in a Supreme Reality and is therefore an obligation superior to one resulting from man's relationship to his fellow man. Peter contends that his opposition to war derives from his acceptance of the existence of a universal power beyond that of man and that this acceptance in fact constitutes belief in a Supreme Being, qualifying him for exemption. We granted certiorari in each of the cases because of their importance in the administration of the Act. 377 U. S. 922.

We have concluded that Congress, in using the expression "Supreme Being" rather than the designation "God," was merely clarifying the meaning of religious training and belief so as to embrace all religions and to exclude essentially political, sociological, or philosophical views. We believe that under this construction, the test of belief "in a relation to a Supreme Being" is whether a given belief that is sincere and meaningful occupies a place in the life of its possessor parallel to that filled by the orthodox belief in God of one who clearly qualifies for the exemption. Where such beliefs have parallel positions in the lives of their respective holders we cannot say that one is "in a relation to a Supreme Being" and the other is not. We have concluded that the beliefs of the objectors in these cases meet these criteria, and, accordingly, we affirm the judgments in Nos. 50 and 51 and reverse the judgment in No. 29.

THE FACTS IN THE CASES.

No. 50: Seeger was convicted in the District Court for the Southern District of New York of having refused to submit to induction in the armed forces. He was originally classified 1–A in 1953 by his local board, but this classification was changed in 1955 to 2–S (student) and he remained in this status until 1958 when he was reclassified 1–A. He first claimed exemption as a conscientious objector in 1957 after successive annual renewals of his student classification. Although he did not adopt verbatim the printed Selective Service System form, he declared that he was conscientiously opposed to participation in war in any form by reason of his "religious" belief; that he preferred to leave the question as to his belief in a Supreme Being open, "rather than answer 'yes' or 'no' "; that his "skepticism or disbelief in the existence of God" did "not necessarily mean lack of faith in anything whatsoever"; that his was a "belief in and devotion to goodness and virtue for their own sakes, and a religious faith in a purely ethical creed." R. 69–70, 73. He cited such personages as Plato, Aristotle and Spinoza for support of his ethical belief in intellectual and moral integrity "without belief in God, except in the remotest sense." R. 73. His belief was found to be sincere, honest, and made in good faith; and his conscientious objection to be based upon individual training and belief, both of which included research in religious and cultural fields. Seeger's claim, however, was denied solely because it was not based upon a "belief in a relation to a Supreme Being" as required by § 6 (j) of the Act. At trial Seeger's counsel admitted that Seeger's belief was not in relation to a Supreme Being as commonly understood, but contended that he was entitled to the exemption because "under the present law Mr. Seeger's position would also include definitions of religion which have been stated more recently," R. 49, and could be "accommodated" under the definition of religious training and belief in the Act, R. 53. He was convicted and the Court of Appeals reversed, holding that the Supreme Being requirement of the section distinguished "between internally derived and externally compelled beliefs" and was, therefore, an "impermissible classification" under the Due Process Clause of the Fifth Amendment. 326 F. 2d 846.

No. 51: Jakobson was also convicted in the Southern District of New York on a charge of refusing to submit to induction. On his appeal the Court of Appeals reversed on the ground that rejection of his claim may have rested on the factual finding, erroneously made, that he did not believe in a Supreme Being as required by § 6 (j). 325 F. 2d 409.

Jakobson was originally classified 1–A in 1953 and intermittently enjoyed a student classification until 1956. It was not until April 1958 that he made claim to noncombatant classification (1–A–O) as a conscientious objector. He stated on the Selective Service System form that he believed in a "Supreme Being" who was "Creator of Man" in the sense of being "ultimately responsible for the existence of" man and who was "the Supreme Reality" of which "the existence of man is the *result.*" R. 44. (Emphasis in the original.) He explained that his reli-

gious and social thinking had developed after much meditation and thought. He had concluded that man must be
"partly spiritual" and, therefore, "partly akin to the Supreme Reality"; and that his "most important religious
law" was that "no man ought ever to wilfully sacrifice
another man's life as a means to any other end . . . ."
R. 45–46. In December 1958 he requested a 1–O classification since he felt that participation in any form of military service would involve him in "too many situations
and relationships that would be a strain on [his] conscience that [he felt he] must avoid." R. 70. He submitted a long memorandum of "notes on religion" in which
he defined religion as the *"sum and essence of one's basic
attitudes to the fundamental problems of human existence,"* R. 72 (emphasis in the original); he said that he
believed in "Godness" which was "the Ultimate Cause for
the fact of the Being of the Universe"; that to deny its
existence would but deny the existence of the universe
because "anything that Is, has an Ultimate Cause for its
Being." R. 73. There was a relationship to Godness, he
stated, in two directions, *i. e.,* "vertically, towards Godness
directly," and "horizontally, towards Godness through
Mankind and the World." R. 74. He accepted the latter one. The Board classified him 1–A–O and Jakobson
appealed. The hearing officer found that the claim was
based upon a personal moral code and that he was not sincere in his claim. The Appeal Board classified him 1–A.
It did not indicate upon what ground it based its decision, *i. e.,* insincerity or a conclusion that his belief
was only a personal moral code. The Court of Appeals
reversed, finding that his claim came within the requirements of § 6 (j). Because it could not determine whether
the Appeal Board had found that Jakobson's beliefs failed
to come within the statutory definition, or whether it had
concluded that he lacked sincerity, it directed dismissal of
the indictment.

No. 29: Forest Britt Peter was convicted in the Northern District of California on a charge of refusing to submit to induction. In his Selective Service System form he stated that he was not a member of a religious sect or organization; he failed to execute section VII of the questionnaire but attached to it a quotation expressing opposition to war, in which he stated that he concurred. In a later form he hedged the question as to his belief in a Supreme Being by saying that it depended on the definition and he appended a statement that he felt it a violation of his moral code to take human life and that he considered this belief superior to his obligation to the state. As to whether his conviction was religious, he quoted with approval Reverend John Haynes Holmes' definition of religion as "the consciousness of some power manifest in nature which helps man in the ordering of his life in harmony with its demands ... [; it] is the supreme expression of human nature; it is man thinking his highest, feeling his deepest, and living his best." R. 27. The source of his conviction he attributed to reading and meditation "in our democratic American culture, with its values derived from the western religious and philosophical tradition." *Ibid.* As to his belief in a Supreme Being, Peter stated that he supposed "you could call that a belief in the Supreme Being or God. These just do not happen to be the words I use." R. 11. In 1959 he was classified 1-A, although there was no evidence in the record that he was not sincere in his beliefs. After his conviction for failure to report for induction the Court of Appeals, assuming *arguendo* that he was sincere, affirmed, 324 F. 2d 173.

BACKGROUND OF § 6 (j).

Chief Justice Hughes, in his opinion in *United States v. Macintosh*, 283 U. S. 605 (1931), enunciated the rationale behind the long recognition of conscientious objec-

tion to participation in war accorded by Congress in our
various conscription laws when he declared that "in the
forum of conscience, duty to a moral power higher than
the State has always been maintained." At 633 (dissenting opinion). In a similar vein Harlan Fiske Stone,
later Chief Justice, drew from the Nation's past when he
declared that

> "both morals and sound policy require that the state
> should not violate the conscience of the individual.
> All our history gives confirmation to the view that
> liberty of conscience has a moral and social value
> which makes it worthy of preservation at the hands
> of the state. So deep in its significance and vital,
> indeed, is it to the integrity of man's moral and
> spiritual nature that nothing short of the self-preser-
> vation of the state should warrant its violation; and
> it may well be questioned whether the state which
> preserves its life by a settled policy of violation of
> the conscience of the individual will not in fact ulti-
> mately lose it by the process." Stone, The Con-
> scientious Objector, 21 Col. Univ. Q. 253, 269 (1919).

Governmental recognition of the moral dilemma posed
for persons of certain religious faiths by the call to arms
came early in the history of this country. Various
methods of ameliorating their difficulty were adopted by
the Colonies, and were later perpetuated in state statutes
and constitutions. Thus by the time of the Civil War
there existed a state pattern of exempting conscientious
objectors on religious grounds. In the Federal Militia
Act of 1862 control of conscription was left primarily in
the States. However, General Order No. 99, issued by
the Adjutant General pursuant to that Act, provided for
striking from the conscription list those who were exempted by the States; it also established a commutation
or substitution system fashioned from earlier state enact-
ments. With the Federal Conscription Act of 1863,

which enacted the commutation and substitution provisions of General Order No. 99, the Federal Government occupied the field entirely, and in the 1864 Draft Act, 13 Stat. 9, it extended exemptions to those conscientious objectors who were members of religious denominations opposed to the bearing of arms and who were prohibited from doing so by the articles of faith of their denominations. Selective Service System Monograph No. 11, Conscientious Objection 40–41 (1950). In that same year the Confederacy exempted certain pacifist sects from military duty. *Id.*, at 46.

The need for conscription did not again arise until World War I. The Draft Act of 1917, 40 Stat. 76, 78, afforded exemptions to conscientious objectors who were affiliated with a "well-recognized religious sect or organization [then] organized and existing and whose existing creed or principles [forbade] its members to participate in war in any form . . . ." The Act required that all persons be inducted into the armed services, but allowed the conscientious objectors to perform noncombatant service in capacities designated by the President of the United States. Although the 1917 Act excused religious objectors only, in December 1917, the Secretary of War instructed that "personal scruples against war" be considered as constituting "conscientious objection." Selective Service System Monograph No. 11, Conscientious Objection 54–55 (1950). This Act, including its conscientious objector provisions, was upheld against constitutional attack in the *Selective Draft Law Cases,* 245 U. S. 366, 389–390 (1918).

In adopting the 1940 Selective Training and Service Act Congress broadened the exemption afforded in the 1917 Act by making it unnecessary to belong to a pacifist religious sect if the claimant's own opposition to war was based on "religious training and belief." 54 Stat. 889. Those found to be within the exemption were

not inducted into the armed services but were assigned
to noncombatant service under the supervision of the
Selective Service System. The Congress recognized that
one might be religious without belonging to an organized church just as surely as minority members of a
faith not opposed to war might through religious reading reach a conviction against participation in war. Congress Looks at the Conscientious Objector (National Service Board for Religious Objectors, 1943) 71, 79, 83, 87,
88, 89. Indeed, the consensus of the witnesses appear-
ing before the congressional committees was that individual belief—rather than membership in a church or
sect—determined the duties that God imposed upon
a person in his everyday conduct; and that "there is a
higher loyalty than loyalty to this country, loyalty to
God." *Id.*, at 29–31. See also the proposals which were
made to the House Military Affairs Committee but rejected. *Id.*, at 21–23, 82–83, 85. Thus, while shifting
the test from membership in such a church to one's individual belief the Congress nevertheless continued its historic practice of excusing from armed service those who
believed that they owed an obligation, superior to that
due the state, of not participating in war in any form.

Between 1940 and 1948 two courts of appeals [1] held
that the phrase "religious training and belief" did not
include philosophical, social or political policy. Then
in 1948 the Congress amended the language of the statute
and declared that "religious training and belief" was to
be defined as "an individual's belief in a relation to a
Supreme Being involving duties superior to those arising
from any human relation, but [not including] essentially
political, sociological, or philosophical views or a merely
personal moral code." The only significant mention of

---

[1] See *United States* v. *Kauten,* 133 F. 2d 703 (C. A. 2d Cir. 1943);
Berman v. *United States,* 156 F. 2d 377 (C. A. 9th Cir. 1946).

163   Opinion of the Court.

this change in the provision appears in the report of the
Senate Armed Services Committee recommending adop-
tion. It said simply this: "This section reenacts substantially the same provisions as were found in subsection
5 (g) of the 1940 act. Exemption extends to anyone who,
because of religious training and belief in his relation to
a Supreme Being, is conscientiously opposed to combatant
military service or to both combatant and noncombatant
military service. (See *United States* v. *Berman* [*sic*],
156 F. (2d) 377, certiorari denied, 329 U. S. 795.)"
S. Rep. No. 1268, 80th Cong., 2d Sess., 14.

INTERPRETATION OF § 6 (j).

1. The crux of the problem lies in the phrase "religious
training and belief" which Congress has defined as "belief
in a relation to a Supreme Being involving duties superior
to those arising from any human relation." In assigning
meaning to this statutory language we may narrow the
inquiry by noting briefly those scruples expressly excepted
from the definition. The section excludes those persons
who, disavowing religious belief, decide on the basis of
essentially political, sociological or economic considerations that war is wrong and that they will have no part
of it. These judgments have historically been reserved for
the Government, and in matters which can be said to fall
within these areas the conviction of the individual has
never been permitted to override that of the state.
United States v. *Macintosh, supra* (dissenting opinion).
The statute further excludes those whose opposition to
war stems from a "merely personal moral code," a phrase
to which we shall have occasion to turn later in discussing
the application of § 6 (j) to these cases. We also pause
to take note of what is not involved in this litigation.
No party claims to be an atheist or attacks the statute
on this ground. The question is not, therefore, one between theistic and atheistic beliefs. We do not deal with

or intimate any decision on that situation in these cases.
Nor do the parties claim the monotheistic belief that there
is but one God; what they claim (with the possible exception of Seeger who bases his position here not on factual
but on purely constitutional grounds) is that they adhere
to theism, which is the "Belief in the existence of a god or
gods; . . . Belief in superhuman powers or spiritual
agencies in one or many gods," as opposed to atheism.[2]
Our question, therefore, is the narrow one: Does the term
"Supreme Being" as used in § 6 (j) mean the orthodox
God or the broader concept of a power or being, or a
faith, "to which all else is subordinate or upon which all
else is ultimately dependent"?   Webster's New International Dictionary (Second Edition).   In considering this
question we resolve it solely in relation to the language
of § 6 (j) and not otherwise.

2. Few would quarrel, we think, with the proposition
that in no field of human endeavor has the tool of language
proved so inadequate in the communication of ideas as it
has in dealing with the fundamental questions of man's
predicament in life, in death or in final judgment and
retribution.   This fact makes the task of discerning the
intent of Congress in using the phrase "Supreme Being"
a complex one.   Nor is it made the easier by the richness
and variety of spiritual life in our country.   Over 250
sects inhabit our land.   Some believe in a purely personal
God, some in a supernatural deity; others think of religion as a way of life envisioning as its ultimate goal the
day when all men can live together in perfect understanding and peace.   There are those who think of God as the
depth of our being; others, such as the Buddhists, strive
for a state of lasting rest through self-denial and inner
purification; in Hindu philosophy, the Supreme Being is

---

[2] See Webster's New International Dictionary (Second Edition);
Webster's New Collegiate Dictionary (1949).

the transcendental reality which is truth, knowledge and bliss. Even those religious groups which have traditionally opposed war in every form have splintered into various denominations: from 1940 to 1947 there were four denominations using the name "Friends," Selective Service System Monograph No. 11, Conscientious Objection 13 (1950); the "Church of the Brethren" was the official name of the oldest and largest church body of four denominations composed of those commonly called Brethren, *id.*, at 11; and the "Mennonite Church" was the largest of 17 denominations, including the Amish and Hutterites, grouped as "Mennonite bodies" in the 1936 report on the Census of Religious Bodies, *id.*, at 9. This vast panoply of beliefs reveals the magnitude of the problem which faced the Congress when it set about providing an exemption from armed service. It also emphasizes the care that Congress realized was necessary in the fashioning of an exemption which would be in keeping with its long-established policy of not picking and choosing among religious beliefs.

In spite of the elusive nature of the inquiry, we are not without certain guidelines. In amending the 1940 Act, Congress adopted almost intact the language of Chief Justice Hughes in *United States* v. *Macintosh, supra:*

"The essence of religion is belief in a relation to *God* involving duties superior to those arising from any human relation." At 633–634. (Emphasis supplied.)

By comparing the statutory definition with those words, however, it becomes readily apparent that the Congress deliberately broadened them by substituting the phrase "Supreme Being" for the appellation "God." And in so doing it is also significant that Congress did not elaborate on the form or nature of this higher authority which it chose to designate as "Supreme Being." By so refraining it must have had in mind the admonitions of the Chief

Justice when he said in the same opinion that even the word "God" had myriad meanings for men of faith:

> "[P]utting aside dogmas with their particular conceptions of deity, freedom of conscience itself implies respect for an innate conviction of paramount duty. The battle for religious liberty has been fought and won with respect to religious beliefs and practices, which are not in conflict with good order, upon the very ground of the supremacy of conscience within its proper field." At 634.

Moreover, the Senate Report on the bill specifically states that § 6 (j) was intended to re-enact "substantially the same provisions as were found" in the 1940 Act. That statute, of course, refers to "religious training and belief" without more. Admittedly, all of the parties here purport to base their objection on religious belief. It appears, therefore, that we need only look to this clear statement of congressional intent as set out in the report. Under the 1940 Act it was necessary only to have a conviction based upon religious training and belief; we believe that is all that is required here. Within that phrase would come all sincere religious beliefs which are based upon a power or being, or upon a faith, to which all else is subordinate or upon which all else is ultimately dependent. The test might be stated in these words: A sincere and meaningful belief which occupies in the life of its possessor a place parallel to that filled by the God of those admittedly qualifying for the exemption comes within the statutory definition. This construction avoids imputing to Congress an intent to classify different religious beliefs, exempting some and excluding others, and is in accord with the well-established congressional policy of equal treatment for those whose opposition to service is grounded in their religious tenets.

3. The Government takes the position that since *Berman* v. *United States, supra,* was cited in the Senate Report on the 1948 Act, Congress must have desired to adopt the *Berman* interpretation of what constitutes "religious belief." Such a claim, however, will not bear scrutiny. First, we think it clear that an explicit statement of congressional intent deserves more weight than the parenthetical citation of a case which might stand for a number of things. Congress specifically stated that it intended to re-enact substantially the same provisions as were found in the 1940 Act. Moreover, the history of that Act reveals no evidence of a desire to restrict the concept of religious belief. On the contrary the Chairman of the House Military Affairs Committee which reported out the 1940 exemption provisions stated:

> "We heard the conscientious objectors and all of their representatives that we could possibly hear, and, summing it all up, their whole objection to the bill, aside from their objection to compulsory military training, was based upon the right of conscientious objection and in most instances to the right of the ministerial students to continue in their studies, and we have provided ample protection for those classes and those groups." 86 Cong. Rec. 11368 (1940).

During the House debate on the bill, Mr. Faddis of Pennsylvania made the following statement:

> "We have made provision to take care of conscientious objectors. I am sure the committee has had all the sympathy in the world with those who appeared claiming to have religious scruples against rendering military service in its various degrees. Some appeared who had conscientious scruples against handling lethal weapons, but who had no

scruples against performing other duties which did
not actually bring them into combat. Others appeared who claimed to have conscientious scruples
against participating in any of the activities that
would go along with the Army. The committee
took all of these into consideration and has written
a bill which, I believe, will take care of all the reasonable objections of this class of people." 86 Cong.
Rec. 11418 (1940).

Thus the history of the Act belies the notion that it was
to be restrictive in application and available only to those
believing in a traditional God.

As for the citation to *Berman*, it might mean a number
of things. But we think that Congress' action in citing
it must be construed in such a way as to make it consistent with its express statement that it meant substantially to re-enact the 1940 provision. As far as we can
find, there is not one word to indicate congressional concern over any conflict between *Kauten* and *Berman*.
Surely, if it thought that two clashing interpretations as
to what amounted to "religious belief" had to be resolved,
it would have said so somewhere in its deliberations.
Thus, we think that rather than citing *Berman* for what
it said "religious belief" was, Congress cited it for what it
said "religious belief" was not. For both *Kauten* and
Berman hold in common the conclusion that exemption
must be denied to those whose beliefs are political, social
or philosophical in nature, rather than religious. Both,
in fact, denied exemption on that very ground. It seems
more likely, therefore, that it was this point which led
Congress to cite *Berman*. The first part of the § 6 (j)
definition—belief in a relation to a Supreme Being—was
indeed set out in *Berman*, with the exception that the
court used the word "God" rather than "Supreme Being."
However, as the Government recognizes, *Berman* took
that language word for word from *Macintosh*. Far from

requiring a conclusion contrary to the one we reach here, Chief Justice Hughes' opinion, as we have pointed out, supports our interpretation.

Admittedly, the second half of the statutory definition— the rejection of sociological and moral views—was taken directly from *Berman*. But, as we have noted, this same view was adhered to in *United States* v. *Kauten, supra*. Indeed the Selective Service System has stated its view of the cases' significance in these terms: "The *United States* v. *Kauten* and *Herman Berman* v. *United States* cases ruled that a valid conscientious objector claim to exemption must be based solely on 'religious training and belief' and not on philosophical, political, social, or other grounds . . . ." Selective Service System Monograph No. 11, Conscientious Objection 337 (1950). See *id.*, at 278. That the conclusions of the Selective Service System are not to be taken lightly is evidenced in this statement by Senator Gurney, Chairman of the Senate Armed Services Committee and sponsor of the Senate bill containing the present version of § 6 (j):

> "The bill which is now pending follows the 1940 act, with very few technical amendments, worked out by those in Selective Service who had charge of the conscientious-objector problem during the war." 94 Cong. Rec. 7305 (1948).

Thus we conclude that in enacting § 6 (j) Congress simply made explicit what the courts of appeals had correctly found implicit in the 1940 Act. Moreover, it is perfectly reasonable that Congress should have selected *Berman* for its citation, since this Court denied certiorari in that case, a circumstance not present in *Kauten*.

Section 6 (j), then, is no more than a clarification of the 1940 provision involving only certain "technical amendments," to use the words of Senator Gurney. As such it continues the congressional policy of providing exemption from military service for those whose opposition is based on grounds that can fairly be said to be "religious."[3] To hold otherwise would not only fly in the face of Congress' entire action in the past; it would ignore the historic position of our country on this issue since its founding.

4. Moreover, we believe this construction embraces the ever-broadening understanding of the modern religious community. The eminent Protestant theologian, Dr. Paul Tillich, whose views the Government concedes would come within the statute, identifies God not as a projection "out there" or beyond the skies but as the ground of our very being. The Court of Appeals stated in No. 51 that Jakobson's views "parallel [those of] this eminent theologian rather strikingly." 325 F. 2d, at 415–416. In his book, Systematic Theology, Dr. Tillich says:

> "I have written of the God above the God of theism . . . . In such a state [of self-affirmation] the God of both religious and theological language disappears. But something remains, namely, the seriousness of that doubt in which meaning within meaninglessness is affirmed. The source of this affirmation of meaning within meaninglessness, of certitude within doubt, is not the God of traditional theism but the 'God above God,' the power of being, which works through those who have no name for it, not even the name God." II Systematic Theology 12 (1957).

---

[3] A definition of "religious training and belief" identical to that in § 6 (j) is found in § 337 of the Immigration and Nationality Act, 66 Stat. 258, 8 U. S. C. § 1448 (a) (1958 ed.). It is noteworthy that in connection with this Act, the Senate Special Subcommittee to Investigate Immigration and Naturalization stated: "The subcommittee realizes and respects the fact that the question of whether or not a person must bear arms in defense of his country may be one which invades the province of religion and personal conscience." Thus, it recommended that an alien not be required to vow to bear arms when he asserted "his opposition to participation in war in any form because of his personal religious training and belief." S. Rep. No. 1515, 81st Cong., 2d Sess., 742, 746.

163   Opinion of the Court.

Another eminent cleric, the Bishop of Woolwich, John A. T. Robinson, in his book, Honest To God (1963), states:

> "The Bible speaks of a God 'up there.' No doubt its picture of a three-decker universe, of 'the heaven above, the earth beneath and the waters under the earth,' was once taken quite literally. . . ." At 11.
> "[Later] *in place of a God who is literally or physically 'up there' we have accepted, as part of our mental furniture, a God who is spiritually or metaphysically 'out there.'* . . . But now it seems there is no room for him, not merely in the inn, but in the entire universe: for there are no vacant places left. In reality, of course, our new view of the universe has made not the slightest difference. . . ." At 13–14.
> "But the idea of a God spiritually or metaphysically 'out there' dies very much harder. Indeed, most people would be seriously disturbed by the thought that it should need to die at all. For it *is* their God, and they have nothing to put in its place. . . . Every one of us lives with some mental picture of a God 'out there,' a God who 'exists' above and beyond the world he made, a God 'to' whom we pray and to whom we 'go' when we die." At 14.
> "But the signs are that we are reaching the point at which the whole conception of a God 'out there,' which has served us so well since the collapse of the three-decker universe, is itself becoming more of a hindrance than a help." At 15–16. (Emphasis in original.)

The Schema of the recent Ecumenical Council included a most significant declaration on religion: [4]

---

[4] Draft declaration on the Church's relations with non-Christians, Council Daybook, Vatican II, 3d Sess., p. 282, N. C. W. C., Washington, D. C., 1965.

"The community of all peoples is one. One is their
origin, for God made the entire human race live on
all the face of the earth. One, too, is their ultimate
end, God. Men expect from the various religions
answers to the riddles of the human condition: What
is man? What is the meaning and purpose of our
lives? What is the moral good and what is sin?
What are death, judgment, and retribution after
death?

.   .   .   .   .

"Ever since primordial days, numerous peoples
have had a certain perception of that hidden power
which hovers over the course of things and over the
events that make up the lives of men; some have
even come to know of a Supreme Being and Father.
Religions in an advanced culture have been able to
use more refined concepts and a more developed
language in their struggle for an answer to man's
religious questions.

.   .   .   .   .

"Nothing that is true and holy in these religions is
scorned by the Catholic Church. Ceaselessly the
Church proclaims Christ, 'the Way, the Truth, and
the Life,' in whom God reconciled all things to Himself. The Church regards with sincere reverence
those ways of action and of life, precepts and teachings which, although they differ from the ones she
sets forth, reflect nonetheless a ray of that Truth
which enlightens all men."

Dr. David Saville Muzzey, a leader in the Ethical Culture Movement, states in his book, Ethics As a Religion
(1951), that "[e]verybody except the avowed atheists
(and they are comparatively few) believes in some kind of
God," and that "The proper question to ask, therefore, is

not the futile one, Do you believe in God? but rather,
What *kind* of God do you believe in?" *Id.*, at 86–87. Dr.
Muzzey attempts to answer that question:

> "Instead of positing a personal God, whose existence
> man can neither prove nor disprove, the ethical con-
> cept is founded on human experience. It is anthro-
> pocentric, not theocentric. Religion, for all the
> various definitions that have been given of it, must
> surely mean the devotion of man to the highest ideal
> that he can conceive. And that ideal is a community
> of spirits in which the latent moral potentialities of
> men shall have been elicited by their reciprocal en-
> deavors to cultivate the best in their fellow men.
> What ultimate reality is we do not know; but we have
> the faith that it expresses itself in the human world
> as the power which inspires in men moral purpose."
> At 95.

> "Thus the 'God' that we love is not the figure on
> the great white throne, but the perfect pattern, en-
> visioned by faith, of humanity as it should be,
> purged of the evil elements which retard its progress
> toward 'the knowledge, love and practice of the
> right.' " At 98.

These are but a few of the views that comprise the
broad spectrum of religious beliefs found among us. But
they demonstrate very clearly the diverse manners in
which beliefs, equally paramount in the lives of their pos-
sessors, may be articulated. They further reveal the difficulties inherent in placing too narrow a construction on
the provisions of § 6 (j) and thereby lend conclusive
support to the construction which we today find that
Congress intended.

5. We recognize the difficulties that have always faced
the trier of fact in these cases. We hope that the test that
we lay down proves less onerous. The examiner is fur-

nished a standard that permits consideration of criteria
with which he has had considerable experience. While the
applicant's words may differ, the test is simple of application. It is essentially an objective one, namely, does the
claimed belief occupy the same place in the life of the
objector as an orthodox belief in God holds in the life of
one clearly qualified for exemption?

Moreover, it must be remembered that in resolving
these exemption problems one deals with the beliefs of
different individuals who will articulate them in a multitude of ways. In such an intensely personal area, of
course, the claim of the registrant that his belief is an
essential part of a religious faith must be given great
weight. Recognition of this was implicit in this language,
cited by the *Berman* court from *State* v. *Amana Society*,
132 Iowa 304, 109 N. W. 894 (1906):

> "Surely a scheme of life designed to obviate [man's
> inhumanity to man], and by removing temptations,
> and all the allurements of ambition and avarice, to
> nurture the virtues of unselfishness, patience, love,
> and service, ought not to be denounced as not per-
> taining to religion *when its devotees regard it as an
> essential tenet of their religious faith.*" 132 Iowa,
> at 315, 109 N. W., at 898, cited in *Berman* v. *United
> States*, 156 F. 2d 377, 381. (Emphasis by the Court
> of Appeals.)

The validity of what he believes cannot be questioned.
Some theologians, and indeed some examiners, might be
tempted to question the existence of the registrant's
"Supreme Being" or the truth of his concepts. But these
are inquiries foreclosed to Government. As MR. JUSTICE
DOUGLAS stated in *United States* v. *Ballard*, 322 U. S. 78,
86 (1944): "Men may believe what they cannot prove.
They may not be put to the proof of their religious doctrines or beliefs. Religious experiences which are as real
as life to some may be incomprehensible to others." Local

boards and courts in this sense are not free to reject beliefs
because they consider them "incomprehensible." Their
task is to decide whether the beliefs professed by a registrant are sincerely held and whether they are, in his own
scheme of things, religious.

But we hasten to emphasize that while the "truth"
of a belief is not open to question, there remains the significant question whether it is "truly held." This is the
threshold question of sincerity which must be resolved
in every case. It is, of course, a question of fact—a prime
consideration to the validity of every claim for exemption
as a conscientious objector. The Act provides a comprehensive scheme for assisting the Appeal Boards in
making this determination, placing at their service the
facilities of the Department of Justice, including the
Federal Bureau of Investigation and hearing officers.
Finally, we would point out that in *Estep* v. *United
States,* 327 U. S. 114 (1946), this Court held that:

> "The provision making the decisions of the local
> boards 'final' means to us that Congress chose not to
> give administrative action under this Act the cus-
> tomary scope of judicial review which obtains under
> other statutes. It means that the courts are not to
> weigh the evidence to determine whether the classi-
> fication made by the local boards was justified. The
> decisions of the local boards made in conformity with
> the regulations are final even though they may be
> erroneous. The question of jurisdiction of the local
> board is reached only if there is no basis in fact for
> the classification which it gave the registrant." At
> 122–123.

APPLICATION OF § 6 (j) TO THE INSTANT CASES.

As we noted earlier, the statutory definition excepts
those registrants whose beliefs are based on a "merely
personal moral code." The records in these cases, how-

ever, show that at no time did any one of the applicants
suggest that his objection was based on a "merely personal moral code." Indeed at the outset each of them
claimed in his application that his objection was based on
a religious belief. We have construed the statutory definition broadly and it follows that any exception to it must
be interpreted narrowly. The use by Congress of the
words "merely personal" seems to us to restrict the exception to a moral code which is not only personal but
which is the sole basis for the registrant's belief and is in
no way related to a Supreme Being. It follows, therefore, that if the claimed religious beliefs of the respective
registrants in these cases meet the test that we lay down
then their objections cannot be based on a "merely personal" moral code.

In *Seeger*, No. 50, the Court of Appeals failed to find
sufficient "externally compelled beliefs." However, it did
find that "it would seem impossible to say with assurance
that [Seeger] is not bowing to 'external commands' in
virtually the same sense as is the objector who defers to
the will of a supernatural power." 326 F. 2d, at 853. It
found little distinction between Jakobson's devotion to
a mystical force of "Godness" and Seeger's compulsion to
"goodness." Of course, as we have said, the statute does
not distinguish between externally and internally derived
beliefs. Such a determination would, as the Court of
Appeals observed, prove impossible as a practical matter,
and we have found that Congress intended no such
distinction.

The Court of Appeals also found that there was no
question of the applicant's sincerity. He was a product
of a devout Roman Catholic home; he was a close student
of Quaker beliefs from which he said "much of [his]
thought is derived"; he approved of their opposition to
war in any form; he devoted his spare hours to the Amer-

ican Friends Service Committee and was assigned to hospital duty.

In summary, Seeger professed "religious belief" and "religious faith." He did not disavow any belief "in a relation to a Supreme Being"; indeed he stated that "the cosmic order does, perhaps, suggest a creative intelligence." He decried the tremendous "spiritual" price man must pay for his willingness to destroy human life. In light of his beliefs and the unquestioned sincerity with which he held them, we think the Board, had it applied the test we propose today, would have granted him the exemption. We think it clear that the beliefs which prompted his objection occupy the same place in his life as the belief in a traditional deity holds in the lives of his friends, the Quakers. We are reminded once more of Dr. Tillich's thoughts:

> "And if that word [God] has not much meaning for you, translate it, and speak of the depths of your life, of the source of your being, of your ultimate concern, *of what you take seriously without any reservation.* Perhaps, in order to do so, you must forget everything traditional that you have learned about God . . . ." Tillich, The Shaking of the Foundations 57 (1948). (Emphasis supplied.)

It may be that Seeger did not clearly demonstrate what his beliefs were with regard to the usual understanding of the term "Supreme Being." But as we have said Congress did not intend that to be the test. We therefore affirm the judgment in No. 50.

In *Jakobson,* No. 51, the Court of Appeals found that the registrant demonstrated that his belief as to opposition to war was related to a Supreme Being. We agree and affirm that judgment.

We reach a like conclusion in No. 29. It will be remembered that Peter acknowledged "some power manifest in nature . . . the supreme expression" that helps man in ordering his life. As to whether he would call that belief in a Supreme Being, he replied, "you could call that a belief in the Supreme Being or God. These just do not happen to be the words I use." We think that under the test we establish here the Board would grant the exemption to Peter and we therefore reverse the judgment in No. 29.

It is so ordered.

Mr. Justice Douglas, concurring.

If I read the statute differently from the Court, I would have difficulties. For then those who embraced one religious faith rather than another would be subject to penalties; and that kind of discrimination, as we held in *Sherbert* v. *Verner,* 374 U. S. 398, would violate the Free Exercise Clause of the First Amendment. It would also result in a denial of equal protection by preferring some religions over others—an invidious discrimination that would run afoul of the Due Process Clause of the Fifth Amendment. See *Bolling* v. *Sharpe,* 347 U. S. 497.

The legislative history of this Act leaves much in the dark. But it is, in my opinion, not a *tour de force* if we construe the words "Supreme Being" to include the cosmos, as well as an anthropomorphic entity. If it is a *tour de force* so to hold, it is no more so than other instances where we have gone to extremes to construe an Act of Congress to save it from demise on constitutional grounds. In a more extreme case than the present one we said that the words of a statute may be strained "in the candid service of avoiding a serious constitutional doubt." *United States* v. *Rumely,* 345 U. S. 41, 47.[1]

---

[1] And see *Crowell* v. *Benson,* 285 U. S. 22, 62; *Ullmann* v. *United States,* 350 U. S. 422, 433; *Ashwander* v. *TVA,* 297 U. S. 288, 341, 348 (concurring opinion).

163   DOUGLAS, J., concurring.

The words "a Supreme Being" have no narrow technical meaning in the field of religion. Long before the birth of our Judeo-Christian civilization the idea of God had taken hold in many forms. Mention of only two—Hinduism and Buddhism—illustrates the fluidity and evanescent scope of the concept. In the Hindu *religion* the Supreme Being is conceived in the forms of several cult Deities. The chief of these, which stand for the Hindu Triad, are Brahma, Vishnu and Siva. Another Deity, and the one most widely worshipped, is Sakti, the Mother Goddess, conceived as power, both destructive and creative. Though Hindu religion encompasses the worship of many Deities, it believes in only one single God, the eternally existent One Being with his manifold attributes and manifestations. This idea is expressed in Rigveda, the earliest sacred text of the Hindus, in verse 46 of a hymn attributed to the mythical seer Dirgha-tamas (Rigveda, I, 164):

"They call it Indra, Mitra, Varuna and Agni
And also heavenly beautiful Garutman:
The Real is One, though sages name it variously—
They call it Agni, Yama, Matarisvan."

See Smart, Reasons and Faiths, p. 35, n. 1 (1958); 32 Harvard Oriental Series, pp. 434–435 (Lanman ed. 1925). See generally 31 and 32 *id.;* Editors of Life Magazine, The World's Great Religions, Vol. 1, pp. 17–48 (1963).

Indian *philosophy*, which comprises several schools of thought, has advanced different theories of the nature of the Supreme Being. According to the Upanisads, Hindu sacred texts, the Supreme Being is described as the power which creates and sustains everything, and to which the created things return upon dissolution. The word which is commonly used in the Upanisads to indicate the Supreme Being is Brahman. Philosophically, the

Supreme Being is the transcendental Reality which is
Truth, Knowledge, and Bliss. It is the source of the
entire universe. In this aspect Brahman is Isvara, a personal Lord and Creator of the universe, an object of worship. But, in the view of one school of thought, that of
Sankara, even this is an imperfect and limited conception
of Brahman which must be transcended: to think of Brahman as the Creator of the material world is necessarily to
form a concept infected with illusion, or *maya*—which is
what the world really is, in highest truth. Ultimately,
mystically, Brahman must be understood as without attributes, as *neti neti* (not this, not that). See Smart, *op.
cit., supra*, p. 133.

Buddhism—whose advent marked the reform of Hinduism—continued somewhat the same concept. As stated
by Nancy Wilson Ross, "God—if I may borrow that word
for a moment—the universe, and man are one indissoluble
existence, one total whole. Only THIS—capital THIS—
is. Anything and everything that appears to us as an
individual entity or phenomenon, whether it be a planet
or an atom, a mouse or a man, is but a temporary manifestation of THIS in form; every activity that takes place,
whether it be birth or death, loving or eating breakfast, is
but a temporary manifestation of THIS in activity.
When we look at things this way, naturally we cannot
believe that each individual person has been endowed
with a special and individual soul or self. Each one of
us is but a cell, as it were, in the body of the Great Self,
a cell that comes into being, performs its functions, and
passes away, transformed into another manifestation.
Though we have temporary individuality, that temporary,
limited individuality is not either a true self or our true
self. Our true self is the Great Self; our true body is the
Body of Reality, or the Dharmakaya, to give it its technical Buddhist name." The World of Zen, p. 18 (1960).

163 DOUGLAS, J., concurring.

Does a Buddhist believe in "God" or a "Supreme Being"? That, of course, depends on how one defines "God," as one eminent student of Buddhism has explained:

"It has often been suggested that Buddhism is an atheistic system of thought, and this assumption has given rise to quite a number of discussions. Some have claimed that since Buddhism knew no God, it could not be a religion; others that since Buddhism obviously was a religion which knew no God, the belief in God was not essential to religion. These discussions assume that *God* is an unambiguous term, which is by no means the case." Conze, Buddhism, pp. 38–39 (1959).

Dr. Conze then says that if "God" is taken to mean a personal Creator of the universe, then the Buddhist has no interest in the concept. *Id.,* p. 39. But if "God" means something like the state of oneness with God as described by some Christian mystics, then the Buddhist surely believes in "God," since this state is almost indistinguishable from the Buddhist concept of Nirvana, "the supreme Reality; . . . the eternal, hidden and incomprehensible Peace." *Id.,* pp. 39–40. And finally, if "God" means one of the many Deities in an at least superficially polytheistic religion like Hinduism, then Buddhism tolerates a belief in many Gods: "the Buddhists believe that a Faith can be kept alive only if it can be adapted to the mental habits of the average person. In consequence, we find that, in the earlier Scriptures, the deities of Brahmanism are taken for granted and that, later on, the Buddhists adopted the local Gods of any district to which they came." *Id.,* p. 42.

When the present Act was adopted in 1948 we were a nation of Buddhists, Confucianists, and Taoists, as well as Christians. Hawaii, then a Territory, was indeed filled with Buddhists, Buddhism being "probably the major

faith, if Protestantism and Roman Catholicism are deemed
different faiths." Stokes and Pfeffer, Church and State in
the United States, p. 560 (1964). Organized Buddhism
first came to Hawaii in 1887 when Japanese laborers were
brought to work on the plantations. There are now
numerous Buddhist sects in Hawaii, and the temple of the
Shin sect in Honolulu is said to have the largest congregation of any religious organization in the city. See
Mulholland, Religion in Hawaii, pp. 44–50 (1961).

In the continental United States Buddhism is found
"in real strength" in Utah, Arizona, Washington, Oregon,
and California. "Most of the Buddhists in the United
States are Japanese or Japanese-Americans; however,
there are 'English' departments in San Francisco, Los
Angeles, and Tacoma." Mead, Handbook of Denominations, p. 61 (1961). The Buddhist Churches of North
America, organized in 1914 as the Buddhist Mission of
North America and incorporated under the present name
in 1942, represent the Jodo Shinshu Sect of Buddhism in
this country. This sect is the only Buddhist group reporting information to the annual Yearbook of American
Churches. In 1961, the latest year for which figures are
available, this group alone had 55 churches and an in-
clusive membership of 60,000; it maintained 89 church
schools with a total enrollment of 11,150. Yearbook of
American Churches, p. 30 (1965). According to one
source, the total number of Buddhists of all sects in North
America is 171,000. See World Almanac, p. 636 (1965).

When the Congress spoke in the vague general terms
of a Supreme Being I cannot, therefore, assume that it
was so parochial as to use the words in the narrow sense
urged on us. I would attribute tolerance and sophistica-
tion to the Congress, commensurate with the religious
complexion of our communities. In sum, I agree with the
Court that any person opposed to war on the basis of a
sincere belief, which in his life fills the same place as a be-

lief in God fills in the life of an orthodox religionist, is
entitled to exemption under the statute.   None comes to
us an avowedly irreligious person or as an atheist; [2] one,
as a sincere believer in "goodness and virtue for their own
sakes."   His questions and doubts on theological issues,
and his wonder, are no more alien to the statutory standard than are the awe-inspired questions of a devout
Buddhist.

[2] If he were an atheist, quite different problems would be presented.
Cf. *Torcaso* v. *Watkins*, 367 U. S. 488.

Appendix B

APPLICATION FOR CONSCIENTIOUS OBJECTOR CLASSIFICATION

This appendix contains Enclosure 1 of Department of Defense Directive 1300.6 and Selective Service Form 150, and this headnote will attempt to answer some of the questions most frequently asked by conscientious objectors or people who are wondering whether to apply for CO status. It is important to note that regulations within the Armed Forces are revised at frequent intervals. Information given here should be checked to see whether it is up-to-date.

Conscientious objection is a legally recognized position. It is not a violation of the law to declare yourself a conscientious objector and request assignment to noncombatant or civilian alternative service. The "burden of proof" is on the applicant, however. Applying for CO should not jeopardize deferments or jobs, but prejudice may be encountered from unsympathetic employers or draft boards. If a man is strongly opposed to participating in war for reasons of conscience, and if he would accept CO status, he should apply. He may not come within the provisions of the present law, or he may meet all the qualifications but not be granted CO status. Even if he is unsuccessful it may be to his advantage to apply, because a denied CO claim may be offered as a defense or in mitigation of sentence if he later violates Selective Service or military law. It is also possible that new court rulings will expand or redefine the way the law is to be interpreted.

In August 1968, the Special Form for Conscientious Objector (SSS Form 150) was substantially changed. Thirty days are allowed before the form must be returned and the questions more directly relate to the provisions of the law. But a CO still faces the difficult task of describing experiences and beliefs which are perceived intuitively and cannot adequately be put into words.

Conscientious objection, according to the present law, is judged by three criteria:

a) religious training and belief (as broadly interpreted by the Seeger decision to include a set of values which are central to the individual's life, see pages 267–299);

b) opposition to participation in war in any form (excluding opposition to a particular war);

c) sincerity (evidenced by attempts to live consistently with one's beliefs, strengthened by filing the claim as early as possible and by letters from references).

Relatively few of the men who currently object to military service fall easily within a narrow application of these criteria. However, there are significant modifications. Church membership is not required. If a CO belongs to a church which does not advocate conscientious objection, his claim should not be denied for that reason. A belief in God is not required if the person has a belief which plays a "parallel" role in his life. A person who would defend himself, his loved ones, his home or church, is not thereby disqualified: you need not be opposed to violence, only to war. CO status is not granted for objection to a particular war although courts have not ruled specifically on this question. (The words "in any form" have been held to apply to "participation" rather than to "war"; thus, it is argued, a man who objects to a particular war might say that he objects to *participation in any form* in that war. See page 258.)

Frequently a CO has had some formal religious background but he has turned away from it or developed views of his own which he does not share with his church. He should mention whatever religious background he had even if it seems totally irrelevant or inadequate to his own perceptions. He may have been sensitized to humane, religious, or ethical values and his present belief may reflect that he took them seriously while rejecting those forms which did not express them. Or he may not reject what he was taught, but extend it to apply to the issues he confronts in his own life. Objection to war on political grounds is sometimes undergirded by a belief in how man should relate to man, the purpose of life, and similar questions which

are what religion is about. In any case, a CO must explain why
participation in war is in conflict with the innermost belief which
guides his life.

The Vietnam war has prompted many people to ask themselves under what circumstances they would be willing to fight.
Sometimes an objection to this particular war is generalized as a
person realizes that he would not fight in Thailand or Guatemala
or any other war he can think of that he is likely to be called on
to fight as an American during the years he is eligible for the
draft. He does not promise about hypothetical wars nor even
about past wars because if he had lived at another time he
would have been a different person, subject to different in-
fluences, and without present-day means of destruction. He
judges whether he could participate in war as he knows it.

Sincerity is established partly by what the applicant says and
partly by what others say about him. It is up to the applicant to
get letters of reference to support his claim. Such letters should
show some understanding of (but not necessarily agreement
with) his religious convictions, attitudes toward participation in
war, good character, and whenever possible should include concrete examples of how he has demonstrated that he lives according to what he says he believes.

The applicant needs to put in enough detail about himself so
that he comes alive as a human being. Rather than confine his
statements to abstractions and generalities, he should mention
specific incidents, depict the formation and development of his
belief, explain changes and the effects of his experience. This is
particularly necessary for an objector who has already participated in a military organization (including ROTC, the Reserves,
or the National Guard).

Conscientious objectors need to state whether they are willing
to do noncombatant service in the Armed Forces, usually as
medical corpsmen. The person who objects only to killing or
carrying weapons may be expected to accept I-A-O (noncombatant) status; a claim for I-O implies opposition to any kind of
military service. One who is not willing to aid the sick and injured in the military must show that to do so would be in conflict

with his basic religious belief. It may be pertinent to consider the context and purpose of service within the Armed Forces (see Senecal headnote, page 244).

Noncombatant service is defined as follows:

1. service in any unit of the Armed Forces which is unarmed at all times;
2. service in the medical department of any of the Armed Forces, wherever performed; or
3. any other assignment the primary function of which does not require the use of arms in combat provided that such other assignment is acceptable to the individual concerned and does not require him to bear arms or to be trained in their use.

Noncombatant training is "Any training which is not concerned with the study, use, or handling of arms or weapons." I-A-Os ". . . because of assignment to medical units will not be allowed to avoid the important or hazardous duties which are the responsibility of all members of the medical organization."

Most men who seek recognition as conscientious objectors request I-O status rather than noncombatant service. Those who are classified I-O are required to serve for two years in civilian alternative service at the time when they otherwise would have been drafted. The conscientious objector himself proposes three kinds of work he is willing to do (preferably after he has lined up specific employers who would be willing to employ him). If none of these choices are acceptable to his draft board they suggest three kinds of work to him. If he rejects all of these a meeting is arranged between himself, his local board members, and a representative of the State Director, and together they try to agree on an assignment. If that fails, the local board issues an order assigning him to a specific job which he must take or he will be in violation of the Selective Service law. A list of agencies which have been approved for alternative service includes some programs outside of the United States. Other jobs can be approved by the State or National Director of Selective Service if they meet certain qualifications. The work must contribute to "the national health, safety, or interest": charitable, welfare, educational, or scientific; either for the government or for a private nonprofit organization, if it is for the benefit of the general public and not just for its own members. Many kinds of social service jobs have been approved, and the CO is well-advised to find a job which relates meaningfully to his life goals, although usually it must be outside the community in which he lives and sometimes only menial work is acceptable.

The best time to apply for CO is as early as possible. Before a draft registrant is classified for the first time he fills out a Classification Questionnaire, SSS Form 100. On that form there is a statement, Series VIII, which is the first opportunity a man has to declare that he is a conscientious objector. If he signs it, the draft board should send him a Form 150 to set forth his CO claim. A registrant may request a Form 150 at any later time, but if he has not declared his objection on the Classification Questionnaire he is considered to be making a "late claim." He should explain how his belief developed or crystallized since the time he returned the Classification Questionnaire. Even if a man expects to be deferred for several years he should apply for CO as soon as it is clear to him that this is what he wants to do: it helps to establish sincerity if it has been on record for months or years that he was a CO, and it fulfills the requirement of the regulations that new information which could affect his classification be submitted within ten days.

The CO claim will not be considered as long as a man has any deferment. The draft board usually classifies him I-A when his last deferment expires; he then writes to the local board and asks them to consider his CO application. Local boards have been instructed to call CO applicants for an interview before deciding on CO claims, but in the past COs have had to request a personal appearance which is the first step in the appeal process.

Normally a classification cannot be reopened after an induction order has been issued unless there was a change due to circumstances beyond the control of the registrant. If a man files a Form 150 after he receives an induction order (or after refusing induction) the local board must determine whether the objection crystallized or came to fruition after the induction order was issued (see Gearey headnote, page 66). The person who is making a CO claim after receiving an induction order may be asked, "Before you received the induction order, what did you think you were going to do?" Unless he intended to apply for CO, didn't his views come to fruition after receiving the order? If he thought he would apply but had not done so, was it because his beliefs had not crystallized? What brought them to fruition or crystallization, or what made him realize he was a CO?

Certain general precautions apply to all dealings with Selective Service. These include observing deadlines, keeping copies of everything, sending everything by certified mail and keeping receipts (or asking for a receipt if delivered in person), submitting new information and changes of address within ten days, and writing reports of any conversations with draft board personnel, sending one copy to the draft board, since only the written record can be reviewed on appeal or in court. Draft counselors should be well-informed about the details of regulations and how they are applied and also take the time to discuss the issues as they bear on each personal situation. Lawyers should be consulted when it is time to prepare a case or take legal action to protect one's rights.

Men who become conscientious objectors after joining the Armed Forces are judged by Selective Service standards. Department of Defense Directive 1300.6 sets forth the policies and procedures for all branches of the Armed Forces and these are implemented by regulations for each service:

> A request for discharge after entering Military Service based solely on conscientious objection which existed but was not claimed prior to induction or enlistment cannot be entertained. Similarly, requests for discharge based on conscientious objection claimed and denied by the Selective Service System prior to induction cannot be entertained. . . . However, claims based on conscientious objection growing out of experiences prior to entering military service, but

which did not become fixed until entry into the service, will
be considered.

Military objectors need experienced help and contacts outside
the military, sometimes to insure their safety as well as to supply
information not readily available within the service. The Central
Committee for Conscientious Objectors (see page 325) can
supply up-to-date information and referral to a counselor or
lawyer. Unlike the personal appearance before a draft board, a
lawyer is permitted at the personal hearing before a military
officer. A chaplain and a psychiatrist also interview CO applicants within the Armed Forces. (See page 300 for information
required of in-service objectors.)

Conscientious objectors who apply for discharge or transfer
to noncombatant service are assigned to noncombatant duties
while their claims are being processed (Executive Order No.
10028). Those who refuse to perform military duty or to wear
the uniform or otherwise to comply with lawful military orders
are barred from veterans' benefits, except insurance, unless it is
established that they were insane. If a man is discharged as a
conscientious objector before he has served 180 days in the
Armed Forces he must do two years of civilian alternative service. Discharges on grounds of conscientious objection have been
extremely rare in recent years but occasionally COs are discharged for medical or other reasons.

Anyone applying for conscientious objection should have
fuller details and personal advice. If immediate steps must be
taken without assistance, it is still advisable to contact an experienced counselor or lawyer with competence in dealing with
such cases as soon as possible. (See Sources of Information,
especially CCCO, pages 325 and following.)

1300.6 (Encl 1)
May 10, 68

Required Information To Be Supplied by Applicants For
Discharge or Non-Combatant Service

Each person seeking release from active service from the Armed Forces,
or assignment to non-combatant duties, as a conscientious objector,
will provide the information indicated below as the minimum required
for consideration of his request. This in no way bars the Military
Departments from requiring such additional information as they
desire. The individual may submit such other information as desired.

A. General Information Concerning Applicant

1. Full name.

2. Military serial number; and Social Security Account
    number.

3. Selective Service number.

4. Service address.

5. Permanent home address.

6. Name and address of each school and college attended,
    together with the dates of attendance, and the type
    of school (public, church, military, commercial, etc.).

7. A chronological list of all occupations, positions,
    jobs, or types of work, other than as a student in
    school or college, whether for monetary compensation
    or not. Include the type of work, name of employer,
    address of employer and the from/to date for each
    position or job held.

8. All former addresses and dates of residence at those
    addresses.

9. Parent's name and addresses. Indicate whether they
    are living or deceased.

10. The religious denomination or sect of both parents.

11. Was application made to the Selective Service System
    (Local Board) for classification as a conscientious
    objector prior to entry into the Armed Forces? To
    which local board? What decision was made by the
    Board, if known?

1300.6 (Encl I)
May 10, 68

12. When the applicant has served less than one hundred
    and eighty (180) days in the military Service, a
    statement by him as to whether he is willing to
    perform work under the Selective Service civilian
    work program for conscientious objectors, if discharged
    as a conscientious objector. Also a statement of the
    applicant as to whether he consents to the issuance
    of an order for such work by his local Selective Service
    Board.

B. Religious Training and Belief.

1. A description of the nature of the belief which is the
   basis of the applicant's claim.

2. An explanation as to how, when, and from whom or from
   what source the applicant received the training and
   acquired the belief which is the basis of his claim.

3. The name and present address of the individual upon
   whom the applicant relies most for religious guidance
   in matters of conviction relating to his claim.

4. A statement as to circumstances, if any, under which
   the applicant believes in the use of force.

5. A description of the actions and behavior in the
   applicant's life which in his opinion most conspicuously
   demonstrates the consistency and depth of his religious
   convictions which gave rise to his claim.

6. A statement as to whether applicant has ever given
   public expression, written or oral, to the views
   expressed in his application as the basis for his
   claim. If so, the applicant will specify when and
   where.

C. Participation in Organizations

1. Information as whether applicant has ever been a
   member of any military organization or establishment
   before entering upon his present term of service. If
   so, the name and address of such organization will be
   given together with reasons why he became a member.

2. A statement as to whether applicant is a member of
   a religious sect or organization. If so, the statement will show the following:

2

1300.6 (Encl 1)
May 10, 68

a. The name of the sect, and the name and location of its governing body or head, if known.

b. When, where, and how the applicant became a member of said sect or organization?

c. The name and location of any church, congregation or meeting which the applicant customarily attends.

d. The name, title, and present address of the pastor or leader of such church, congregation or meeting.

e. A description of the creed or official statements, if any, and if they are known to him, of said religious sect or organization in relation to participation in war.

3. A description of applicant's relationships with and activities in all organizations with which he is or has been affiliated, other than military, political, or labor organizations.

D. References

The name, full address, occupation or position and relationship to applicant, concerning persons who could supply information as to the sincerity of applicant's professed convictions regarding participation in war.

3

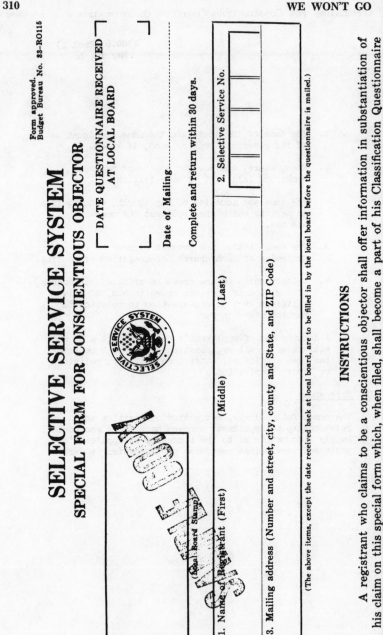

Form approved,
Budget Bureau No. 33-RO115

SELECTIVE SERVICE SYSTEM
SPECIAL FORM FOR CONSCIENTIOUS OBJECTOR

DATE QUESTIONNAIRE RECEIVED
AT LOCAL BOARD

Date of Mailing..........

Complete and return within 30 days.

(Local Board Stamp)

2. Selective Service No.

1. Name of Registrant (First)   (Middle)   (Last)

3. Mailing address (Number and street, city, county and State, and ZIP Code)

(The above items, except the date received back at local board, are to be filled in by the local board before the questionnaire is mailed.)

INSTRUCTIONS

A registrant who claims to be a conscientious objector shall offer information in substantiation of his claim on this special form which, when filed, shall become a part of his Classification Questionnaire

Section 6(j) of the Military Selective Service Act of 1967 provides:

"Nothing contained in this title shall be construed to require any person to be subject to combatant training and service in the Armed Forces of the United States who, by reason of religious training and belief, is conscientiously opposed to participation in war in any form. As used in this subsection, the term 'religious training and belief' does not include essentially political, sociological, or philosophical views, or a merely personal moral code. Any person claiming exemption from combatant training and service because of such conscientious objections whose claim is sustained by the local board shall, if he is inducted into the Armed Forces under this title, be assigned to noncombatant service as defined by the President, or shall, if he is found to be conscientiously opposed to participation in such noncombatant service, in lieu of such induction, be ordered by his local board, subject to such regulations as the President may prescribe, to perform for a period equal to the period prescribed in section 4(b) such civilian work contributing to the maintenance of the national health, safety, or interest as the local board pursuant to Presidential regulations may deem appropriate and any such person who knowingly fails or neglects to obey any such order from his local board shall be deemed, for the purposes of section 12 of this title, to have knowingly failed or neglected to perform a duty required of him under this title."

SSS Form 150 (Revised 8-30-68). (Previous Printings Obsolete)

Series I.—CLAIM FOR EXEMPTION

INSTRUCTIONS.—The registrant should sign his name to either statement A or B in this series. If he cannot sign either one, he must indicate why.

A I am, by reason of my religious training and belief, conscientiously opposed to participation in war in any form. I, therefore, claim exemption from combatant training and service in the Armed Forces, but am prepared to serve in a noncombatant capacity if called. (Registrants granted this status are classified I-A-O.)

(Signature of registrant)

B I am, by reason of my religious training and belief, conscientiously opposed to participation in war in any form and I am further conscientiously opposed to participation in noncombatant training and service in the Armed Forces. I, therefore, claim exemption from both combatant and noncombatant training and service in the Armed Forces, but am prepared to perform civilian alternative service if called. (Registrants granted this status are classified I-O.)

(Signature of registrant)

Series II.—RELIGIOUS TRAINING AND BELIEF

INSTRUCTIONS.—If more space is needed use extra sheets of paper.

1. Describe the nature of your belief which is the basis of your claim and state why you consider it to be based on religious training and belief.

SAMPLE USE

2. Explain how, when and from whom or from what source you received the religious training and acquired the religious belief which is the basis of your claim. (Include here, where applicable, such information as religion of parents and other members of family; childhood religious training; religious and general education; experiences at school and college; organizational memberships and affiliations; books and other readings which influenced you; association with clergymen, teachers, advisers or other individuals which affected you; and any other material which will help give the local board the fullest possible picture of how your beliefs developed.)

(2)

3. To what extent does your religious training and belief restrict you from ministering to the sick and injured, either civilian or military, or from serving in the Armed Forces as a noncombatant without weapons?

_____

_____

_____

_____

_____

4. Have you ever given expression publicly or privately, written or oral, to the views herein expressed as the basis for your claim? Give examples.

_____

_____

_____

_____

_____

Series III.—REFERENCES

You may provide your local board with any additional evidence from any source that would support your claim of conscientious objection. You may, if you choose, provide in the space below the names of references who could provide the local board with information regarding your religious training and belief. You may wish to suggest that these references, if given, write directly to the local board in support of your claim.

NAME	FULL ADDRESS	OCCUPATION OR POSITION	RELATIONSHIP TO YOU

(3)

REGISTRANT'S CERTIFICATE

INSTRUCTIONS.—Every registrant claiming to be a conscientious objector shall make this certificate.

NOTICE.—Imprisonment for not more than 5 years or a fine of not more than $10,000, or both such fine and imprisonment, is provided by law as a penalty for knowingly making or being a party to the making of any false statement or certificate regarding or bearing upon a classification. (Military Selective Service Act of 1967.)

I, _____, certify that I am the registrant named and described in the foregoing statements in this form; that I have read (or have had read to me) the statements made by and about me, and that each and every such statement is true and complete to the best of my knowledge, information, and belief. The statements made by me in the foregoing _____ (are, are not) in my own handwriting.

Registrant sign here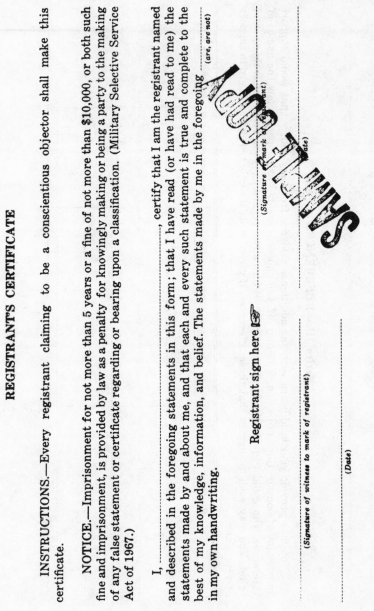

_____
(Signature or mark of registrant)

_____
(Date)

_____
(Signature of witness to mark of registrant)

_____
(Date)

If another person has assisted the registrant in completing this form, such person shall sign the

(Signature of person who has assisted)

(Occupation of person who has assisted)

(Address of person who has assisted)

(Date)

(4)

Appendix C

DOCUMENTS RELATED
TO WAR CRIMES

The following documents are frequently cited to challenge the legality of the Vietnam war, most notably in *Mitchell* v. *U.S.* and *Mora et al.* v. *McNamara et al.*

KELLOGG-BRIAND PACT (46 Stat. 2343)

A treaty between the United States of America and sixty-one other powers, more formally identified as the General Treaty for the Renunciation of War of August 27th, 1928:

Article I. The High Contracting Parties solemnly declare in the names of their respective peoples that they condemn recourse to war for the solution of international controversies, and renounce it as an instrument of national policy with one another.

Article II. The High Contracting Parties agree that the settlement or solution of all disputes or conflicts of whatever nature or of whatever origin they may be, which may arise among them, shall never be sought except by pacific means.

President Hoover's proclamation of said treaty (July 24, 1929) stated:

Now Therefore, be it known that I, Herbert Hoover, President of the United States of America, have caused the said treaty to be made public, to the end that the same and every article and clause thereof may be observed and fulfilled with good faith by the United States and the citizens thereof.

CHARTER OF THE UNITED NATIONS (59 Stat. 1031)

Signed June 26, 1945: ratified by the United States Senate and proclaimed by President Harry S Truman to be effective October 24, 1945.

Article 2, Section 4: All members shall refrain in their international relations from the threat or use of force against the territorial integrity or political independence of any state or in any manner inconsistent with the Purposes of the United Nations.

Chapter XVI, Article 103: In the event of a conflict between the obligations of the Members of the United Nations under the present Charter and their obligations under any other international agreement, their obligations under the present Charter shall prevail.

THE NURNBERG PRINCIPLES

The Treaty of London, August 8, 1945 (59 Stat. 1544), provided for the creation of the International Military Tribunal and the Charter of the Tribunal. The first session of the General Assembly of the United Nations unanimously affirmed the principles of international law recognized by the Charter and Judgment of the Nurnberg Tribunal and directed the International Law Commission to formulate them into an International Criminal Code (Res. 95 [1], 11 December 1946). "The Nurnberg Principles" were adopted by the International Law Commission, June–July 1950:

Principle I. Any person who commits an act which constitutes a crime under international law is responsible therefor and liable to punishment.

Principle II. The fact that internal law does not impose a penalty for an act which constitutes a crime under international law does not relieve the person who committed the act from responsibility under international law.

Principle III. The fact that a person who committed an act which constitutes a crime under international law acted as Head of State or responsible government official does not relieve him from responsibility under international law.

Principle IV. The fact that a person acted pursuant to order of his Government or of a superior does not relieve him from responsibility under international law, provided a moral choice was in fact possible to him.

Principle V. Any person charged with a crime under international law has the right to a fair trial on the facts and law.

Principle VI. The crimes hereinafter set out are punishable as crimes under international law:

(a) Crimes against peace:

(i) Planning, preparation, initiation, or waging of aggression or a war in violation of international treaties, agreements or assurances;

(ii) Participation in a common plan or conspiracy for the accomplishment of any of the acts mentioned under (i).

(b) War crimes:

Violations of the laws or customs of war which include, but are not limited to, murder, ill-treatment or deportation to slave-labour or for any other purpose of civilian population of or in occupied territory, murder or ill-treatment of prisoners of war or persons on the seas, killing of hostages, plunder of public or private property, wanton destruction of cities, towns, or villages, or devastation not justified by military necessity.

(c) Crimes against humanity:

Murder, extermination, enslavement, deportation, and other inhuman acts done against any civilian population, or persecutions on political, racial, or religious grounds, when such acts are done or such persecutions are carried on in execution of or in connexion with any crime against peace or any war crime.

Principle VII. Complicity in the commission of a crime against peace, a war crime, or a crime against humanity as set forth in Principle VI is a crime under international law.

GENEVA CONVENTION OF 1949.

Article 12: Prisoners of war are in the hands of the enemy power, but not of the individuals or military units who have captured them. Irrespective of the individuals' responsibilities that may exist, the Detaining Power is responsible for the treatment given them.

Article 17: No physical or mental torture nor any other form of coercion may be inflicted on prisoners of war to secure from them information of any kind whatsoever. Prisoners of war who refuse to answer may not be threatened, insulted, or exposed to unpleasant or disadvantageous treatment of any kind.

EXCERPTS FROM THE
FINAL DECLARATION OF THE GENEVA CONFERENCE
(JULY 21, 1954)

4. The Conference takes note of the clauses in the agreement on the cessation of hostilities in Vietnam prohibiting the introduction into Vietnam of foreign troops and military personnel as well as of all kinds of arms and munitions. . . .

5. The Conference takes note of the clauses in the agreement on the cessation of hostilities in Vietnam to the effect that no military base under the control of a foreign State may be established in the regrouping zones of the two parties, the latter having the obligation to see that the zones allotted to them shall not constitute part of any military alliance and shall not be utilized for the resumption of hostilities or in the service of an aggressive policy. . . .

6. The Conference recognizes that the essential purpose of the agreement relating to Vietnam is to settle military questions with a view to ending hostilities and that the military demarcation line is provisional and should not in any way be interpreted as constituting a political or territorial boundary. . . .

7. The Conference declares that, so far as Vietnam is concerned, the settlement of political problems, effected on the basis of respect for the principles of independence, unity, and territorial integrity, shall permit the Vietnamese people to enjoy the fundamental freedoms, guaranteed by democratic institutions established as a result of free general elections by secret ballot. In order to ensure that sufficient progress in the restoration of peace has been made, and that all the necessary conditions obtain for free expression of the national will, general elections shall be held in July, 1956, under the supervision of an international commission composed of representatives of the Member States of the International Supervisory Commission, referred to in the agreement on the cessation of hostilities. Consultations will be held on this subject between the competent representative authorities of the two zones from July 20, 1955, onward.

8. The provisions of the agreements on the cessation of hostilities intended to ensure the protection of individuals and of property must be most strictly applied and must, in particular, allow everyone in Vietnam to decide freely in which zone he wishes to live.

12. In their relations with Cambodia, Laos, and Vietnam, each member of the Geneva Conference undertakes to respect the sovereignty, the independence, the unity, and the territorial integrity of the above-mentioned States, and to refrain from any interference in their internal affairs.

EXCERPT FROM THE
CLOSE OF THE GENEVA CONFERENCE (JULY 21, 1954)

Mr. Bedell Smith (United States): . . . my Government is not prepared to join in a Declaration by the Conference such as is submitted. However, the United States makes this unilateral declaration of its position in these matters . . .

The Government of the United States of America

Declares with regard to the aforesaid Agreements and paragraphs that (i) it will refrain from the threat or the use of force to disturb them, in accordance with Article 2 (Section 4) of the Charter of the United Nations dealing with the obligation of Members to refrain in their international relations from the threat or use of force; and (ii) it would view any renewal of the aggression in violation of the aforesaid Agreements with grave concern and as seriously threatening international peace and security.

In connexion with the statement in the Declaration concerning free elections in Vietnam, my Government wishes to make clear its position which it has expressed in a Declaration made in Washington on June 29, 1954, as follows:

"In the case of nations now divided against their will, we shall continue to seek to achieve unity through free elections, supervised by the United Nations to ensure that they are conducted fairly."

With respect to the statement made by the Representative of the State of Vietnam, the United States reiterates its traditional position that peoples are entitled to determine their own future and that it will not join in an arrangement which would hinder this. Nothing in its declaration just made is intended to or does indicate any departure from this traditional position.

We share the hope that the agreement will permit Cambodia, Laos, and Vietnam to play their part in full independence and sovereignty, in the peaceful community of nations, and will enable the peoples of that area to determine their own future.

THE LAW OF LAND WARFARE

(Department of the Army Field Manual, FM 27–10, July 1956.)

Chapter 1, Section 1, Paragraph 2:

The conduct of armed hostilities on land is regulated by the law of land warfare which is both written and unwritten. It is inspired by the desire to diminish the evils of war by:

(a) Protecting both combatants and non-combatants from unnecessary suffering;

(b) Safeguarding certain fundamental human rights of persons who fall into the hands of the enemy, particularly prisoners of war, the wounded and sick, and civilians; and

(c) Facilitating the restoration of peace.

Chapter 1, Section 1, Paragraph 7b:

Force of Treaties Under the Constitution. Under the Constitution of the United States, treaties constitute part of the "supreme Law of the Land" (Art. VI, Cl. 2).

In consequence, treaties relating to the law of war have a force equal to that of laws enacted by the Congress. Their provisions must be observed by both military and civilian personnel with the same strict regard for both the letter and spirit of the law which is required with respect to the Constitution and statutes enacted in pursuance thereof.

Chapter 1, Section 1, Paragraph 9:

Applicability of Law of Land Warfare in Absence of a Declaration of War. As the customary law of war applies to cases of international armed conflict and to the forcible occupation of enemy territory generally as well as to declared war in its strict sense, a declaration of war is not an essential condition of the application of this body of law. Similarly, treaties relating to "war" may become operative notwithstanding the absence of a formal declaration of war.

Chapter 8, Section II, Paragraph 498:

Any person, whether a member of the armed forces or a civilian, who commits an act which constitutes a crime under international law is responsible therefor and liable to punishment. Such offenses in connection with war comprise:

a. Crimes against peace.

b. Crimes against humanity.

c. War crimes.

Although this manual recognizes the criminal responsibility of individuals for those offenses which may comprise any of the foregoing types of crimes, members of the armed forces will normally be concerned only with those offenses constituting "war crimes."

Chapter 8, Section IV, Paragraph 509(a):

The fact that the law of war has been violated pursuant to an order of a superior authority, whether military or civil, does not deprive the act in question of its character of a war crime, nor does it constitute a defense in the trial of an accused individual, unless he did not know and could not reasonably have been expected to know that the act ordered was unlawful. In all cases where the order is held not to constitute a defense to an allegation of war crime, the fact that the individual was acting pursuant to orders may be considered in mitigation of punishment.

Chapter 8, Section IV, Paragraph 511:

The fact that domestic law does not impose a penalty for an act which constitutes a crime under international law does not relieve the person who committed the act from responsibility under international law.

SOURCES OF INFORMATION

THERE ARE two organizations which for years have specialized in providing expert counsel, assistance, and literature for conscientious objectors:

1. Central Committee for Conscientious Objectors
   2016 Walnut Street
   Philadelphia, Pennsylvania 19103
and regional offices in San Francisco and Chicago.

This Committee publishes the *Handbook for Conscientious Objectors*, which is the most comprehensive guide readily available. It includes information for noncooperators as well as for those who wish to qualify for status as conscientious objectors. Request the latest edition; $1.00.

CCCO also distributes copies of some Selective Service forms and detailed memoranda on many problems related to deferments, conscientious objection, and draft refusal, such as "The CO and the Armed Forces," "Refusal of Induction," "The CCCO Counselor and the Law," etc. These are free on request. "News Notes" includes lists of indictments, sentences, who is in prison where, etc. CCCO recommends and assists counselors and lawyers in all parts of the United States. Applicants for conscientious objectors status may send tentative answers to the written questions to CCCO for evaluation.

2. National Service Board for Religious Objectors
   Washington Building
   15th and New York Avenue, N.W.
   Washington, D.C. 20005
NSBRO publishes a very concise and easy-to-read booklet entitled "Questions and Answers on the Classification and Assignment of Conscientious Objectors." Request the latest edition; $.35.

They have also compiled *Statements of Religious Bodies on the Conscientious Objector,* which may provide supporting evidence to attach to Series III of the new Form 150.

NSBRO can also provide assistance with Selective Service appeals and alternative service placements and can recommend local counselors and lawyers.

News and articles regarding the law, alternative service, etc.,

are published monthly in "The Reporter for Conscience' Sake,"
$1.00/year.

Organizations which are keenly concerned with protecting the
constitutional rights of selective service and military objectors
include:

1. American Civil Liberties Union
   156 Fifth Avenue
   New York, N.Y. 10010

The ACLU is interested in test cases, which they handle without charge.

2. National Lawyers Guild
   Box 673
   Berkeley, California 94701

and chapters in Detroit, New York, San Francisco, Los Angeles,
and Philadelphia. (The address given is a permanent address for
publications. The national office changes with the presidency of
the NLG.)

The NLG provides information to lawyers particularly in the
areas of civil rights, civil liberties, welfare, and selective service
law.

The "Civil Liberties Docket" is a supplement to the *Civil
Rights and Liberties Handbook* and lists all pertinent cases on
selective service, demonstrations against war, tax refusal, and
similar topics, annually.

The Guild Practitioner is a quarterly magazine which has
issues devoted to problems such as the Nurnberg War Crimes
Trials (Summer 1966 and Winter 1968), and Selective Service
(Summer 1967).

A book edited by Ann Fagan Ginger discusses due process
requirements in selective service procedures, lists possible areas
of test cases and has other portions which may be of general
interest: *The New Draft Law, a manual for lawyers and counselors,* 1967; $10.00; $5.00 for nonlawyers.

The NLG has prepared a book which includes details about
penalties for desertion, AWOL, and missing movement as well
as for violations of Selective Service law.

3. National Emergency Civil Liberties Committee
   25 East 26th Street
   New York, N.Y. 10010

presents legal assistance without charge in test cases, and refers any persons needing legal aid in the civil rights or civil liberties field to lawyers who charge according to the client's ability to pay.

4. A number of private lawyers, some of whom are mentioned in this book, specialize in Selective Service and military law. Their counsel may be particularly valuable if they are consulted before the law is violated.

Various religious and pacifist organizations have specialized services for conscientious objectors.

1. American Friends Service Committee
   160 North Fifteenth Street
   Philadelphia, Pennsylvania 19102

and regional offices in Baltimore, Md.; Cambridge, Mass.; Chicago, Ill.; Dayton, Ohio; Des Moines, Iowa; High Point, N.C.; Houston, Texas; New York, N.Y.; Pasadena, Calif.; Portland, Ore.; San Francisco, Calif.; and Seattle, Wash., all of which offer counseling, literature, and in some cities counselor training.

Through seminars and camps the American Friends Service Committee provides opportunities for young people to become acquainted with and to discuss peaceful alternatives.

2. Mennonite Central Committee, Peace Section
   21 South Twelfth Street
   Akron, Pennsylvania 17501

Oriented to traditional conscientious objectors who perform alternative service, MCC publishes *A Manual of Draft Information for Ministers and Other Counselors* which contains copies of most of the Selective Service forms that a registrant might encounter.

3. Fellowship of Reconciliation
   Box 271
   Nyack, New York 10960

and subsidiaries at the same address, which provide local contacts and brochures explaining conscientious objection from Catholic, Jewish, and denominational viewpoints as follows: Baptist, Disciples, Episcopal, Liberal (Unitarian-Universalist), Lutheran, Methodist, New Church, Presbyterian U.S. and Presbyterian U.S.A., and Ethical Culture. The FOR promotes peace education especially among clergy and young people. Provides assistance in setting up draft information centers. Maintains bibliographies on religion and pacifism; publishes *Fellowship* magazine, Peace Information edition, $4.00/year.

4. War Resisters League
   5 Beekman Street
   New York, N.Y. 10038
and regional offices in San Francisco, Los Angeles, and Monterey,
Calif.; Portland, Ore.; and Atlanta Workshop in Nonviolence,
Atlanta, Ga. Affiliated with
   War Resisters International
   88 Park Avenue
   Enfield, Middlesex
   England
which may be of help to objectors overseas.

WRL represents a nonreligious pacifist viewpoint; provides
counseling and excellent literature. It sells tape recordings on
prison experience and other topics of interest to war resisters.

"WRL News," sent free to people on the mailing list, reports
on tax refusal and other forms of anti-war activity.

WIN magazine and other aspects of the Committee for Nonviolent Action have been transferred to the War Resisters League.
WIN has full news coverage of peace actions; $5.00/year.

5. New England Committee for Nonviolent Action
   Box 197-B
   Voluntown, Conn. 06384
In 1968, the Committee for Nonviolent Action merged with the
War Resisters League but local CNVA groups continue in New
England and Philadelphia. Conducts nonviolent training pro-
grams and action projects to confront war-related enterprises.

6. Peacemakers
   10208 Sylvan Avenue
   Cincinnati, Ohio 45241
Maintains a "Sharing Fund" for support of families in need as
a result of imprisonment for conscience' sake. Libertarian, pacifist;
emphasis upon noncooperation with war and war taxes. Publishes *Peacemaker* every three weeks; $3.00/year.

7. Catholic Worker
   175 Chrystie Street
   New York, N.Y. 10002
These Christian pacifists live in voluntary poverty, seek to do
works of mercy through houses of hospitality in a number of
cities. They publish the *Catholic Worker* newspaper which covers
among other things their participation in resistance to war and
war taxes. $.25/year.

Information on emigration to Canada is available from counseling services in the United States such as CCCO. However, it is advisable to contact one of the groups in Canada for up-to-date information and temporary assistance. Both Vancouver and Montreal have published brochures entitled "Immigration to Canada and its relation to the Draft." Request the latest edition.

1. Toronto Anti-Draft Programme
   2279 Yonge St., Suite 15
   Toronto 12, Ontario
   Canada

This group publishes a handbook, edited by Mark Satin, entitled *Manual For Draft-Age Immigrants To Canada;* $2.00.

2. Committee to Aid American War Objectors
   P.O. Box 4231
   Vancouver 9, British Columbia
   Canada

3. Montreal Council to Aid War Resisters
   P.O. Box 231, Westmount Station
   Montreal 6, Quebec
   Canada

This group provides information and temporary assistance to antiwar immigrants.

For news and contacts among radical war resisters the following provide up-to-date literature and local contacts:

1. Students for a Democratic Society
   1608 West Madison Street
   Chicago, Illinois

SDS has extensive literature on draft resistance and nationwide contacts; publishes *New Left Notes* weekly, $1.00/year for members, $10.00/year for nonmembers.

2. National Black Anti-War Anti-Draft Union
   100 Fifth Avenue, Room 803
   New York, N.Y. 10011

NBAWADU was set up in 1968 as a clearinghouse for anti-war organizing in black communities.

3. Resist
   763 Massachusetts Avenue
   Cambridge, Massachusetts 02139

An adult support group, Resist assists local draft resistance groups throughout the country. Their *Newsletter* and mailings serve to coordinate resistance efforts nationally.

4. *The Movement*
   449 14th Street
   San Francisco, California 94103
Affiliated with the Student Nonviolent Coordinating Committee, monthly newspaper includes news of anti-war activity; $2.00/year.

5. *Guardian*
   197 East 4th Street
   New York, N.Y. 10009
Formerly *The National Guardian;* newsweekly with national circulation, international coverage, gives sympathetic reporting of resistance and liberation struggles; $7.00/year.

Other magazines which often carry pertinent articles include:

1. *Liberation*
   5 Beekman Street
   New York, N.Y. 10038
This radical pacifist magazine offers reprints of excellent articles such as "The New Conscientious Objector" by noted attorney Francis Heisler which suggests approaches to the filing of Form 150 for men who do not hold strictly pacifist or religious views. $5.00/year.

2. *Ramparts*
   301 Broadway
   San Francisco, California 94133
This magazine has published stirring articles such as the one exposing CIA involvement in the National Student Association and most significantly for the purposes of this book, the article by Donald Duncan, "A 'Green Beret' Blasts the War" in February 1966. $7.00/year.

Selective Service Regulations can be found in libraries designated as "depositories for government publications." (A list of such libraries is published yearly in the September issue of the *Monthly Catalog of U.S. Government Publications.*) Look up the "Code of Federal Regulations, Title 32 (National Defense), part 1600–1700." For recent amendments look in the index of the *Federal Register* for amendments to Code of Federal Regulations 1600–1700. Individuals can enter a subscription to the

Selective Service Regulations and Amendments by sending the subscription price ($5.00) to the Superintendent of Documents, Government Printing Office, Washington, D.C. 20402. Local Board Memorandums, which are advisory and interpretive elaborations on the regulations, may be obtained by subscription in the same manner as the Regulations; $4.00.

The *Selective Service Law Reporter* is an invaluable resource for counselors and draft information centers as well as lawyers. It contains photoreproductions of the Act, Regulations, many Selective Service forms, Local Board Memorandums, selected Operations Bulletins; pertinent chapters from the Medical Fitness Standards (AR 40-501), procedures regulating Armed Forces Examining and Entrance Stations (AR 601-270), Personnel Security Clearance (AR 604-10), and regulations governing discharge from the armed forces for conscientious objection (DoD 1300.6 and AR 635-20); also a practice manual, reports of recent cases, interpretive articles, a comprehensive composite index, bibliography and newsletter. Changes are reported and new documents issued months before they are supplied through government subscriptions. Begun in April 1968, the *SSLR* is available by subscription from the Public Law Education Institute, 1029 Vermont Avenue, N.W., Washington, D.C. 20005; looseleaf, updated monthly $18.00/year for legal defense and education organizations (higher rates for libraries and established attorneys).

Some Army regulations are available from the Government Printing Office; others are ordered from the U.S. Army Adjutant General Publications Center, 2800 Eastern Boulevard, Baltimore, Maryland 21220.

For bibliographies of books on war resistance and pacifism:
1. *Handbook for Conscientious Objectors,* Part 5. (See CCCO, p. 325.)
2. *The Pacifist Conscience,* Peter Mayer, editor, Holt Rinehart and Winston, 1966, includes a "Bibliography of Books on War, Pacifism, Nonviolence and Related Studies." This was compiled in 1965 by a Bibliography Committee of the Fellowship of Reconciliation, to be revised and published by the FOR in subsequent years. (See FOR, p. 327.)

Forthcoming books similar in nature to this one are in preparation and will probably be publicized through the vehicles already mentioned.

A few accounts of World War I and World War II objectors are included in *The Pacifist Conscience,* cited above, and *Nonviolence in America: A Documentary History,* Staughton Lynd, editor, The Bobbs-Merrill Co., Indianapolis, Indiana, 1966.